Environment and Ecology in the History of Economic Thought

This volume proposes a reconsideration of ecological and environmental aspects of the work and ideas of various heterodox authors and traditions in the history of economic thought, including the field of economic development.

Many of the contributors to this book focus on thinkers and works which are not typically considered as part of the ecological sphere, while others consider such economists in a new light or domain. Thus, the book elucidates a new and useful research field of reconsidering ecological dimensions in the traditional history of economic thought as well as helping to delineate alternative views for ongoing debates on ecological themes. Did Veblen, Keynes, Sraffa, C. Furtado and other key economists and schools of thought of our age have relevant and useful insights with respect to environmental issues? Which aspects of their intellectual legacies should eventually be discarded in the face of our new environmental challenges? On the contrary, what aspects of their economic theories can be updated and adapted to a better interpretation of our present ecological concerns? How do they differ, and why? The essays contained in this book will help to answer these questions, by means of recovering, analysing and updating the work of some of the most relevant heterodox economists and schools of thought of our time.

This book will be of great interest for readers in the history of economic thought, ecological economics, environmental economics and economic development.

Vitor Eduardo Schincariol holds a PhD in economic history from the University of São Paulo and is Associate Professor of Economic History and Political Economy at the Federal University of ABC, São Paulo, Brazil.

Routledge Studies in the History of Economics

Adam Smith on the Ancients and the Moderns
Gloria Vivenza

James Mill, John Stuart Mill, and the History of Economic Thought
Edited by Masatomi Fujimoto, John Vint and Taro Hisamatsu

Léon Walras's Economic Thought
The General Equilibrium Theory in Historical Perspective
Kayoko Misaki

Adam Smith's Theory of Value and Distribution
Economics as a Moral Science Once Again
Jeffrey T. Young

Arthur Spiethoff and the German Historical School
Continuities and Discontinuities
Vitantonio Gioia

The Economic Thought of Hilaire Belloc
A Christian alternative to the Servile State
Alfonso Díaz Vera

Schumpeter's General Theory of Capitalism
Tristan Velardo
Translated by Katya Long

Slavery and Colonialism in the History of Economic Thought
The Cases of France and Great Britain
Simona Pisanelli

For more information about this series, please visit: www.routledge.com/series/SE0341

Environment and Ecology in the History of Economic Thought

Reassessing the Legacy of the Classics

Edited by Vitor Eduardo Schincariol

Routledge
Taylor & Francis Group

LONDON AND NEW YORK

First published 2025
by Routledge
4 Park Square, Milton Park, Abingdon, Oxon OX14 4RN

and by Routledge
605 Third Avenue, New York, NY 10158

Routledge is an imprint of the Taylor & Francis Group, an informa business

British Library Cataloguing-in-Publication Data
A catalogue record for this book is available from the British Library

ISBN: 978-1-032-45109-1 (hbk)
ISBN: 978-1-032-45110-7 (pbk)
ISBN: 978-1-003-37542-5 (ebk)

DOI: 10.4324/9781003375425

Typeset in Times New Roman
by Apex CoVantage, LLC

Contents

Figures

Contributors

Marcio Alvarenga Junior is Master in Economics and PhD candidate, Universidade Federal do Rio de Janeiro, Brazil.

Shachi Amdekar holds an MPhil and PhD from the University of Cambridge and is Policy Fellow at the Centre for Science & Policy.

Muhammad Ba is Lecturer in Economics at University Gaston Berger, Sénégal.

Chandni Dwarkasing is Lecturer in Economics, School of Oriental and African Studies, University of London, United Kingdom.

Ramon Vicente Garcia Fernandez is Professor of Economics, Universidade Federal do ABC, São Bernardo do Campo, Brazil.

Marco P. Vianna Franco is EUTOPIA-SIF COFUND Marie Skłodowska-Curie Fellow at CY Cergy Paris Université.

Matthew Fright holds an MPhil and PhD from the University of Cambridge.

(late) Paolo Sylos Labini is former Professor of Political Economy at the Sapienza University of Rome, Italy.

Manuel Ramon Souza Luz is Lecturer in Economics, Universidade Federal do ABC, São Bernardo do Campo, Brazil.

Abdourahmane Ndiaye is Lecturer in Economics, University Bordeaux Montaigne, France.

David Philippy is a SNSF postdoctoral research fellow, Sciences Po Paris, Centre for the Sociology of Organisations, Paris, France.

Gabriel Porcile is Economic Affairs Officer at the Economic Commission for Latin America and the Caribbean, Chile.

Alessandro Roncaglia is Emeritus Professor of Economics, Sapienza University of Rome, Italy.

Vitor Eduardo Schincariol is Lecturer in Economics, Universidade Federal do ABC, São Bernardo do Campo, Brazil.

Leo Steeds is Research Associate, School of Social and Political Sciences, University of Glasgow, Scotland.

Miguel Torres is Economic Affairs Officer at the Economic Commission for Latin America and the Caribbean, Chile.

Carlos Eduardo Frickmann Young is Professor of Economics, Universidade Federal do Rio de Janeiro, Brazil.

Acknowledgements

I would like to express my gratitude to all those who somehow helped me to edit this volume. Firstly, my gratitude to all of the contributors who kindly accepted to join this project and who cooperated with me in several ways during the whole editing process: in alphabetical order, Abdourahmane Ndiaye; Alessandro Roncaglia; Carlos Eduardo Frickmann Young; Chandni Dwarkasing; David Philippy; Gabriel Porcile; Leo Steeds; Manuel Ramon Souza Luz; Marcio Alvarenga Junior; Marco P. Vianna Franco; Matthew Fright; Miguel Torres; Muhammad Ba; Ramon Vicente Garcia Fernandez; and Shachi Amdekar. Their contributions formed an interesting and provocative selection of essays in the boundaries between the history of economic thought and ecology. Thank you!

I also want to thank the following people whose help, cooperation and ideas have also allowed me to edit this volume: the Routledge team, particularly Andy Humphries, Christiana Mandizha and Holly Martin, for their kind support and agility during the whole editing process; Wendy Harcourt for providing me with useful ideas and contacts; Fernanda Graziella Cardoso for reading and commenting on my chapter on Celso Furtado; Fernando Martins Ustariz and Marcia Maria de Queiroz for their constant kind support at the Federal University of ABC (UFABC) in São Bernardo do Campo, Brazil; my colleagues and classmates at the UFABC; Susana Catino, José Antonio Schincariol and Claudio Schincariol for their valuable help under several ways; my wife María Cecilia Ipar, as well as my friends Demétrio Gaspari Cirne de Toledo, Gabriel Almeida Antunes Rossini and Muryatan Santana Barbosa for discussing and debating with me some of the ideas presented in my chapter and the introduction of this volume; and my children Olivia Schincariol and Valentino Schincariol for their patience and love.

Vitor Eduardo Schincariol
São Paulo, Brazil
December 2023

Acronyms

CCAG	Climate Crisis Advisory Group
CEPAL	Comisión Económica para la América Latina y el Caribe (Economic Commission for Latin America and the Caribbean)
CFA franc	West African CFA franc, adopted in eight West African countries, and the Central African CFA franc, adopted in six Central African countries
CPEF	centre-periphery environmental frontier
EEA	European Environment Agency
ECLAC	Economic Commission for Latin America and the Caribbean
EITI	Extractive Industries Transparency Initiative
ELRR	Economic and Labour Relations Review
FAO	United Nations Food and Agriculture Organization
FOEN	Federal Office for the Environment, Switzerland
ESAM	Enquête Sénégalaise Auprès des Ménages (Senegalese Household Survey)
GND	Green New Deal
IPCC	Intergovernmental Panel on Climate Change
ISEW	Index of Sustainable Economic Welfare
OECD	Organization for Economic Cooperation and Development
PED	Principle of Effective Demand
RSTT	Réseau Sénégalais des Think Tanks
UN	United Nations
UNEP	United Nations Environmental Program
USAD	United States Department of Agriculture
WN	The Wealth of Nations

Part I

Classical political economy and the surplus approach

1 Introduction

Vitor Eduardo Schincariol

Man cannot create material things. In the mental and moral world indeed he may produce new ideas; but when he is said to produce material things, he really only produces
utilities; or in other words, his efforts and sacrifices result in changing the form or ar-
rangement of matter to adapt it better for the satisfaction of wants. All that he can do in
the physical world is either to readjust matter so as to make it more useful, as when he
makes a log of wood into a table; or to put it in the way of being made more useful by
nature, as when he puts seed where the forces of nature will make it burst out into life.
                                      Alfred Marshall, *Principles of Economics*, 1920

1. The incorporation of ecological and environmental themes by economic theory as a cumulative process

There has been real progress in social and economic theory as regards the multifaceted relations between society and nature—a progress which has also helped to
change policies and attitudes. This process is obviously connected with the growing awareness of the biophysical limits to human activities—a perception which
is widely shared by different theoretical and political positions in present times; as
with philosophy, progress could also be here defined, in Ayer's words, as a 'change
in the fashion in which the problems are posed, and in an increasing measure of
agreement concerning the character of their solution' (Ayer, 1990, p. 14). Contributions from different theoretical schools of thought could be mutually assimilated
towards more comprehensive approaches (an example is Lange's Marxist assimi-
lations of neoclassical perspectives; see Lange, 1963, 1970; for the classical and
broader argument for feasible objectivity in social sciences, see Mannheim (1960
[1936])). A refined perception by the economic theory of the environmental limits
to economic activity has been fostered by escalating and multiple ecological crises
(losses in biodiversity, growing pollution and waste, global warming, deforestation, depletion of natural resources, natural disasters).[1] The advancement and refinement of economic ideas concerning the environment came up from the gradual
discussion of these themes by economic theory in the face of biophysical problems
generated by human economic activity on Earth. In this sense, Marx's claim that
economic conditions determine economic ideas is perfectly appropriate. This progressive awareness led to the improvement of the existing tools of analysis and

DOI: 10.4324/9781003375425-2

epistemological premises; contradictions and theoretical disputes led to the gradual discarding of outdated conceptions, with the incorporation of partial achievements in higher theoretical frameworks or even the creation of new 'paradigms', in a 'Kuhnian' sense (as the very ecological economics).[2]

For most of past economists and schools of thought in economics, the extraction and destruction of natural resources and the human impacts on the environment have been generally assumed as non-problematic conditions in broader terms. Intergenerational conflict, carrying capacity, ecological footprint, natural resources accounts, substitutability between natural and man-made resources, pollution havens, resource intensity, etc.—most of these terms refer to notions that neither Adam Smith, Karl Marx or Alfred Marshall directly incorporated into their theoretical frameworks. But even today, admirable efforts in reinstating the so-called 'heterodox' approach, such as made by Shaikh's lengthy and scholarly *Capitalism—competition, conflict, crises* (Shaikh, 2016), may be written without a single mention to the environmental issues—a blatant contrast with the above-mentioned tendency in economic theory.

Several histories of the environment as well as of environmental and ecological ideas have appeared over the last several years. Let us briefly mention the main examples. Martinez Alier and Klaus Schlüpmann's *Ecological Economics* (1990) is maybe the most quoted work of this genre. By revisiting the works of Sergei Podolinsky, Otto Neurath, Rudolf Clausius, Patrick Geddes, Henry Adams and other scientists and intellectuals, the authors wrote a history of ecological ideas and a critique of what they define as 'conventional' economics. These included, according to the authors, neoclassicals, Keynesians and Marxists. The work concluded with an anarchist proposal for ecological crises and with a suggested dismissal of the entire legacy of the old schools of economics—which cover the interlude from Adam Smith to John M. Keynes.

Erhun Kula's *History of Environmental Economic Thought* was first published in 1998; in a more conventional way, the author intended to 'bring together in a historical context the major ideas on population growth, resource scarcity and environmental contamination' (Kula, 1998, p. xii). The book mixed analyses of 'classical' economists in the history of economic thought—Malthus, Ricardo, Marx, Marshall, Keynes—with more contemporary ones such as K. Boulding, Georgescu-Roegen and Dennis Meadows. Although lacking deeper concerns with regard to the methodology of the history of economic thought, the book offered an useful account of the evolution of the environmental and ecological ideas, with brief analyses of each selected topic. Donald Worster's *Wealth of the Nature* made a descriptive and lengthy account of the emergence of environmental ideas in the United States (Worster, 1993). However, the book left aside the tradition of European economic thought, focusing on a regional history of environmentalism in that nation. More recently, Missemer and Franco (2022) explored, with much detail, 'the history of ideas from the Renaissance to the 1940s', covering topics which ranged from

French botanists of the 18th century with the proposals of Russian utopians of the late 19th century or with the valuations of natural environments proposed by North American economists in the 1930s.

(p. 8)

This book makes a rich account of the several trends in the formation of ecological thought in the Western world (including Russia). However, as the other previously mentioned works, the book left untouched the legacy of classical economists, particularly in methodological terms. A methodological evaluation of some classical authors in the history of economic thought was made by Peter Victor's *Managing without Growth* (2018).

In fact, a specialised literature on environmental and ecological issues has also thrived over the last several years, with a rise in the number of works, themes and journals. To quote a few examples in the history of economic thought, many works revisiting past economist's views on nature have been written. John Toye has analysed Keynes' views on population growth (Toye, 1997); Bellamy Foster has analysed Marx's views on nature (Foster, 2000); similarly, the work *Post Keynesian and Ecological Economics*, edited by Holt, Pressman and Spash (2009), gave new steps in combining post-Keynesian and Institutionalist theories with ecological concerns. These theoretical efforts, including the history of economic thought, have also led to operational recommendations, such as *Finance and the Macroeconomics of Environmental Policies* (Arestis and Sawyer, 2015). In the same line, the present author has discussed Joan Robinson's views on population, environment and ecology (Schincariol, 2017, 2021).

However, a reconsideration of the legacy of different past economists and schools of thought with regard to environmental themes is still to be deepened on a more systematic level. Most traditional authors of histories of economic thought such as Joseph Schumpeter (1994 [1954]), Maurice Dobb (1973), Eric Roll (1992 [1938]), Mark Blaug (1997) and Alessandro Roncaglia (2005) do not stress this perspective, despite the quality and wide scope of their works. Therefore, a more focused reconsideration of environmental themes inside the 'traditional' history of economic thought becomes a fertile and useful research field. This orientation guided the several essays presented in this volume. Accordingly, did Veblen, Keynes, Sraffa, Celso Furtado—and other important economists and schools of thought—have relevant and useful insights with respect to environmental issues? Which aspects of their intellectual legacies should eventually be discarded in the face of our current stocks of knowledge? Additionally, which aspects of their economic theories can be updated and adapted to a better interpretation of our present ecological concerns? How do they differ, and why? The several essays contained in this book tackle these questions with more attention by means of recovering, analysing and updating the work of classical economists and schools of thought in economics. The next sections trace a brief historical and theoretical account of the questions concerning environmental issues in the history of economic thought as an introductory step to the other more specialised chapters contained in this volume.

2. Some historical remarks

2.1. *Classical political economy*

In their classic work, Alier and Schlüpmann (1993) argued that Adam Smith, Malthus and Ricardo cannot be blamed for not 'spending their time' interpreting the flows of matter and energy in the economic activity (p. 15). According to them, this is because thermodynamics still did not exist at that time. On the contrary, they suggest that Marxists, neoclassicals and Keynesians should not be saved from critiques for ignoring energy and matter flows in the economic activity, as their works were contemporary or even succeeded the modern works of Rudolf Clausius, James Maxwell and Ludwig Boltzmann. Therefore, if their frameworks were to be interpreted in energetic terms, they would be outdated in ecological terms.

These were interesting and provocative critiques. However, they ignored two fundamental aspects in the history of economic thought: (a) changes in economic theory are related to the changes of historical circumstances; (b) progress in economic theory does not erase past achievements. As Schumpeter observed in his *History of Economic Analysis*, 'the economics of different epochs deal with different sets of facts and problems'; at the same time, scientific economics does not lack historical continuity' (Schumpeter, 1994 [1954], pp. 6–7). As ecological problems were still not relevant over the 19th century or even the first half of the last century—at least if compared to our present age—this type of 'rational reconstruction' (that is, treating past economists as if they were contemporary to us)[3] is not entirely legitimate; in fact, it cannot be made without the resource of historical contextualization, with the risk of falling into anachronism. The underlying claim that scientific revolutions erase past achievements is also wrong if we adopt a dialectical point of view, as the new always incorporates the old in a higher theoretical level.[4]

Given that, it is a fertile intellectual challenge to return to the past economists and see what they thought on topics such as depletion and externalities. Were they completely unaware of them? Should their broader theoretical perspectives be discarded as old-fashioned, or could they be taken under a new and useful light? These answers refer to the methodological challenges for researchers in the field of the history of economic thought which show ecological concerns. A dialectical perspective in the history of economic thought would suggest that there is no need to assume—as Hegel once did with philosophy—that all economic theories are a part of a 'whole, a circle coming closure to itself' (*Encyclopaedia of the Philosophical Sciences in Basic Outline. Part I. Science of Logic*, introduction; Hegel, 2010 [1827]), so as to accept that theoretical achievements depend on past knowledge.[5] Similarly, it is not necessary to accept Hegel's metaphysical claim that nature is a 'manifestation of the Idea'[6] to accept that reality is made of contradiction, movement and progress arising from 'critical reaction[s] against traditional doctrine and an integrated system of related concepts' (Dobb, 1973, p. 247). Here, the role of Marx and Engels in reinterpreting Hegel's dialect in objective ('materialist') terms should still be stressed as a great epistemological achievement—although, as we will see, their own conceptions on nature and even economic theory should also be criticised towards new syntheses.

It is often mentioned that Thomas Malthus and David Ricardo have already discussed—although, under a preliminary form—some economic problems nowadays considered to have obvious environmental relevance, as the problem of decreasing returns in agriculture and the question of population growth. Ricardo famously claimed that the decreasing fertility of soil as production expands leads to the fact that 'the natural tendency of profits then is to fall; for in the progress of society and wealth, the additional quantity of food required is obtained by the sacrifice of more and more labour' (Ricardo, 1971 [1817], p. 140). By its turn, Malthus' well-known argument regarding population growth was that 'population, when unchecked, goes on doubling itself every twenty-five years, or increases in a geometrical ratio', while 'it may be fairly said, therefore, that the means of subsistence increase in an arithmetical ratio' (Malthus, 1988 [1798], pp. 20–22). As we know, these hypotheses, proposed in a time of still-low technical progress and high population growth in Europe, were bypassed by technical improvements and the exploitation of new lands in the new nations of the world, as well as by wars and a deceleration of population growth in the old capitalist nations. However, over the following century, overall economic growth and rising numbers particularly in the post-colonial regions reinstated the questions posed by Malthus and Ricardo on a larger scale. As Joan Robinson observed:

> For Ricardo, the trouble lies in the limitation of natural resources. In the simplest version of his theory, capital accumulates, offering employment to an ever-growing labour force (supplied by increasing population) at a fixed wage rate in terms of corn (which stands for agricultural produce in general). To increase the output of corn, it is necessary to extend cultivation to inferior lands. The profit per man employed is the excess over the corn-wage of the net product per man on the land of lowest yield (the advantage of superior land going entirely to its owners in the form of rent). Since the net product per man falls as cultivation is extended, and the corn-value of capital per man employed is more likely to rise than to fall, the rate of profit on capital is falling as time goes by. In the end, the motive for further investment will disappear and accumulation will come to an end. Considering the rate at which the population of the world is growing, all aspiring to attain to the *per capita* level of destruction of natural resources now prevailing in the United States, it seems as though Ricardo's problem may well become actual before long.
> (Robinson, 2021 [1962], pp. 93–94)

For a dialectical view of the history of economic thought, where progress incorporates the old ideas in a superior theoretical framework, this kind of preliminary steps in treating environmental problems could be taken as real advancements towards new syntheses, as they anticipated natural limits for the economic growth or even social reproduction of large societies without economic growth. However, these steps meant only relative progress, as their insights were not conceived for an ecological critique as such. In fact, Ricardo aimed to criticise landowners and trade protectionism in order to argue for a liberal order where capitalists could profit and freely expand capital accumulation. Writing in a time of rapid population growth and political changes, Malthus did not contest population growth with the aim of saving natural resources. Guided by conservative principles and not seeing that the so-called 'poor laws' in England served as a way of overcoming the insufficient aggregate demand which he had detached as a capitalist problem, he blamed the poor for their poverty (for a discussion, see Deane, 1978 and Robinson and Eatwell, 1974).[7] He also did not foresee that agricultural production would be able to overcome numbers for many years ahead. On the other hand, their stress on the centrality of natural resources as an impediment to unlimited accumulation was a right clue.

2.2. *Marx, Engels and Mill*

Marx and Engels were, together with Stuart Mill, the major heirs of Ricardo's legacy. If, departing from what we know today, we were to establish a direct conversation with them rather than with their critics (an exercise in 'rational reconstruction'), the following vignettes could be developed.

As we know, Marx attempted to contest Malthus's views on population growth. He also tried to improve Ricardo's value theory, particularly with his dialectical interpretation of labour exploitation and capitalist crises. For Marxists, Marx's critiques of Ricardo were obviously considered as a 'positive' step, 'for which he has sometimes been called, if in a special, almost Hegelian sense of *Aufhebung*, the last of the classical economists' (Dobb, 1973, p. 142). The broad range of Marx's interests and readings has led Bellamy Foster to argue that Marx also anticipated modern ecology (Foster, 2000). By means of reconstructing Marx's intellectual environment and putting together his several excerpts on biology, chemistry, physics, etc., Foster argued that Marx 'exhibited deep ecological awareness' (Foster, 2000, p. vi). According to him, Marx 'developed and transformed an existing Epicurean tradition with respect to materialism and freedom, which was integral to the rise of much of modern scientific and ecological thought' (Foster, 2000, p. 1).

This claim may render useful insights, as many of Marx's theoretical observations can, indeed, contribute to a renewed economic theory in ecological terms, particularly when departing from his broad critique of the irrationality of capitalist accumulation as an end in itself and its consequences to the environment (the 'second contradiction', in the words of James O'Connor) as well as his analyses of inequality and power. But Marx's theoretical analysis of capitalism can only establish general hints, not a definite *corpus* of ideas that can be automatically transplanted from the 19th century to our present conditions.

As sensitive and encyclopaedic thinkers, Marx and Engels were aware of the negative consequences of capitalist expansion to the quality of land, the fate of forests and urban conditions of living. But their theory of value did not analyse how economic activity is based on underlying stocks and flows of energy and matter. A more adequate interpretation of the economic consequences of thermodynamics would have led Marx and Engels to the perception that the higher the level of economic activity—by means of a higher utilisation of water, raw materials, land, as well as waste disposal, pollution, etc.—the higher tended to be the entropy on Earth. The apparent 'progress' of civilization meant the acceleration of energetic—and probably material—'disorder'.

An incorporation of the second law of thermodynamics, whose main features Marx and Engels knew by reading, could have led them to the development of different economic categories. Thus, raw materials, machines and other elements defined by Marx as 'constant capital' could only be defined as such from the capitalist's accounting point of view, in which prices do not incorporate ('internalise') negative externalities or, say, the invisible costs of depleted natural resources to the living conditions of the next generations. In fact, when raw materials are removed from Earth's crust and transformed by labour into means of production, they can be defined as 'constant capital' only as long as their monetary values reappear in prices. But from the exploration of the stocks of low entropy of coal to its burning as a fuel, coal disappeared, with the released heat being scattered over the universe; the fate of raw materials is similar, although recycling and other means can postpone entropic depletion.[8] Similarly, a machine made of iron is a complex result of the transformation of raw materials by human labour, but it becomes ruined by its economic utilisation over time. In accounting terms, a machine can be defined as 'constant capital'; but not in material terms. Besides, 'capital' can be made of different types of material resources—some recyclable; others not.

Marx's observations on the negative consequences of economic expansion to the environment contradict his claim that a higher population growth is not an economic problem *per se* but only a *relative* one in face of the degree of accumulation. This argument, contained in the first volume of *Das Capital*, drove many to a blind view on the subject, particularly in the so-called Third World, where population growth—and the very size of population—are obvious problems *in absolute terms*, particularly in China and India, as observed by Myrdal (1972), Robinson (1979) and Nove (1991).

Engels is also well-known for his encyclopaedism, in the tradition of Hegel and German philosophy. He also took the trouble of studying chemistry, physics and biology to interpret the scientific developments of that time considering historical materialism and, inversely, in order to enrich it in light of new scientific discoveries. His *Anti-Dühring* and *Dialectics of Nature* are full of complex analyses and useful hints. However, it is a curious fact, which can be only interpreted considering his lack of ecological concerns in a broader sense, how Engels also did not develop the logical conclusions of an economic interpretation of thermodynamics. He was not able to interpret economic activity considering energetic and material flows, despite his several readings in chemistry and physics and despite some already existing suggestions in this regard (as argued by Alier and Schlüpmann, 1993; for an alternative view, see Burkett, 2006). Thus, Engels observed in *Anti-Dühring*,

> Matter without motion is just as inconceivable as motion without matter. Motion is therefore as uncreatable and indestructible as matter itself; as the older philosophy (Descartes) expressed it, the quantity of motion existing in the world is always the same. Motion therefore cannot be created; it can only be transferred.
>
> (Engels, 1987 [1882?], p. 56)

This is right, but he could not take a step further to see that the *practical* means of exploring natural sources, which allow us to convert matter into useful goods, motion and heat, change as we use these resources. Coal, oil, raw materials, water and even air are converted from their original conditions of *stocks* of low entropy to *flows* with higher entropy as their final conditions, such as later pointed out by Boulding (1966) and Georgescu-Roegen (1971). Engels' remarks on the laws of thermodynamics, if correct when criticising Dühring, are limited from an economic point of view, for he was not able to discuss the fundamental economic fact that, even if total energy (and matter) is conserved, the transformation of matter from one state into another (from states of low entropy to higher ones) implies a rise in the total disorder.[9] As observed, this can be partially reversed with recycling, reutilisation and a larger use of sunlight by means of extended agricultural activities, but it cannot be totally prevented.

Therefore, Marx and Engels did not grasp how the apparent creation of 'value' by human labour implied a negative impact on the available stocks of low entropy, the 'creation of value' being, in fact, a misnomer in entropic terms, as all 'values' will deteriorate by consumption or the passage of time. The current velocity taken by capital accumulation, particularly in Asia, as well as the very magnitude already reached by the world economic growth turned this apparent long-run problem into a question concerning a much shorter time frame. Taking a wrong track regarding Ricardo's (correct) view that land is a major limit to capitalist expansion, Marx claimed in a famous passage of *Das Capital* (Volume 3) that:

> The *true barrier* to capitalist production is *capital itself*. It is that capital and its self-valorisation appear as the starting and finishing point, as the motive and purpose of production; production is production only for *capital*, and not the reverse, i.e. the means of production are not simply means for a steadily expanding pattern of life for the *society* of the producers.
>
> (Marx, 1992 [1894])

We do not know if Marx would have maintained such eloquent statements had he lived through the following century. As he aged, he apparently became more aware of the role of natural resources for economic activity. He observed in the *Critique of the Gotha Program*:

> Labour is *not the source* of all wealth. *Nature* is just as much the source of use values (and it is surely of such that material wealth consists?) as labour, which itself is only the manifestation of a force of nature, human labour power. The above phrase[10] is to be found in all children's primers and is correct insofar as it is *implied* that labour is performed with the pertinent objects and instruments. But a socialist program cannot allow such bourgeois phrases to pass over in silence the *circumstances* that alone give them meaning. Only insofar as the human being from the beginning behaves toward nature, the primary source of all objects and instruments of labour, as an owner, treats her as belonging to him, his labour becomes the source of use values, therefore also of wealth.
>
> (Marx, 2023 [1875]), p. 51)

However, he reinstated the bulk of his economic theory in the *Critique* without making concrete suggestions over the practical implementation of a socialist society and without other references to nature as a source of wealth (not to mention the broader notion of 'environment'). It is ironic that Mill's visions of the so-called 'stationary state' anticipated, with more clarity, a society based on equality and a low ecological footprint (this in 1848!). To take a few excerpts of Mill's classic *Principles of Political Economics*:

But in contemplating any progressive movement, not in its nature unlimited, the mind is not satisfied with merely tracing the laws of the movement; it cannot but ask the further question, to what goal? Towards what ultimate point is society tending by its industrial progress? . . . Even in a progressive state of capital, in old countries, a conscientious or prudential restraint on population is indispensable, to prevent the increase of numbers from outstripping the increase of capital, and the condition of the classes who are at the bottom of society from being deteriorated. . . . The same determination would be equally effectual to keep up their condition in the stationary state, and would be quite as likely to exist. . . . Where there is an indefinite prospect of employment for increased numbers, there is apt to appear less necessity for prudential restraint. If it were evident that a new hand could not obtain employment but by displacing, or succeeding to, one already employed, the combined influences of prudence and public opinion might, in some measure, be relied on for restricting the coming generation within the numbers necessary for replacing the present. . . . It is only in the backward countries of the world that increased production is still an important object: in those most advanced, what is economically needed is a better distribution, of which one indispensable means is a stricter restraint on population. . . . It is not good for man to be kept perforce at all times in the presence of his species. A world from which solitude is extirpated is a very poor ideal. Solitude, in the sense of being often alone, is essential to any depth of meditation or of character; and solitude in the presence of natural beauty and grandeur, is the cradle of thoughts and aspirations which are not only good for the individual, but which society could ill do without. Nor is there much satisfaction in contemplating the world with nothing left to the spontaneous activity of nature; with every rood of land brought into cultivation, which is capable of growing food for human beings; every flowery waste or natural pasture ploughed up, all quadrupeds or birds which are not domesticated for man's use exterminated as his rivals for food, every hedgerow or superfluous tree rooted out, and scarcely a place left where a wild shrub or flower could grow without being eradicated as a weed in the name of improved agriculture. If the earth must lose that great portion of its pleasantness which it owes to things that the unlimited increase of wealth and population would extirpate from it, for the mere purpose of enabling it to support a larger, but not a better or a happier population, I sincerely hope, for the sake of posterity, that they will be content to be stationary, long before necessity compels them to it.

(Mill, 2004 [1848], pp. 188–193)

These excerpts anticipated crucial aspects of an economic policy centred around a balance between economic (and social) development and environmental concerns: a critique to 'uneconomic' growth; population growth as a source of unemployment and reduced real wages; 'de-growth' as a means of avoiding environmental depletion; destruction of nature and overcrowded cities as sources of alienation. By its turn,

Marx appears to have believed that technical progress already made under capitalism had fundamentally *solved* the problem of production, but that the shackles imposed on the forces of production by the capitalist system prevented this from being realised in practice.

(Nove, 1991, p. 16)

Accordingly, in face of the modern developmentalist and environmentalist approaches, his claim that the 'true barrier' to capitalist expansion was 'the capitalist process itself' was only partially correct, given the biophysical limits to economic growth and social reproduction that lie *outside* the social relations. That is, limits to economic growth should be found not only in social relations—as they partially do—but also in the broader notion of *absolute* scarcity (decreasing returns in agriculture, lack of energy sources, limited stocks of raw materials and water, etc.). As the history of socialist planning showed, the transformation of social relations and the abolition of private property did not solve these problems. (For a discussion, see Nove (1991), Kornai (1992) and Ellman (2014).)

In all these senses, or 'rational reconstructions', Alier and Schlüpmann are correct; however, it is still possible to reconsider Marxian categories for a renewed ecological critique, as argued by Burkett (2006; see also Harrys-White, 2012). But this should be made by retaining the rational and correct contents of Marx's approach, in parallel with a reconsideration of his outdated aspects. Accordingly, theoretical aspects of Marx's *Capital* could be revised and adapted to the modern notions of ecology and sustainability. For example, an update of Marx's 'schemes of reproduction' should obviously include depletion, pollution and other externalities as negative values and contrasted to the apparent 'creation' of 'value', as given by the old notion of Gross Domestic Product. We could wonder what the utility of concepts such as the 'equalisation of the rate of profit' would be in face of the fact that some sectors are more energy-intensive than others; for example, as energy input for sugar-cane production relies primarily on sunlight, its utilisation seems apparently more sustainable than fossil fuels; however, sugar-cane's opportunity costs as a source of energy *vis-à-vis* its use for food supply should also be considered. They may render the same rate of profit per unit of capital employed; but beneath similar rates, there are different types of environmental impacts and different opportunity costs of each production. What are the operational consequences of this? Is there a reasonable way of comparing both options to achieve a better choice both in ecological and social terms? Marx's detailed analysis of the ground rent could also be the basis for an extended analysis of the utilisation of other natural resources.

2.3. *From marginalism to Keynes*

The so-called neoclassical school (or schools) reacted against the labour-value theory. The theoretical emphasis shifted from the side of production to the demand aspects of the economic activity. This implied several setbacks in the economic analysis (for a discussion, see Dobb, 1973), but 'marginalists' have also contributed with useful notions and instruments of analysis. As an example, Stanley Jevon's *The Coal Question* anticipated modern debates on energy and scarcity in 1866. He warned on the negative consequences for England from the exhaustion of her coal mines. Jevons observed:

> Day by day it becomes more evident that the Coal we happily possess in excellent quality and abundance is the mainspring of modern material civilization. As the source of fire, it is the source at once of mechanical motion and of chemical change. Accordingly it is the chief agent in almost every improvement or discovery in the arts which the present age brings forth. It is to us indispensable for domestic purposes, and it has of late years been found to yield a series of organic substances, which puzzle us by their complexity, please us by their beautiful colours, and serve us by their various utility. . . . Coal in truth stands not beside but entirely above all other commodities. It is the material energy of the country—the universal aid—the factor in everything we do. With coal almost any feat is possible or easy; without it we are thrown back into the laborious poverty of early times. . . . Geologists of eminence, acquainted with the contents of our strata, and accustomed, in the study of their great science, to look over long periods of time with judgement and enlightenment, were long ago painfully struck by the essentially limited nature of our main wealth. And though others have been found to reassure the *p*ublic, roundly asserting that all anticipations of exhaustion are groundless and absurd, and "may be deferred for an indefinite period", yet misgivings have constantly recurred to those really examining the question.
>
> (Jevons, 1866, p. 3)

Jevons was not an ecologist. He was writing to protect England's national interests. His warnings directly contradicted the feature of optimising that marked the new marginalist theory, which could be defined, in the words of Dobb, as 'the child of the marriage of utility with the technique of marginal increments and decrements' (Dobb, 1973, p. 174). The coal question was a perfect example of how 'the assumed maximizing behaviour (of utility on the part of consumers and profit by *entrepreneurs*) yielded the result that under conditions of competition in all markets the (net) value produced was maximized' (Dobb, 1973, p. 174). In the case of coal, as in other markets, physical exhaustion could lead to higher prices, then to higher profitability and consequently to extended exploitation of mines until the end of reserves. This process would subsequently be defined as the 'Jevons Paradox' (for a discussion, see Mayumi (2001), Polimeni et al. (2008) and Victor (2008)).

Despite the striking contradiction between the maximisation of private utilities and the finitude of Earth's resources, Jevons was pointing to a real problem. Coal extraction in the United Kingdom would decrease over the following century, given the exhaustion of the most productive reserves and then campaigns for the use of 'cleaner' types of energy. Over the following century, the massive use of coal would be followed by the use of an even powerful source of energy: crude oil. Mankind, and particularly the so-called 'developed' nations, would spend about half of all known oil reserves in one century—reserves which were formed by natural events over millions of years. The use of crude oil allowed for a huge liberation of energy which was naturally contained in this resource of low entropy; the burning of oil drove up by artificial means the levels of 'productivity' of human labour, if compared to the use of the thin but constant (and eternal for human purposes) flow of sunlight that reaches Earth every day. The search for crude oil would determine geopolitics.

Neoclassicals were pioneers in developing their own approaches to environmental issues, with important contributions, as their critique to monopolist tendencies, the cost-benefit analysis, the analysis of negative externalities and the so-called 'market failures', the measuring of environmental values and the theories on the optimal allocation of resources.[11] The several authors under this label helped to change the usual vocabulary and premises of economic theory by means of the new approach of welfare economics (a detailed account of welfare economics was made by Blaug, 1997; see also Kula 1998). From the point of view of the progress of economic history, Marshall's value theory could be considered as an attempt of synthesis between an approach based on production costs, as developed by Ricardo, and the ones based on the influence of demand, by the marginalists.[12]

However, despite the creation of new, useful tools and highly developed in technical terms, those authors were often subsumed under a rigid *Weltanschauung*, which assumed that the 'free' pursuit of private interests conducted to the maximisation of 'general utility', eventually after some corrections of 'market failures' by public authorities. Excluding reformists as Knut Wicksell, the correlated set of 'recommendations' did not go much beyond the introduction of taxes as the most adequate tools to deal with 'externalities' and 'market failures'—with eventual necessary structural changes in institutions and attitudes being discarded.[13] For example, Garret Hardin defined collective property—'commons'—as a 'tragedy' that, without private property, would lead to the exhaustion of natural resources. This should be corrected with private property, as if it really could prevent environmental depletion. Similarly, Ronald Coase has also argued that 'clear' property rights would solve conflicts involving negative externalities (for a modern discussion, see Daly and Farley, 2011). Subsequently, an adaptation of the original Kuznets' curve argued that *per capita* environmental impacts would decline over time as economies 'developed'—the 'environmental' Kuznets curve. This was argued even when common sense showed that modernisation and industrialisation led to higher demands of natural resources and energy as well a higher pollution on a *per capita* basis, when compared to the 'traditional' societies. This does not mean that poor nations necessarily know better how to preserve their environmental heritage but that 'development' tends to be more material intensive if compared to the lifestyle of rural communities. Robert Solow subsequently argued that manmade capital could be a substitute for 'natural capital' (Solow, 1974)—a hypothesis which is of limited or even null practical application for exhausted mines, deforestation, polluted rivers and biomes under risk or even extinct. The current mainstream approach in economics can still be summarised in the claim that 'demand for environmental quality rises rapidly with per capita income' (Samuelson and Nordhaus, 2010, p. 356), a statement which contradicts the second law of thermodynamics (for this line of approach, see Daly and Farley, 2011).

2.4.   *'What is growth for?': the critique of Joan Robinson*

In 1930, John M. Keynes—who was beginning to review his past neoclassical credentials—speculated about 'mankind solving its economic problem' in the long run, in the fine but too optimistic *The Economic Possibilities of our Grandchildren* (Keynes, 1963 [1930]). Keynes suggested that, in the long run, capital accumulation and material affluence could eventually reach a level which would be enough to finally liberate mankind to the dedication to the most important things of life: mankind would be

> free, therefore, to return to some of the most sure and certain principles of religion and traditional virtue—that avarice is a vice, that the exaction of usury is a misdemeanour, and the love of money is detestable, that those walk most truly in the paths of virtue and sane wisdom who take least thought for the morrow.
>
> (Keynes, 1963 [1930], p. 20)

Some years later, the relevant issues would be related to the economic depression and then a new world war. Keynes started to worry about England's decreasing population, both as a matter of national interest and of decreasing effective demand (see Keynes, 1978 [1937]; for a discussion see also Toye [1997]). Decreasing numbers could, in fact, allow for a rise in welfare but could also mean a lower level of employment. In any case, Keynes maintained an optimistic point of view regarding the physical limits to economic growth and welfare.[14]

It was only after the horrors of the Second World and the subsequent conflicts between the two major superpowers (United States and Soviet Union) that ecological thought began to exert more influence on social sciences and public opinion. The second war was not followed by enduring peace; instead, rearmament was the rule, in parallel with ongoing conflicts in the peripheral nations. A fast universalisation of the 'capitalist rules of the game' on a world scale accelerated ecological threats, mostly ignoring academic debates. The hypothesis of a contradictory progress of modern societies, whose roots could already be found in Marx's brilliant philosophical reflections, was developed by Theodor Adorno and Max Horkheimer, from the 'Frankfurt School'. They observed that the implementation of the rationalist ideals of Enlightenment, of liberation and freedom, had led to the opposite results of a renewed alienation and a deeper destructive mastery over nature. 'To dominate nature boundlessly, to turn the cosmos into an endless hunting ground, has been the dream of millennia' (Adorno and Horkheimer, 2002 [1947], p. 206). However, '[in] the mastery of nature, without which mind does not exist, enslavement to nature persists' (Adorno and Horkheimer, 2002 [1947], pp. 31–32). In the cryptic fashion that often characterised their style, they claimed that

> Society perpetuates the threat from nature as the permanent, organized compulsion which, reproducing itself in individuals as systematic self-preservation, rebounds against nature as society's control over it. Science is repetition, refined to observed regularity and preserved in stereotypes. The mathematical formula is consciously manipulated regression, just as the magic ritual was; it is the most sublimated form of mimicry. In technology the adaptation to lifelessness in the service of self-preservation is no longer accomplished, as in magic, by bodily imitation of external nature, but by automating mental processes, turning them into blind sequences. With its triumph human expressions become both controllable and compulsive. All that remains of the adaptation to nature is the hardening against it. The camouflage used to protect and strike terror today is the blind mastery of nature, which is identical to farsighted instrumentality.
>
> (Adorno and Horkheimer, 2002 [1947], p. 149)

Some years later, Jean Paul Sartre mused on the category of *scarcity*, attributing to it a new ontological status in his philosophy of history. By claiming that 'Marx says very little about scarcity' (Sartre, 2004 [1960], p. 147), that, for Marxism, 'scarcity is not a scarcity of goods, or of tools or of men, but of *time*' (p. 145), Sartre sought to find in the notion of scarcity a decisive aspect of the history of mankind.

> [It] is always *scarcity*, as a real and constant tension both between man and his environment and between man and man, which explains fundamental structures (techniques and institutions)—not in the sense that it is a real force and that it has produced them, but because they were produced in the *milieu of scarcity* bey men whose *praxis* interiorises this scarcity even when they try to transcend it.
>
> (Sartre, 2004 [1960], p. 127)

This 'truth' would 'reappear later on when new contradictions will arise in a socialist society owing to the gigantic struggle against scarcity' (p. 148). Some years later, Hans Jonas, drawing on a mix of Kantian, Marxist and Heideggerian themes, interpreted the necessity of avoiding the destruction of nature's resources as a matter of 'responsibility' with the next generations (Jonas, 1985). He raised doubts over the hypothesis that liberal democracies could manage to solve the entropic problem (as implied by the modern several methods 'contingent valuations'). Jonas added disturbing conclusions on environmental themes to the modern philosophical reflections.

After his departure from neoclassical economics and then also from Keynesianism, Kenneth Boulding's institutionalist article 'The economics of the coming Spaceship Earth' (Boulding, 1966) constituted another important landmark in the history of economic thought, with a ground-breaking discussion of the limits of resources of our planet by means of the concept of a 'closed Earth'. Matter and information were considered as the main inputs and outputs. According to Boulding, these were, more or less, subject to the availability of stocks of low entropy, with the former (energy) having 'no escape from the grim Second Law of Thermodynamics' (Boulding, 1966, p. 6), while, according to him, 'there is, fortunately, no law of increasing material entropy, as there is in the corresponding case of energy, as it is quite possible to concentrate diffused materials if energy inputs are allowed' (p. 5).

The incorporation of ecological dimensions by schools of economic thought became more frequent. Georgescu-Roegen has also left behind his past neoclassical overtones with *The Entropy Law and the Economic Process* (1971). A true landmark, the work was a reaction against 'conventional' approaches where underlying matter and energy—under the perspective of the entropy law—were not taken into account. Dwelling on an attempt of applying the entropy laws to the interpretation of the economic activity, this scholarly work showed how energetic *and* material stocks of low entropy are the prerequisite to the economic activity as well as being depleted by it over time. This aspect, which had been more or less overlooked by all previous schools of economy, brought a gloomy perspective to the nature of modern industrial societies. Mill's old critiques of 'economic growth' were now reinstated on a much higher level of complexity. On the face of it, development without economic growth should now be pursued, at least for the old, industrialised nations.

> There is no necessary association between development and growth; conceivably, there could be development without growth. Because of the failure to observe the preceding distinctions systematically, it was possible for environmentalists to be accused of being against development. Actually, the true environmentalist position must focus on the total rate of resource depletion (and the rate of the ensuing pollution).
>
> (Georgescu-Roegen, 1976, p. 20)

Under these intellectual changes in economic theory, Joan Robinson criticised what she defined as the so-called 'bastard Keynesianism'. She opened a crack in traditional Keynesian thought by claiming that the achievement of full employment by means of private investments had led to superfluous consumption and negative externalities, not to mention militarisation and the constant threats of war.

> The *laissez-faire* bias that still clings around orthodoxy also helps to falsify true values. When Keynes (in his "moderately conservative" mood) maintained that, provided overall full employment is guaranteed "there is no objection to be raised against the classical analysis of the manner in which private self-interest will determine what in particular is produced," he had forgotten that in an earlier chapter he had written "There is no clear evidence from experience that the investment policy which is socially advantageous coincides with that which is most profitable." At that point he was considering the bias of private enterprise in favour of quick profits. There is a still more fundamental bias in our economy in favour of products and services for which it is easy to collect payment. Goods that can be sold in packets to individual customers, or services that can be charged for at so much per head, provide a field for profitable enterprise. Investments in, say, the layout of cities, cannot be enjoyed except collectively and are not easy to make any money out of; while negative goods, such as dirt and noise, can be dispensed without any compensation being required.
>
> (Robinson, 2021 [1962], p. 122)

In 1972, Robinson now claimed that the mainstream economic theory now faced a 'second crisis', also because of its failure in recognizing environmental threats.

> Then consider the notorious problem of pollution. Here again the economists should have been forewarned. The distinction that Pigou made between private costs and social costs was presented by him as an exception to the benevolent rule of *laissez faire*. A moment's thought shows that the exception is the rule and the rule is the exception. In what industry, in what line of business are the true social costs of the activity registered in its accounts? Where is the pricing system that offers the consumer a fair choice between air to breathe and motor cars to drive about in? The economists were the last to realise what is going on and when they did recognize it they managed to hush it up again. *Laissez-faire* and consumer sovereignty were still absolute except for a few minor points discussed under the heading of "externalities" that could easily be put right.
>
> (Robinson, 1972, p. 7)

Hopes of abundance were also progressively turned down by the works of biologists and geographers alike; works such as Rachel Carson's *Silent Spring* (1972) were disruptive analyses of environmental consequences of modern industrial production. It became hard to maintain an optimistic perspective after the decisive and well-known events of the second part of the last century. The US atomic bombs in Japan (1945) and all subsequent threats of nuclear war; the high population growth in peripheral nations; the disappointing results of the Soviet economy regarding ecology; extreme consumerism and waste of resources in the so-called 'developed nations'; the American war on Vietnam, with all its modern technologies for killing and destroying (nature included, as with *napalm*); the oil crises of 1974–1979; pollution and general loss of biodiversity; global warming: these events explain why ecological concerns developed more quickly within the economic theory and public debate over the second half of the last century.

There would be resistances to these new approaches to economic thinking. This included the Soviet economic theory, which supposedly should have been more advanced, given the alleged socialist nature of that nation. A Soviet official guide on socialist planning claimed in 1977 that 'the facts on geological reserves of minerals, timber reserves, and land and water resources indicate that in the long run the Soviet economy will be sure of all the main types of natural resources', despite the fact that 'the scale of the mining and extraction of natural raw materials and fuels has attained gigantic dimensions', with the growth of the economy 'causing a rapid growth of consumption of various kinds of minerals and necessitating the mining of deposits in remote, out-of-the-way, and underdeveloped areas' (Berri, 1977, pp. 216–217). There was no mention of the depletion of these 'remote, out-of-the-way and underdeveloped areas' over the next rounds of capital accumulation; they were supposed to last forever.

2.5. *Some consequences to the surplus approach*

As Georgescu-Roegen observed, a relevant share of the *concrete* forms production, investment and consumption relied on fossil fuels and other non-renewable sources of raw materials. Modern industrial societies achieved an apparent 'development' by a massive depletion of a large stock of energy of low entropy, formed by millions of years by nature. The lifestyle of modern societies implied a rapid utilisation of a highly energetic resource of low entropy—fossils—in order to 'produce', transport and consume all kinds of goods. All potential competitors to fossils have a lower energetic intensity by a given physical unit or involve higher economic, logistic, environmental and even ethical costs, such as nuclear energy. In this sense, part of the industrial 'production' comes indeed from human labour; but the other part comes from the extraction and transformation of natural resources which already existed for millions of years. Therefore, according to Georgescu-Roegen, the term 'production' should be reconsidered in light of the second law of thermodynamics—as well as economic surplus—as society did not 'produce' fossils or raw materials.

The fact that the apparent abundance of the modern societies—capitalist or allegedly socialist—depended on a large and rapid depletion of fossil fuels became an upsetting element. Ninety-four percent of all energy consumption in 1970 came from fossil fuels; this value dropped to 79% in 1989 and was then increased again, reaching 80% in 2014, mainly because of China's high economic growth.[15] The so-called energetic revolution in the United States over the last several years involves nothing more than the extraction of fossils and other non-renewable resources at a higher speed and often with more environmental costs.

In the last instance, these aspects lead us to the surplus approach, with its detachment of the physical aspects of distribution, as first discussed by François Quesnay and his *Tableau Économique* in 1758. Entropic degradation showed that the traditional notion around 'economic surplus' and its related categories suffered from limitations. They were too abstract for a society that relied so much on a *specific* type of energy source (fossils)—crude oil being also highly used as a source for material goods; in a broader sense, classical political economy had not developed its categories with an eye on the entropic degradation of material and energetic sources of production.

Joan Robinson often stressed the importance of Piero Sraffa's critique to the marginalist approach and for a renewed political economy deprived of 'metaphysical' aspects.

[In Sraffa's *Production of Commodities by Means of Commodities*] corn is the only commodity consumed by workers and . . . the corn-wage rate is fixed. Corn is required also as a seed, and there is no other commodity or equipment necessary to produce corn. Then a stock of corn in existence at the beginning of a year has reproduced itself with a surplus at the end of the year.
(Robinson, 1980, p. 144)

She added: 'Why do we need *value* to show that profits can be made in industry by selling commodities for more than they cost to produce [. . .]?' (p. 144). Robinson returned to these questions in other works, although without making use of all theoretical possibilities of the post-Keynesian 'capital critique' to a renewed revaluation of neoclassical discourse (for a discussion, see Schincariol, 2021). Sraffa's emphasis on the physical aspects of production and distribution, where prices have allocative roles but without necessarily expressing a proportional quantity with regard to labour values, seemed to be a more adequate point of departure if entropic aspects were to be incorporated by political economy.

Piero Sraffa defined economic surplus as the resources which constitute 'more than the minimum necessary for replacement' (Sraffa, 1960, p. 6). He then observed that the ratios which satisfy the conditions of production of his system should be more properly called 'costs of production' instead of 'values' (p. 8). By means of the 'standard-commodity' and the 'standard-system', involving determined fixed ratios between means of production, the final production and the economic surplus, he proved that there is an inverse relation between profits and wages without appealing to 'labour values'. From the fact that prices do not directly reflect 'labour time', we can conclude that they also do not reflect other underlying environmental variables, as negative externalities, or the fact that natural resources and ecological systems have an intrinsic value which is 'independent of any value placed on them by humans' (Thirwall, 1999, p. 287). Moreover, labour values do not express the strategic value of natural resources for any national entity as well as their value in intergenerational terms; following Sraffa's system, prices could be taken as reflecting these conflicting aspects in operational terms, without the illusion that distributive or ecological contradictions could be bypassed.

Given the approaching end of material abundance of the so-called 'free goods',[16] it is not even possible anymore to state that 'water and air are abundantly useful [and that] under ordinary circumstances, nothing can be obtained in exchange for them' (Ricardo, 1971 [1821], p. 55). Entropic material scarcity is creating conditions for rising the 'value' of many goods on the basis of 'scarcity alone', even before their absorption by market. Accordingly, Sraffa's stress on the physical aspects of distribution between classes, with the rate of profit as a share of the total corn produced in his original model, seems more adequate if entropic degradation of energy and matter are to be considered by an update of the value theory. However, an updated 'ecologic' version of Sraffa's model should consider the fact that, in modern societies, the economic surplus does not take only the form of reproducible goods whose production is mostly based on the 'free' availability of sunlight—corn, wear, rice—but also on fossils, whose total available supply should be taken as limited stock. This line of interpretation, originally allowed by Sraffa's work, was subsequently developed by Charles Perrings in mathematical terms (see Perrings, 1987, and chapter 3). But much is still to be done on these lines, as the following chapters suggest.

2.6. Economic development

In 1979, Joan Robinson observed in her Aspects of Development and Under-development:

> There is another problem which is of urgent importance today that cannot be well represented in terms of *value*. Marx assumes that the depletion of a pre-existing stock of means of production (represented by *c*) is continually made good by current labour. But some depletion, in particular that of minerals, can never be made good. The increase in productivity that comes about with technical change is very largely due to the use of energy to supplement human work.
> (Robinson, 1979, p. 39)

The book concluded with practical recommendations for a realistic program for development, which should consider not only the availability of financial resources but also environmental ones.

The concern over environmental questions posed many dilemmas to the so-called developing process. Many debates were triggered by the much-cited *The Limits to Growth* (Meadows et al., 1972). Despite the several critiques to the methodological foundations of this work (see for example Myrdal, 1972), this work discussed important matters and indirectly led to many new problematic questions. To quote some of them:

• Are there enough resources for a universalisation of industrialisation and 'modern' lifestyles? What would be the environmental consequences of industrialisation of all peripheral nations in terms of pollution and negative externalities?
• What are the 'fair' prices for raw materials exported by the South nations?

- What are the 'unequal exchanges' between the South and North in environmental terms?
- Should South nations really deplete their environment and export 'raw' materials?
- How could environmental services made by the South territories be charged?
- Should the population growth be taken only as a sign of national strength and consolidation?
- Are the industrialised nations, highly dependent on fossils, really 'developed'?

As we know, these themes were successively raised by Meadows' work, and subsequently by Celso Furtado (2020 [1974]), the Brandt Report (1980), the Economic Commission for Latin America and the Caribbean (see Sunkel and Gligo, 1980) and the South Commission (1990). The several problems involving the distributive ecological conflicts between the so-called 'South' and 'North' were also discussed on a renewed basis by Alier and Schlüpmann in their introductory book on ecological economics (1990). These conflicts and problematic issues became a central part of the modern discussion around economic and social development, and most of them do not have easy solutions. They often lead to impasse, with ecological concerns conflicting with short run necessities. Despite the critique that environmental issues are used against the interests of the poor nations—a statement which is often true—the questions posed by these works cannot not be ignored. Environmental issues also pressed the theory of economic development to readapt its premises and to lower its degree of certainties.

3.   A new research field for the history of economic thought

Almost one century after Keynes' poetic vision of future, we now face a scenario of global warming, decreasing stocks of mineral reserves, destruction of biomes (the Amazon Forest in Brazil is one of the worst examples), the melting of polar ice caps and other several ecological problems that pose new 'limits to growth'. These limits are not faced only by the South nations, as German manufacturers realised after the rise in gas prices in the aftermath of the recent war between Russia and Ukraine. At the same time, most of so-called 'developing' nations did not reach 'development', with large and impoverished populations, rural exodus, deindustrialisation and other 'underdeveloped' features that turned Keynes' speculations on abundance into a sad illusion. However, this gloomy perspective is not shared by all. As previously observed, even if, today, it became generally accepted that there are natural limits to economic activity, the dimensions of these limits are still a matter of heated theoretical and political discussions. Great hope is still posed on 'technology', which is supposed to 'substitute' natural resources and help to postpone exhaustion.[17]

In fact, economic theory will never reach a stage where all theoretical perspectives converge in their diagnostics of how to cope with mounting environmental problems. As long as conflicting economic interests remain in society, this is not possible. Although most of the economists now accept that environmental issues should be taken seriously, there is not a definite and neutral 'synthesis' which may guide our actions. Ironically, both neoclassical and Marxist perspectives of an alleged unlimited power of technology to revert ecological destruction and scarcity still exist, with the former dominating the academic teaching and the minds of businessmen.[18] Therefore, in order to avoid obscurantism and dogmatism, different theoretical positions must coexist, and learn with each other. Gunnar Myrdal's plea for 'lifting up valuations into the full light' (Myrdal, 1968) is still an adequate perspective in a world where different theories coexist and diverge, while one subgroup still prevails over the rest.

The several essays of this 'pluralist' book help to challenge the dominant perspectives on the relations between economic theory, history of economic thought and ecological issues. An edited volume with different accounts of how nature is tackled in the history of economic thought should perform several methodological roles: (a) they should evaluate wrong conceptions, departing from our present knowledge; (b) they should debate with past thinkers, in order to enlighten our current conceptions; (c) they should retake contributions which are still useful, rescuing them from history; (d) finally, they should contribute to a free debate among the existing different theoretical perspectives, helping the readers to decide with autonomy. In more formalist terms, the essays will adopt methodological perspectives that may mix, according to the classification of Mark Blaug (1990), the methodology of '*Geistesgeschichten*', 'historical reconstructions' and 'rational reconstructions'. The first means 'to identify the central questions that past thinkers have posed and to show how they came to be central to their systems of thought'; the second one refers to the methodological option of 'making accounts of past thinkers' systems in their own terms'; and last one means to treat 'the great dead thinkers of the past as contemporaries with whom we exchange views' (Blaug, 1990, p. 27). This should contribute both to the literature on the history of economic thought and economic theory, as the past thinkers should now figure as the main subjects of analysis regarding ecological and environmental themes.

The several essays in this book argue, in several different ways, that, even if past economists were not completely aware of the importance of underlying energetic and material flows beneath the monetary processes, many aspects of their theories or theoretical frameworks can be adapted to economic analysis. In this sense, it is a useful exercise to reassess the ecological dimensions of the classical authors of the history of economic thought. In fact, as readers can see by analysing this book's table of contents, the work does not intend to cover all authors and schools of thought in economics; the underlying idea of its organisation is that the methodological contributions here presented can stimulate similar approaches to the other topics which were not covered here. Although the new debates around environmental issues are now being made with a higher awareness of environmental themes, this should still incorporate tradition. In this sense, it is hoped that these exercises in the history of economic thought may help to consolidate the update of the economic theory.

Notes

1 For data on the world environment situation, see the United Nations Environment Program on https://wesr.unep.org/.

2 '[E]conomic ideas are always and intimately a product of their own time and place; they cannot be seen apart from the world they interpret. And that world changes -is, indeed, in a constant process of transformation- so economic ideas, if they are to retain relevance, must also change' (Galbraith, 1987, p. 2).

3 'Analytic philosophers who have attempted "rational reconstructions" of the arguments of great dead philosophers have done so in the hope of treating these philosophers as contemporaries, as colleagues with whom they can exchange views. They have argued that unless one does this one might as well turn over the history of philosophy to historians -whom they picture as mere doxographers, rather than seekers after philosophical truth. Such reconstructions, however, have led to charges of anachronism. Analytic historians of philosophy are frequently accused of beating texts into the shape of propositions currently being debated in the philosophical journals. It is urged that we should not force Aristotle or Kant to take sides in current debates within philosophy of language or metaethics. There seems to be a dilemma: either we anachronistically impose enough of our problems and vocabulary on the dead to make them conversational partners, or we confine our interpretive activity to making their falsehoods look less silly by placing them in the context of the benighted times in which they were written. Those alternatives, however, do not constitute a dilemma. We should do both of these things, but do them separately' (Rorty, 1984, p. 49).

4 'The dialectic has a positive result, because it has a determinate content or because its result is in truth not an empty, abstract nothing, but instead the negation of definite determinations that are contained in the result precisely because it is not an immediate nothing, but a result instead' (Hegel, 2010 [1827], p. 307).

5 As Keyne's modern reinterpretation of Malthus's theory of aggregate demand, or, more recently, the discard of the outdated notion of Gross Domestic Product in favour of an Index of Sustainable Economic Welfare (ISEW); for a discussion, see respectively Robinson and Eatwell (1974) and Daly and Farley (2011, p. 265); for a system of environmental-economic accounting, see United Nations (2014).

6 'The idea, which is for itself, considered in terms of this, its unity with itself, is the process of intuiting [*Anschauen*] and the idea insofar as it intuits is nature. As intuiting, however, the idea is posited by external reflection in a one-sided determination of immediacy or negation. Yet the absolute freedom of the idea is that it does not "merely pass over into life or let life shine in itself as finite knowing, but instead, in the absolute truth of itself, resolves to release freely from itself the moment of its particularity or the first determining and otherness, the immediate idea, as its reflection [*Widerschein*], itself as nature' (Hegel, 2010 [1827], p. 680).

7 'A labour who marries without being able to support a family, may in some respects be considered as an enemy to all his fellow-labourers. [. . .] I have no doubt whatever that the parish laws of England have contributed to raise the price of provisions, and to lower the real price of labour' (Malthus, 1988 [1798], p. 86).

8 This is the argument of Kenneth Boulding, who argued that '[the second law of thermodynamics] may be offset by the recreation of potential through anti-entropic processes. Water exhausts its gravitational potential as it flows downstream, but then it rains upstream because the earth is an open system of constant throughput of energy from the sun. Soil erodes and is then replaced by the decomposition of rock and the activity of the soil organisms. Biological potential is exhausted by ageing, but every time a new egg is fertilised it is re-created. Organisations rigidify and decay, and the occupants of their essential roles then retire or die and are replaced by younger people who may rejuvenate the organization' (Boulding, 1985, p. 17). For the hypothesis that some economic activities can reverse entropy ('negentropic production'), see, for example, Leff, 2021).

9 'In some places there even appears to be not a little desire to re-import the thermodynamical category of work back into political economy (as with the Darwinists and the struggle for existence), the result of which would be nothing but nonsense. Let someone try to convert any SKILLED LABOUR into kilogram-metres and then to determine

wages on this basis! Physiologically considered, the human body contains organs which in their totality, *from one aspect,* can be regarded as a thermodynamical machine, where heat is supplied and converted into motion. But even if one presupposes constant conditions as regards the other bodily organs, it is questionable whether physiological work done, even lifting, can be at once fully expressed in kilogram-metres, since within the body *internal* work is performed at the same time which does not appear in the result. For the body is not a steam-engine, which only undergoes friction and wear and tear. Physiological work is only possible with continued chemical changes in the body itself, depending also on the process of respiration and the work of the heart. Along with every muscular contraction or relaxation, chemical changes occur in the nerves and muscles, and these changes cannot be treated as parallel to those of coal in a steam-engine. One can, of course, compare two instances of physiological work that have taken place under otherwise identical conditions, but one cannot measure the physical work of a man according to the work of a steam-engine, etc.; their external results, yes, but not the processes themselves without considerable reservations' (Engels, 1987 [1882?], p. 587). He cautiously added: 'All this has to be thoroughly revised'.

10 'Labour is the source of all wealth and all culture', from the Gotha Program.

11 Arthur C. Pigou's *The Economics of Welfare* (1932) was a landmark. 'The possibility of conflict between the effects of economic causes upon economic welfare and upon welfare in general, which these considerations emphasise, is easily explained. The only aspects of conscious life which can, as a rule, be brought into relation with a money measure, and which, therefore, fall within economic welfare, are a certain limited group of satisfactions and dissatisfactions' (Pigou, 1932, p. 15).

12 'Thus we may conclude that, as a general rule, the shorter the period which we are considering, the greater must be the share of our attention which is given to the influence of demand on value; and the longer the period, the more important will be the influence of costs of production on value' (Marshall, 1986 [1920], p. 291).

13 'Pigou set out the argument of his *Economics of Welfare* in terms of exceptions to the rule that *laisser faire* ensures maximum satisfaction; he did not question the rule' (Robinson, 2021 [1962], p. 69).

14 Commenting on Jevons' *The Coal Question*, Keynes observed in 1933: 'There is not much in Jevons's scare which can survive cool criticism [regarding the exhaustion of coal in England]. His conclusions were influenced, I suspect, by a psychological trait, unusually strong in him, which many other people share, a certain hoarding instinct, a readiness to be alarmed and excited by the idea of the exhaustion of resources' (Keynes, 1933 [1951], p. 266). He then added, in a caricatural vein, that Jevons' 'own notes were mostly written on the backs of old envelopes and odd scraps of paper, of which the proper place was the waste-paper basket', as he 'held similar ideas as to the approaching scarcity of paper as a result of the vastness of the demand in relation to the supplies of suitable material'. History showed that Jevons' insights seemed less unimportant than Keynes suggested.

15 See World Bank, 'Fossil fuel energy consumption (% of total)', available on https://data. worldbank.org/.

16 Defined by Marshall as those 'afforded by Nature without requiring the effort of man' (Marshall, 1986 [1920], p. 46).

17 'If resource owners are optimists, they believe new discoveries will be made and substitutes invented. This means that their resource will not become scarce, and its price will not go up (and may even go down). Under such circumstances, it makes sense to extract the resources as quickly as possible and invest the returns. If the resources are being extracted quickly, aboveground supply is large, and the price is low. This reduces the incentives for exploration and the development of substitutes. The problem is that developing substitutes requires technology, technological advance re- quires time, and the less warning we have of impending resource exhaustion, the less time there is to develop substitutes' (Daly and Farley, 2011, p. 204).

18 'Generally, mainstream economists tend to lie between the environmentalist and the cornucopian [optimist] extremes. They recognize that humans have been drawing upon the earth's resources for ages. Economists tend to emphasise that *efficient management of the economy requires proper pricing of natural and environmental resources*' (Samuelson and Nordhaus, 20100, p. 268).

References

Adorno, T., and Horkheimer, M. (2002 [1947]) *Dialectic of Enlightenment*. Stanford: Stanford University Press.

Alier, J. M., and Schlüpmann, K. (1990) *Ecological Economics. Energy, Environment and Society*. London: Blackwell.

Alier, J. M., and Schlüpmann, K. (1993) *La ecología y la economía*. Mexico City: Fondo de Cultura Económica.

Arestis, P., and Sawyer, M. (eds.) (2015) *Finance and the Macroeconomics of Environmental Policies*. London: Palgrave Macmillan.

Ayer, A. J. (1990) *Philosophy in the Twentieth Century*. London: Unwin Paperbacks.

Berri, L. (ed.) (1977) *Planning a Socialist Economy*. Moscow: Progress Publishers.

Blaug, M. (1990) 'On the Historiography of Economics', *Journal of the History of Economic Thought*, 12: 27–37.

Blaug, M. (1997) *Economic Theory in Retrospect*. Cambridge: Cambridge University Press.

Boulding, K. (1966) 'The Economics of the Coming Spaceship Earth', in H. Jarrett (ed.), *Environmental Quality in a Growing Economy*, pp. 3–14. Baltimore: Resources for the Future/Johns Hopkins University Press.

Boulding, K. (1985) *The World as a Total System*. Beverly Hills: Sage Publications.

Brandt Report. (1980) *North-South: A Programme for Survival*. London: Pan Books.

Burkett, P. (2006) *Marxism and Ecological Economics. Toward a Red and Green Political Economy*. Leiden: Brill.

Daly, H., and Farley, J. (2011) *Ecological Economics*. Washington, DC: Island Press.

Deane, P. (1978) *The Evolution of Economic Ideas*. Cambridge: Cambridge University Press.

Dobb, M. (1973) *Theories of Value and Distribution Since Adam Smith. Ideology and Economic Theory*. Cambridge: Cambridge University Press.

Ellman, M. (2014) *Socialist Planning*. 3rd ed. Cambridge: Cambridge University Press.

Engels, F. (1987 [1882?]) *Dialectics of Nature*. Moscow: International Publishers.

Foster, B. (2000) *Marx's Ecology. Materialism and Nature*. New York: Monthly Review Press.

Furtado, C. (2020 [1974]) *The Myth of Economic Development*. Cambridge: Polity Press.

Galbraith, J. K. (1987) *Economics in Perspective. A Critical History*. Boston: Houghton Mifflin Company.

Georgescu-Roegen, N. (1971) *The Entropy Law and the Economic Process*. Cambridge, MA: Harvard University Press.

Georgescu-Roegen, N. (1976) *Energy and Economic Myths*. New York: Pergamon Press.

Harrys-White, B. (2012) 'Ecology and the Environment', in B. Fine, A. Saad Filho and M. Boffo (eds.), *The Elgar Companion to Marxist Economics*, pp. 102–111. Cheltenham: Edward Elgar.

Hegel, G. W. F. (2010 [1827]) *Encyclopaedia of the Philosophical Sciences in Basic Outline. Part I. Science of Logic*. Cambridge: Cambridge University Press. Epub Version.

Holt, R., Pressman, S., and Spash, C. (eds.) (2009) *Post Keynesian and Ecological Economics, Confronting Environmental Issues*. Cheltenham: Edward Elgar.

Jevons, W. S. (1866) *The Coal Question. An Inquiry Concerning the Progress of the Nation, and the Probable Exhaustion of Our Coal Mines*. London: MacMillan and Co.

Jonas, H. (1985) *The Imperative of Responsibility. In Search of an Ethics for the Technological Age*. Chicago: University of Chicago Press.

Keynes, J. M. (1951 [1933]) *Essays in Biography*. New York: The Norton Library.

Keynes, J. M. (1963 [1930]) 'Economic Possibilities for Our Grandchildren', in *Essays in Persuasion*, pp. 358–374. New York: W.W. Norton & Company.

Keynes, J. M. (1978 [1937]) 'Economic Consequences of a Declining Population', *Population and Development Review*, 4 (3): 517–523.

Kornai, J. (1992) *The Socialist System*. Princeton, NJ: Princeton University Press.

Kula, E. (1998) *History of Environmental Economic Thought*. London: Routledge.

Lange, O. (1963) *Political Economy. Volume 1. General Problems*. Oxford: Pergamon Press.

Lange, O. (1970) *Papers in Economics and Sociology*. Oxford: Pergamon Press.

Leff, E. (2021) *Political Ecology. Deconstructing Capital and Territorializing Life*. London: Palgrave Macmillan.

Malthus, T. (1988 [1798]) *An Essay on the Principle of Population*. New York: Prometheus Books.

Mannheim, K. (1960 [1936]) *Ideology and Utopia*. London: Routledge & Kegan Paul Ltd.

Marshall, A. (1986 [1920]) *Principles of Economics. An Introductory Volume*. London: Macmillan.

Marx, K. (1991 [1867]). Capital. Volume 1. A Critique of Political Economy. London: Penguin Books.

Marx, K. (1992 [1894]). Capital. Volume 3. The process of Capitalist Production as a whole. London: Penguin Books.

Marx, K. (2023 [1875]) *Critique of Gotha Program*. Oakland: PM Press.

Mayumi, K. (ed.) (2001) *The Origins of Ecological Economics. The Bioeconomics of Georgescu-Roegen*. London: Routledge.

Meadows, D., et al. (1972) *The Limits to Growth*. New York: Universe Books.

Mill, J. S. (2004 [1848]) *Principles of Political Economy, with Some of Their Applications to Social Philosophy. Abridged*. Indianapolis, IN: Hackett Publishing Company.

Missemer, A., and Franco, M. P. V. (2022) *A History of Ecological Economic Thought*. London: Routledge.

Myrdal, G. (1968) *Asian Drama. An Inquiry into the Poverty of Nations*. New York: Pantheon Books.

Myrdal, G. (1972) 'Economics of an Improved Environment', *World Development*, 1 (1–2): 102–104.

Nove, A. (1991) *The Economics of Feasible Socialism—Revisited*. London: Harper-Collins.

Perrings, C. (1987) *Economy and Environment. A Theoretical Essay on the Interdependence of Economic and Environmental Systems*. Cambridge: Cambridge University Press.

Pigou, A. C. (1932) *The Economics of Welfare*. 4th ed. London: Macmillan.

Polimeni, J. M., et al. (2008) *The Jevons Paradox and the Myth of Resource Efficiency Improvements*. London: Earthscan.

Ricardo, D. (1971 [1817]) *On the Principles of Political Economy and Taxation*. London: Penguin.

Robinson, J. (1972) 'The Second Crisis of Economic Theory', *The American Economic Review*, 62 (1/2): 1–10.

Robinson, J. (1979) *Aspects of Development and Underdevelopment*. Cambridge: Cambridge University Press.

Robinson, J. (1980) *Further Contributions to Modern Economics*. Oxford: Basil Blackwell.

Robinson, J. (2021 [1962]) *Economic Philosophy*. London: Routledge.

Robinson, J., and Eatwell, J. (1974) *Introduction to Modern Economics*. London: MacGraw-Hill.

Roll, E. (1992 [1938]) *A History of Economic Thought*. London: Faber & Faber.

Roncaglia, A. (2005) *The Wealth of Ideas. A History of Economic Thought*. Cambridge: Cambridge University Press.

Rorty, R. (1984) 'The Historiography of Philosophy: Four Genres'. In R. Rorty, et al. (eds.), *Philosophy in History*. Cambridge: Cambridge University Press.

Samuelson, P., and Nordhaus, W. (2010) *Economics*. 19th edition. New York: MacGraw-Hill Irwin.

Sartre, J. P. (2004 [1960]) *Critique of Dialectical Reason*. London: Verso.

Schincariol, V. E. (2017) 'Joan Robinson on Population Growth', *Review of Political Economy*, 29 (2): 1–25.

Schincariol, V. E. (2021) 'Joan Robinson on Environment and Ecology', *Agrarian South, Journal of Political Economy*, 10 (3): 1–23.

Schumpeter, J. (1994 [1954]) *History of Economic Analysis*. New York: Oxford University Press.

Shaikh, A. (2016) *Capitalism. Competition, Conflict, Crises*. Oxford: Oxford University Press.

Solow, R. (1974) 'The Economics of the Resources or the Resources of Economics', *American Economic Association*, 64 (2): 1–14.

South Commission. (1990) *The Challenge to the South. The Report of the South Commission*. Oxford: Oxford University Press.

Sraffa, P. (1960) *Production of Commodities by Means of Commodities*. Cambridge: Cambridge University Press.

Sunkel, O., and Gligo, N. (1980) *Estilos de Desarrollo y Medio Ambiente em América Latina*. Mexico City: Fondo de Cultura Económica.

Thirwall, A. P. (1999) *Growth and Development*. London: Macmillan.

Toye, J. (1997) 'Keynes on Population and Economic Growth', *Cambridge Journal of Economics*, 21 (1): 1–26.

United Nations. (2014) *System of Environmental-Economic Accounting 2012—Framework*. New York: United Nations.

Victor, P. (2008) *Managing Without Growth*. Cheltenham: Edward Elgar.

Worster, D. (1993) *The Wealth of Nature. Environmental History and the Ecological Imagination*. Oxford: Oxford University Press.

2 Adam Smith as ecological economist

Leo Steeds

1. Introduction

To some, it might seem strange to find a chapter on Adam Smith within a volume on environment and ecology in the history of economic thought. Smith was not—and could not have been—an environmental or ecological thinker in a modern sense. Writing in the second half of the 18th century, his work significantly predated key scientific and cultural developments that inform environmental and ecological thought today, including the development of thermodynamics and ecological science and the birth of modern environmentalism. Moreover, the general consensus amongst historians of ecological economic thought is that Smith was a thinker who was either unaware of or ignored issues of environmental limits to economic progress, and it was only through subsequent developments in economics that these began to be recognised. This chapter challenges this interpretation of Smith's thought and the history of economics, making the case that Smith was, instead, deeply interested in human relations to the environment—in fact, in a way that goes well beyond many of his 19th-century (and indeed 20th-century) successors—and that he deserves to be included within the canon of ecological economics.

To date, most efforts to identify a canon of ecological economic thinkers have not devoted attention to Smith. Where he is mentioned, it is generally to set the 'real' ecological economists in relief by indicating a kind of economics that absolutely fails to take account of environmental issues. Martínez-Alier and Schlüpmann's classic text, for example, refers to Smith only in order to locate him as the starting point of a tradition of economic theory which 'does not pay attention (in principle) to the physical characteristics of commodities', but rather, is concerned solely with 'the pattern of quantities transacted and the accompanying prices' (1987, p. 157). Other surveys contain not a single mention of the putative founder of economics (Fragio, 2022). Instead, the first real awareness of environmental limits in the history of economics is frequently located in the 'discovery' of diminishing returns in agriculture in the work of Malthus and Ricardo in the early 19th century.

This pattern of either treating Smith as irrelevant or regarding his political economy as actively antithetical to an understanding of ecological issues is mirrored also within broader critical environmental scholarship. John Bellamy Foster, for

DOI: 10.4324/9781003375425-3

example, has contrasted the 'abstract' and 'simplistic' (2007) understanding of the nonhuman environment supposedly shared by Smith and other classical economists with the avowedly much richer and more nuanced account provided by Karl Marx and Friedrich Engels. Taking aim at the environmentally destructive, neoliberal ideology of which Smith is popularly taken as a figure-head, Naomi Klein has talked of 'slapping the invisible hand' (2014, p. 105). In a similar vein, but even more forcefully, Richard A. Smith has gone as far to denounce the supposedly 'eco-suicidal economics of Adam Smith' (2007). Such dismissive, if not actively hostile, takes on Smith's ecological credentials, however, appear to be based on a very limited engagement with his work and the problematic assumption that his thought can be aligned straightforwardly either with the 'classical' economics of Malthus, Ricardo and others or, alternatively, with neoliberalism such as it developed since the mid-20th century (Mirowski and Plehwe, 2009).

Somewhat surprisingly, even within the now vast specialist literature on the thinker, Smith's understanding of the environment has not been a topic of any sustained consideration (though some relevant reference points are mentioned later). By contrast, environmental historians have, for some time, regarded Smith as a notable contributor to the development of understandings of human-environment relations (Thomas, 1984; Worster, 1994), and the past two decades has seen growing attention paid to Smith's thought around the environment from intellectual historians. Margaret Schabas (2005) has emphasised the importance of ideas of 'nature' in Smith's work, and especially, his interest in contemporary natural history, botany and agricultural chemistry. Building on this, Frederic Jonsson (2010) has stressed the specificity of Smith's 'liberal' ecology and the way this contrasted the more interventionist environmental management demanded by Karl Linnaeus' botanical science and political economy. More recently, Nathaniel Wolloch (2020) has even argued that there exists a protean concept of 'natural capital' in Smith's work.

Here, I will pick up, in particular, on Jonsson's (2014, p. 53) suggestive but not fully elaborated comment that Smith's political economy 'looks surprisingly like a forerunner of ecological economics'. While Jonsson, nevertheless, maintains a fairly critical perspective, emphasising the limitations of Smith's ecological credentials, I want to make a more positive case for reading Smith as an ecological thinker, exploring some of the theoretical foundations on which his ecological thought rests. Elsewhere, I have made the argument that Smith's approach to political economy should be read as a kind of 'social ecology' (Steeds, 2022). The impetus of this chapter is very much the same, though here I engage more directly with some of the specific concerns within the (history of) ecological economics literature, specifically, around matter, energy and limits. In doing so—and in keeping with the aims of this volume—I adopt a mixed method, leaning towards rational reconstruction in order to bring out the links between Smith's thought and today's debates, whilst (being aware of the limitations of this approach) also paying attention to specific words, concepts and context.

I put forward two sets of claims. Firstly, I make two claims about the history of ecological economic thought: 1) that Smith *should* be regarded as a thinker in the canon of ecological economics; 2) that the ways in which he should be considered as an ecological thinker are not reducible to his credentials as a 'classical' econo-mist, and indeed, his work should be understood as grounded on significantly different theoretical foundations to the political economists of the early 19th century. Secondly, I make three claims about the nature of Smith's ecological thought: 1) he was a ho-listic thinker who grounded his political economy in an account of evolving human-environment relations and understood the economy as a subset of the environment; 2) even whilst this conceptual language was unavailable to him, he showed an awareness of the material and energetic foundations of economic processes and of biophysical limits and demonstrated a concern for sustainable resource use; 3) finally, and perhaps most controversially, his was what might be called an 'optimistic ecology' in the sense that he was hopeful about the capacity of humans to 'improve' the earth, although he saw this as increasingly conditional on the perfection of political systems.

The chapter is structured in four sections. The first looks at Smith's well-known anti-mercantilism, showing how this was, in fact, framed as an attempt to de-centre a myopic focus on money by stressing the materiality of trade and shifting focus towards a broader notion of 'wealth', conceived as access to resources. The sec-ond section suggests that Smith's arguments can be understood as founded on an account of the material and energetic foundations of the pre-industrial 'organic' economy, leading Smith to emphasise the centrality of agriculture in economic development. The third section shows how this approach was, in turn, grounded in a developmental account of human societies that focused on progressive changes in the 'mode of subsistence', with shifting regimes of property acting as the pri-mary mediation of human-environment relations. In light of this, the final section assesses the reasoning behind Smith's ecological optimism and the limitations that his theory implicitly placed on his conclusions.

2. Wealth beyond money: Smith's anti-mercantilist critique

Smith has often been read by historians of economics as a thinker of increasing returns (e.g. Negishi, 1985, chap. 2)—a reading which has undoubtedly influenced, in turn, historians of *ecological* economics. In this view, Smith emphasised the expanding riches that growing markets and division of labour would bring with-out taking into accounts either limits to this growth or its negative environmen-tal consequences. Histories of ecological economics therefore tend, in somewhat Whiggish fashion, to read a progression from Smith's ecological ignorance to the burgeoning ecological awareness of Malthus and Ricardo in the early 19th century, with their theories of *diminishing* returns in agriculture.

Such a reading is consistent with the view that Smith's economics represents or even inaugurated a tradition of economic thought that pays attention solely to 'the pattern of quantities transacted and the accompanying prices' (Martínez-Alier and Schlüpmann, 1987, p. 157). It is, after all—so the criticism goes—a myopic focus on monetary metrics that renders the ecological dimension of economic processes invisible. As a critique of much of subsequent economic thought, this may well be justified. But as a reading of Smith, it is misguided and, indeed, somewhat ironic, given that one of the central threads of *The Wealth of Nations* is a repudiation of what Smith termed the 'mercantile system' of political economy as a system that was, itself, too narrowly focused on money. Smith's 'system of natural liberty' was pitched as an alternative to this flawed mode of economic thinking.

Whilst his anti-mercantilism is well known, the character of Smith's opposition is seemingly less well understood. As he noted in the entire chapter devoted to the 'Principle of the commercial, or mercantile System',

> That wealth consists in money, or in gold and silver, is a popular notion which naturally arises from the double function of money, as the instrument of commerce, and as the measure of value.
> (A. Smith 2014 [1776], IV.i.1; hereafter *WN*)[1]

This was a grave error, in Smith's view. According to him, mercantilism (in which, rightly or wrongly, he included nearly all preceding thought and policy in Europe since the early modern period) had developed a fixation on the 'balance of trade'—that is, the need to create a trade surplus that ensured a net inflow of money into the country. According to this logic, the increased quantity of money in the country would give rise to investment and improvements in industry. For Smith, such arguments were 'sophistical' (*WN* IV.i.9) and their logic was precisely backwards. Rather, it was that the expansion of trade and industry would, by a mechanism of supply and demand, *cause* money to be drawn to a country. This, however, left the obvious question of how, then, trade and industry might be increased.

The way Smith constructed his anti-mercantilist critique is instructive, for the present purposes, on two levels. Firstly, Smith sought to provide some perspectives on mercantilist debates by interrogating the materiality of money, such as it was at the time, with international trade based around gold and silver. Much to the frustration of some readers, *The Wealth of Nations* thus contains extensive passages on the history of the mining of precious metals—most notably, in the infamously long 'Digression concerning the Variations in the Value of Silver during the Course of the Four last Centuries' (*WN* I.xi.e-m). The point he sought to make here is that the absolute price rises observed in recent centuries were purely a historical accident—a product of European colonialism—and not, as some of his mercantilist adversaries had argued, the cause of improvements in industry seen during the same period.

> The increase of the quantity of gold and silver in Europe, and the increase of its manufactures and agriculture, are two events which, though they have happened nearly about the same time, yet have arisen from very different causes, and have scarce any natural connection with one another.
> (*WN* I.xi.m.1)

Money, instead, for Smith, was merely a facet of circulation—the 'wheel' (*WN* II.ii.14), as he termed it, figuratively, that circulates goods.

The second, and more positive element of Smith's answer to mercantilism was to put forward a more systematic account of wealth. Unsurprisingly for a book titled, in full, *An Inquiry into the Nature and Causes of the Wealth of Nations*, Smith gave this careful consideration. In the work, he put forward a dualistic notion of wealth: at the level of individuals, this could be understood as access to the 'necessaries and conveniences of life' (*WN* I.intro.1); at the societal level, instead, wealth was understood to be equivalent to the 'annual produce of the land and labour of the society' (*WN* I.intro.9). It seems that, for Smith, these were mutually compatible, and indeed, complimentary ways of understanding the nature of wealth.

This is not to say that he did not pay attention to money or recognize its importance. On the contrary, *The Wealth of Nations* contains significant sections devoted to the topic, beyond the discussion of mining. Book I, chapter iv, for example, provides Smith's well-known (if not universally well-regarded)[2] account 'Of the Origin and Use of Money', which sites the origin of money in the need to overcome the problem of the unlikeliness of a double coincidence of wants—that is, that the goods that any two potential trading partners have available to exchange will be a sufficient match for their respective needs to allow a bilateral trade to take place. Book II, chapter ii, meanwhile, conducts a detailed analysis of contemporary banking practices, including the use of paper money and fractional reserve banking. The important point for the present purposes, however, is that the impetus of Smith's analysis, as a whole, is to move decisively *away* from a straightforward conflation of money with wealth by providing a more sociological perspective on the use of money.

Smith's commentary on price dynamics, then, is conducted with an eye to the nature of money as a material commodity and as a set of social practices and sits within a much more expansive account of the nature of wealth. The text famously opens with its commentary on labour. The very first words of the introduction read,

> THE annual labour of every nation is the fund which originally supplies it with all the necessaries and conveniences of life which it annually consumes, and which consist always, either in the immediate produce of that labour, or in what is purchased with that produce from other nations.
>
> (*WN* I.intro.1)

This emphasis on labour has led some historians of economics to read Smith as a thinker who pivoted economic thought away from land and towards labour (Heilbroner, 2000, p. 49), but this interpretation is misleading. Whilst it is true that, in comparison to the physiocrats (with whose work he was clearly familiar—see *WN* IV.ix), Smith shifted the focus from agricultural labour specifically to labour in general, land and agriculture nevertheless played a crucial role within his theoretical system as whole.

Smith was clear that the physiocrats erred to the extent that they viewed agriculture as the *sole* form of productive industry, but he nevertheless insisted that their theoretical system, 'with all its imperfections is, perhaps, the nearest approximation to the truth that has yet been published upon the subject of political œconomy' (*WN* IV.ix.38). As he elaborated,

> The industry of merchants, artificers, and manufacturers, though in its own nature altogether unproductive, yet contributes in this manner indirectly to

increase the produce of the land. It increases the productive powers of productive labour, by leaving it at liberty to confine itself to its proper employment, the cultivation of land; and the plough goes frequently the easier and the better by means of the labour of the man whose business is most remote from the plough.

(*WN* IV.ix.15)

The physiocrats main error, then, was failing to take into account the beneficial effects of an extended division of labour in a commercial society on agricultural productivity. Far from pivoting away from land, then, he continued to insist that

The land constitutes by far the greatest, the most important, and the most durable part of the wealth of every extensive country.

(*WN* I.xi.m.9)

Unsurprisingly, therefore, land and agriculture remain a central focus throughout the text.

3.   Matter and energy in the organic economy

How should we interpret Smith's views on the primacy of agriculture? The prevailing view amongst historians of economics has seemingly been a mixture of confusion and embarrassment. Samuel Hollander (2016 [1992], p. 175), for example, referred to Smith's commentary on agriculture as 'physiocratic residues which, fortunately, do not have serious consequences for Smithian applied economics'. Takashi Negishi (1985, p. 23), meanwhile, condemned Smith's arguments for the primacy of agriculture as 'not systematic, not persuasive; rather, they are ambiguous, confusing, and mutually inconsistent'.

Negishi was at least partially right: Smith was not especially systematic in the way he developed his arguments around agriculture. Perhaps seeking to add rhetorical weight to his case for the primacy of agriculture in economic development, he was seemingly at pains to include a range of somewhat disparate arguments. Appealing to psychology, for example, he suggested that individuals with a capital to invest will naturally favour investment in nearby land over more risky investments at a distance (such as the foreign carrying trade), embellishing this with additional arguments about 'the pleasures of a country life, the tranquillity of mind' (*WN* III.i.3) that owning land brings, even whilst he strongly criticized landlords elsewhere in the text (e.g. *WN* I.vi.8). From a societal perspective, he stressed that investments in land were the best way to secure mobile capitals, saying of mercantile capital that

No part of it can be said to belong to any particular country, till it has been spread as it were over the face of that country, either in buildings, or in the lasting improvement of lands.

(*WN* III.iv.24).

This line of reasoning, he further buttressed with a supposed historical example, suggesting that the improvement of land in ancient Roman times was the principle reason that the countries of Italy still continued to be 'among the most populous and best cultivated in Europe' (Ibid.).

All of these arguments, however, are only supplementary, I suggest, to Smith's most fundamental reason for assigning a central place to agriculture within his theoretical system. As economic historian Anthony Wrigley (2016, chap. 2) has argued, whilst Smith has often been taken as heralding a burgeoning industrial revolution, the dramatic energetic paradigm shift that this entailed—with the rise of the fossil fuel use—registers nowhere in Smith's work. This should, perhaps, hardly be surprising. As remarkably foresightful as Smith was in many respects in his analysis of the dynamics of the emerging market economy, steam power was still very much in its developmental phase during the years in which *The Wealth of Nations* was composed, with James Watt's condenser engine being released commercially only around the time of the publication of the book in 1776, so it is perhaps asking too much that Smith should have foreseen the profound transformations that steam power would entail. Rather, as Wrigley suggests, Smith's work is much more accurately read as a more-or-less convincing model of the pre-industrial 'organic economy'—one whose material and energetic limits were prescribed by the annual photosynthetic yield of the available land area. Agriculture was, thus, in a very real sense, the foundation on which all other forms of industry rested.

Though Smith had no access to the conceptual language of modern thermodynamics, it nevertheless seems clear that he had at least an intuitive understanding of these material and energetic foundations of economic processes. This is, in fact, I suggest, the basic reason—seemingly lost on many interpreters of Smith's work—that he spends so much of the text discussing the relationship between the town and country, especially in Books III and IV (notably the areas of the work most frequently dismissed or simply ignored by economists). For Smith, understanding the reasons that societies had established this kind of spatial division of labour and the relation between these contrasting geographical zones was foundational to a good understanding of political economy.

Smith's more substantial justification for the primacy of agriculture rests on two related fundamental arguments: one concerning its natural temporal priority in the development of societies and one concerning its conceptual priority as a site of human labour. Broadly, it might be helpful to say that these correspond respectively to material and energetic dimensions, even if this is perhaps only approximate. The first is laid out clearly in the opening chapter of Book III, 'Of the natural Progress of Opulence'. It is worth stressing that the emphasis for Smith is on the word 'natural' here—this is what form societal progress *should* take, absent human interventions to the contrary (whereas, in fact, the chapter serves to set up an extended discussion of the ways in which the nations of Europe have developed in an 'unnatural and retrograde order' [*WN* III.i.9]).

Smith opened this chapter with a very clear statement of the logic underpinning his reflections in the following two books:

> The great commerce of every civilized society, is that carried on between the inhabitants of the town and those of the country. It consists in the exchange of rude for manufactured produce. . . . The country supplies the town with the

means of subsistence, and the materials of manufacture. The town repays this supply by sending back a part of the manufactured produce to the inhabitants of the country. The town, in which there neither is nor can be any reproduction of substances, may very properly be said to gain its whole wealth and subsistence from the country.

(*WN* III.i., p. 1)

He went on to explain that this is not to overlook the fact that some towns have, at different times, obtained much of their subsistence not from their 'neighbourhood' but from 'very distant countries' (*WN* III.i., p. 2); however, he sees this—at his time at least—as the exception rather than the rule and as something that does not alter his fundamental point.

The key point here, for our purposes, is that Smith recognized that in towns there cannot be any 'reproduction of substances'. The use of the word 'substance' here is, itself, a clear indication of the fact that Smith is reasoning in material terms. The established spatial division of labour meant that towns were centres of commerce and manufacturing, whilst the raw materials for the goods produced and traded there—as well as the foodstuffs and other subsistence goods consumed by inhabitants—originated in the countryside. As he elaborated:

It is the surplus produce of the country only, or what is over and above the maintenance of the cultivators, that constitutes the subsistence of the town, which can therefore increase only with the increase of this surplus produce.

(*WN* III.i.2)

It is on this basis that Smith reasoned that

Had human institutions, therefore, never disturbed the natural course of things, the progressive wealth and increase of the towns would, in every political society, be consequential, and in proportion to the improvement and cultivation of the territory or country.

(*WN* III.i.4)

Agriculture, therefore, is naturally the first form of industry to develop as it is only on the basis of the prior accumulation of material surpluses here that other sectors can grow.

The second argument for the primacy of agriculture is related to this but is developed less systematically. The ideas are recapitulated in various ways, but the clearest statement appears just before the above passage, at the end of Smith's discussion of capital in Book II, where he stated that

In agriculture . . . nature labours along with man; and though her labour costs no expence, its produce has its value, as well as that of the most expensive workmen.

(*WN* II.v.12)

Today, the idea of nature 'labouring' along with man may seem somewhat quaint, and, indeed, even only 40 years later, Ricardo quoted this passage in his *Principles of Political Economy and Taxation*, seemingly mocking Smith on this point (2004 [1817], p. 76n). Yet, it played an important role within Smith's thought, grounding his arguments about the superior productivity of agricultural labour and, in turn, capital invested in agriculture.

As much as Ricardo, like many readers of Smith, seems not to have grasped the full significance of this within Smith's work, his comments are nevertheless instructive. Ricardo's point was to question why agriculture should be seen as uniquely productive in this sense.

> Does nature nothing for man in manufactures? Are the powers of wind and water, which move our machinery, and assist navigation, nothing? The pressure of the atmosphere and the elasticity of steam, which enable us to work the most stupendous engines—are they not the gifts of nature?
>
> (Ibid.)

The mentions of wind and water power notwithstanding, it is not difficult to detect here an important shift in perspective resulting from the recognition of the enormous potential of fossil fuels to transform human industry. Without, himself, being able to identify clearly the nature of this change, Ricardo's comments nevertheless help us today identify this shift in thought corresponding to an epochal shift in energy regime.

Smith's comments on how nature adds her labour to that of man in agriculture appear within his discussion of capital in Book II, in the concluding chapter which provides an analysis 'Of the different Employment of Capitals' (*WN* II.v), immediately after his assertion that '[n]o equal capital puts into motion a greater quantity of productive labour than that of the farmer' (*WN* II.v.12) and is offered as an explanation for this. Over the course of this chapter, Smith argued that there is a hierarchy of productivity in the employments in capital. Procuring raw materials is the most productive, followed by manufacturing, followed by transportation and commerce.

The integration of a theory of capital into his political economic analysis was one of the most novel and important features of Smith's text and is a key part of what justifies its reputation as a, if not *the*, founding text of modern economics. Yet the specificity of Smith's understanding of capital is often overlooked. Historians of economics have debated the extent to which Smith's is best understood as 'materialist' or a 'fundist' theory of capital (Hicks, 1974). According to this distinction, materialists were those who understood capital as a specific class of physical goods; fundists, by contrast, are those who stress that value is the essence of capital, the outward form of which is liable to change. But, in fact, Smith's understanding of capital was 'material' in a much more thoroughgoing sense that brings him closer to ecological economics.

Capital, or 'stock', as Smith often called it, is employed, maintained and must ultimately be replaced. But, again, here, he is clear about the foundational role of agriculture. In a passage in the chapter 'Of the Division of Stock' that seems to echo the *Tableau Économique* of Francois Quesnay, he stated that

> Land, mines, and fisheries, require all both a fixed and a circulating capital to cultivate them; and their produce replaces with a profit, not only those capitals, but all the others in the society. Thus the farmer annually replaces to the manufacturer the provisions which he had consumed and the materials which he had wrought up the year before; and the manufacturer replaces to the farmer the finished work which he had wasted and worn out in the same time.
>
> (*WN* II.i., p. 28)

Shortly after, he qualified this, however, suggesting that of land, mines and fisheries, it is land that is most important.

> Land even replaces, in part, at least, the capitals with which fisheries and mines are cultivated. It is the produce of land which draws the fish from the waters; and it is the produce of the surface of the earth which extracts the minerals from its bowels.
>
> (Ibid.)

Land, Smith recognized, therefore played a foundational role in all economic processes in the organic economy, supplying not only raw materials and energy used directly to produce goods but facilitating other primary production, and thus, underpinning all accumulation of capital.

4.   A developmental history of societies

Smith's analysis of the dynamics of a market society, therefore, was premised on an appreciation of the material and energetic centrality of agriculture within the functioning of the organic economy, and this alone would be grounds to reconsider his place within the canon of ecological economics. Yet, this far from exhausts the ways in which an understanding of the relationship between human societies and the environment registers in Smith's work.

There has been, for some time, within the specialist scholarship, a recognition of the importance in Smith's work of a stadial account of human societal development. An older tradition interpreting Smith's stadial theory as a precursor of that of Marx has now largely been rejected by a majority of specialists on the grounds that it implies a deterministic view of history that leaves no space for political agency (Salter, 1992). Today the role of the stadial theory in Smith's thought continues to be debated, though its significance is often downplayed (e.g., Paganelli, 2022). I suggest that, whilst Smith scholars have been right to reject deterministic readings of Smith, the dismissal of the Marxist interpretation has been too absolute. Nevertheless, this chapter is not the place to engage in detail with these debates, the content of which goes well beyond the scope of the concerns of this volume. Here, it is sufficient to say that, whilst rejecting implications of determinism, I nevertheless agree with the emphasis in the Marxist interpretation on the centrality of the stadial model within Smith's thought as a whole, and within his political economy in particular, and suggest that this crucial for grasping the environmental content of his work.

One problem for interpretation arises from the fact that, although Smith did lay out his stadial theory in significant detail, this was not done within *The Wealth of Nations*, but rather, in lectures that he gave whilst at the University of Glasgow in the 1760s and which have survived, fortunately, in the form of two sets of student notes discovered long after Smith's death—today published as the *Lectures on Jurisprudence* (Meek, Raphael and Stein, 2014 [1978]; hereafter *LJ*).[3] Here, Smith instructed his students that

> There are four distinct states which mankind passes through:—first, the Age of Hunters; second, the Age of Shepherds, third, the Age of Agriculture; and fourth, the Age of Commerce.
>
> (*LJ(A)*, i.27)

He proceeded to outline aspects of law and government that corresponded to these various 'modes of subsistence'.[4]

Although *The Wealth of Nations* lacks a systematic treatment of this theory, references to hunting, shepherding, agricultural and commercial societies abound throughout its pages, as does the language of stages and the broad *longue durée* developmental approach. Moreover, many of the reflections on property and government that appear within the *Lectures* are repeated and elaborated here (see, for example, Smith's account 'Of the Expences of the Sovereign or Commonwealth'— *WN* V.i). It seems, therefore, entirely appropriate to read the *Lectures* and *The Wealth of Nations* in continuity, with the former providing additional insights into the theoretical foundations of the latter.

Drawing on the natural law theories of Hugo Grotius, Samuel von Pufendorf and (especially, I suggest) John Locke (Steeds, 2023), Smith provided an account of evolving relations of property through the development of societies. Smith, however, went further than these other authors in detailing how particular institutions of property and government related to a given mode of subsistence. In keeping with other Scottish Enlightenment contemporaries, his investigation expanded well beyond the remit of purely jurisprudential investigation, taking on a much broader sociological character (Meek, 1971).

The significance for the present purposes of Smith's stadial theory is that, as I have argued elsewhere (Steeds, 2023), this can (and, indeed, should) be read as an account of shifting relationships between human societies and the nonhuman world. The most essential characteristic of hunting societies was their reliance on what Smith termed the 'spontaneous productions of the earth' (*WN* II.iii.3). These were societies in which 'there is scarce any property, or at least none that exceeds the value of two or three days labour' (*WN* V.i.b.2). This changed in the shepherding phase, the definitive feature of which was the development of property rights over domesticated animals. This was, for Smith, a crucial development, since extended property in live animals—as opposed to the natural property granted in the carcass of a hunted wild animal —necessitated, for the first time, a 'regular administration of justice' (WN V.i.b.2), and thus, saw the instantiation of permanent forms of government. From a jurisprudential point of view, this shift from a hunting to a pastoral mode of subsistence constituted 'the greatest in the progression of society, for by it the notion of property is extended beyond possession, to which it is in the former state confined' (*LJ(A)* ii.97).

The crucial factor in this stadial development was the growth of population (C. Smith, 2020, p. 91). Smith comments on this a number of times within *The Wealth of Nations*; for example, in Book V, where, discussing the development of modern armies, he noted:

> An army of hunters can seldom exceed two or three hundred men. The precarious subsistence which the chace affords could seldom allow a greater number to keep together for any considerable time. An army of shepherds, on the contrary, may sometimes amount to two or three hundred thousand.
>
> (*WN* V.i.a.5)

Elsewhere, he emphasised, again, that

> the difference is very great between the number of shepherds and that of hunters whom the same extent of equally fertile territory can maintain.
>
> (*WN* IV.vii.c.100)

Such comments make clear the extent to which Smith appreciated that relationships between humans and the environment were crucially mediated by social institutions. The development of social institutions was thus inextricably and fundamentally linked to the expansion of population.

The essential reason for the capacity of shepherding societies to sustain much greater populations was their enhanced command over nonhuman life. As Smith noted, in a shepherding society,

> The chase [i.e. hunting] can no longer be depended on for the support of any one. All the animalls fit for the support of man are in a great measure appropriated.
>
> (*LJ(A)*, iv.21)

Shepherding societies were, thus, no longer solely dependent on the animals 'spontaneously' provided by nature. Nevertheless, such societies were limited by the fact that a shepherd 'should frequently change his situation, or at least the place of his pasturing, to find pasture for his cattle' (LJ(A) i.48–49).

In Smith's schema, the instantiation of agriculture therefore sees another key shift in the relations between humans, instantiating fixed habitation and extending human command over the environment beyond animals to plants. As he notes,

> The most important operations of agriculture seem intended, not so much to increase, though they do that too, as to direct the fertility of nature towards the production of the plants most profitable to man.
>
> (*WN* II.v.12)

Whereas shepherding societies were still reliant on undirected plant growth, agriculture constituted a much more extensive form of command over the earth's natural fertility. Exercising this command, 'the labourers and labouring cattle' (Ibid.) were able to produce well in excess of their own subsistence, allowing the further extension of a division of labour, as expressed, in particular, in the separation of town and country.

Smith was well aware that not only did the development of agriculture have important implications for the structure of human societies; it also, in turn, implied a profound transformation of the environment. He conjectured that,

> In its rude beginnings the greater part of every country is covered with wood. . . . As agriculture advances, the woods are partly cleared by the progress of tillage, and partly go to decay in consequence of the increased number of cattle. . . . [These], when allowed to wander through the woods, though they do not destroy the old trees, hinder any young ones from coming up, so that in the course of a century or two the whole forest goes to ruin.
>
> (*WN* I.xi.c.16)

Such comments, again, reflect Smith's deep concern with population dynamics and the complex interactions between humans and the environment.

As we see here, it was not only human population that interested Smith, though comments on this are scattered throughout *The Wealth of Nations*, but also animal populations. Interestingly, in an aspect of the work that normally receives very little attention, Smith actually tries to use historical price records as a way of empirically verifying patterns of environmental change. The following passage is worth quoting at length, showing how Smith uses the logic of supply and demand to try and ascertain information about the state of agricultural development at a given time.

> But though the low money price either of goods in general, or of corn in particular, be no proof of the poverty or barbarism of the times, the low money price of some particular sorts of goods, such as cattle, poultry, game of all kinds, &c. in proportion to that of corn, is a most decisive one. It clearly demonstrates, first, their great abundance in proportion to that of corn, and consequently the great extent of the land which they occupied in proportion to what was occupied by corn; and, secondly, the low value of this land in proportion to that of corn land, and consequently the uncultivated and unimproved state of the far greater part of the lands of the country. It clearly demonstrates that the stock and population of the country did not bear the same proportion to the extent of its territory, which they commonly do in civilized countries, and that society was at that time, and in that country, but in its infancy.
>
> (*WN* I.xi.m.4)

Elsewhere, Smith pays attention to the value of hides in proportion to meat (*WN* I.xi.l.1) and the prices of game, wild fowl and birds of passage (*WN* I.xi.k.1). These reflections are developed most systematically in the chapter on rent (*WN* I.xi), but Smith refers back to them throughout the work (e.g., *WN* IV.vii.b.29).

Whilst *The Wealth of Nations* makes many references to these first three stages of societal development, it is undoubtedly the fourth 'commercial' stage that is the work's main focus. By commercial society—a concept that may indeed have been his own invention (Pauchant, 2017)—Smith referred not to societies based primarily around international trade, but rather, to what we might today call the 'market economy'. Unlike previous stages, the emergence of commercial society did not imply directly an enhanced of command over the nonhuman world through an expansion of property relations. As we have seen previously, agriculture, in Smith's theoretical apparatus, remained the foundation of all forms of trade. Nevertheless, he did think that the growth of commerce had profound implications for the direction of nature's fertility, and it was on this assessment that his cautious optimism about the prospects of commercial society was founded.

5.   Smith's optimistic ecology

At this point, therefore, it is possible to situate Smith's comments on the economic primacy of agriculture within the much broader account of the development of societies contained within his stadial theory. It is in this sense that we can interpret Jonsson's (2014, p. 53) comment that 'Smith's political economy looks surprisingly like a forerunner of ecological economics, premised on the recognition that the economy formed a subset of the environment'. In fact, Smith has no concept of *the* economy, as such, which is, in any case, a much later invention (Tribe, 2015). But his account of what we would now term economic processes fits within the broader sociological/anthropological understanding of human societies, which is itself, I have suggested, grounded in an account of evolving human-environment relations.[5]

Whilst acknowledging the way that Smith's account of economic processes fitted within an understanding of human relations to the environment, Jonsson's work nevertheless casts doubt on Smith's ecological credentials, emphasising how his work can be read as opposed both to the model of environmental management by enlightened expertise advocated by Karl Linnaeus and his disciples (Jonsson, 2010) and to a nascent conservation movement in his native Scotland (Jonsson, 2014). On this reading, in both cases, Smith's reply was to emphasise ideas of natural balance, with Jonsson suggesting that Smith's political economy implied a 'quasi-providential fit between markets and nature' (Jonsson, 2010, p. 1362). As we have seen, ideas of natural balance play an important role in Smith's stadial theory and, to the extent that he saw the emergence of commercial societies as itself a natural part of human progress, such reasoning underpinned his famous advocacy of free trade and laissez faire. But focusing narrowly on Smith's conclusions gives insufficient credit both to the reasoning underpinning these, which hinged on Smith's perception of environmental change in the burgeoning commercial society of his day, and to the limitations that his political economic theory implied to his ecological optimism.

As I have argued elsewhere (Steeds, 2022), Smith's cautious optimism about the prospects for commercial society hinged on a model of land use change that, besides a brief flurry of interest amongst geographers in the 1970s (Watson, 1976; Grigg, 1979), has received remarkably little commentary. In Smith's stadial history, agriculture appeared as an important shift in subsistence relations, signifying a dramatic extension of human command over the environment. Yet, Smith was well aware that, in practice, individuals in the feudal societies of Europe—which he took as the archetypical expression of the agricultural phase of development— were not, in fact, able to cater for the entirety of their needs through cultivation. He understood that, for most individuals in such societies, tenancy arrangements were such that allocations of cultivable land for a family to grow crops were crucially supplemented by access to surrounding 'wastes'—uncultivated areas of wood or grassland that would provide utilities such as timber, firewood and space to graze animals (Thompson, 1982 [1963]). The transition from such subsistence dwelling to marketised production, with the gradual emergence of commercial societies, implied an important shift in the mechanism of societal subsistence, one which involved, in turn, a further transformation of the environment.

He observed that the poorest occupiers of land could often maintain 'a few poultry, or a sow and a few pigs' (*WN* I.xi.k.10) at minimal expense.

> The little offals of their own table . . . supply those animals with a part of their food, and they find the rest in the neighbouring fields without doing any sensible damage to any body.
>
> (Ibid.)

Smith theorised that the decline of these traditional forms of land use meant that the availability of goods that had been derived from such uncultivated areas would also decline. According to the logic of supply and demand, this would increase their market price, and thus, make it sufficiently profitable for landowners to devote their land to previously unprofitable uses such as the pasturing of cattle (*WN* I.xi.k.3) or the production of timber (*WN* I.xi.c.16) that would previously have been supplied by wastes. Thus, progressively, ever more goods would come to be provided not by the spontaneity of nature but by the allocation of specific plots to their cultivation as commodities.

One good, above all, however, held special interest for Smith. With the decline of wastes, he thought that the price of 'butcher's-meat' had risen sufficiently to justify, for the first time, the dedication of plots of land to the pasturing of cattle (*WN* I.xi.b.13). The significance of this lay in an issue that demonstrates Smith's attention to contemporary agricultural chemistry and farming practices. Cultivated soil, he suggested, could become 'entirely exhausted' (*WN* I.xi.k.3) after only a few years without proper fertilisation. Traditional fertilisation practices relied on the use of dung from cattle kept for tillage and on the use of 'night soils' from surrounding towns. But Smith judged these to be woefully insufficient, representing a key limiting factor not only on the development of agriculture but—by extension—the progress of industry, in general. But keeping cattle in barns or directly on pasture made it possible to harvest the power of their manure to replenish soils (Ibid.). The decline of wastes and the accompanying rise in beef prices therefore provided a mechanism for the generalisation of good soil fertility practices throughout the country as a whole. As empirical evidence of this, Smith used the example of the rapid development of Scotland after the union with England in 1707. In Smith's analysis, the single most decisive factor in this development had been the extension in the market for cattle and the accompanying rise in prices, which had been 'the principal cause of the improvement of the low country' (Ibid.).

As much as Smith thought about such issues of land use, soil fertility and (implicitly, at least) the material and energetic foundations of economic processes, he did not share modern environmentalism's conservationist impulse. On the contrary, apart from notable exceptions, human transformation of the environment, for the most part, appeared to Smith unambiguously as an improvement of the natural order. In leaning on this notion of 'improvement', Smith's thought drew on the by then well-established English discourse on agricultural improvement (Linklater, 2014) as well as the broader interest amongst Enlightenment elites in improving the natural order (Drayton, 2000). In keeping with this, Smith talks both of technical improvements in agriculture and, more broadly, of conversion of wastes to cultivated land as a form of improvement. The great promise of commercial society, then, was that it offered a path towards the 'compleat improvement and cultivation of the country', which Smith said, with conviction, was 'most certainly . . . the greatest of all publick advantages' (*WN* I.xi.k.12).

This positive assessment fitted with the tenor of his stadial theory, which emphasised the tendency of human societies to adapt—and adapt to—their environment in a way that would tend towards an equilibrium at a given stage of development. As I have argued elsewhere (Steeds, 2023), to the extent that he emphasised the capacity of human societies to overcome environmental limits through technological and socio-political innovation, Smith can be considered a thinker of abundance. This does not mean, however, that he thought in terms of endless growth. On the contrary, Smith was well aware that there existed ultimate limits to growth.

> the annual produce of the land and labour of the country, how great soever, can never be infinite, but must have certain limits.
>
> (*WN* II.iii.3)

The conversion of the 'unimproved wilds' (*WN* I.xi.b.6) that accompanied the progress of commercial society, thus, had its endpoint in 'compleat improvement', at which point—unlike modern growth theorists—Smith concluded that the nation would be 'fully peopled' (*WN* I.ix.14) and a 'stationary state' reached (*WN* I.viii.43).

Whilst, as Jonsson (2014, p. 53) notes, Smith's theory implied 'that advanced economies were subject to diminishing returns and would eventually settle into a mature form close to the ecological limits of production', this did not translate into an emphasis on scarcity in the same way as it did in the political economy of Malthus and Ricardo a generation later. In keeping with the approach of his stadial theory, Smith discussed limits in conditional terms, not simply as immutable facts of nature but as a reflection of human institutions and the way in which these mediated societal relations to the environment. In a passage in which he discusses China, for example, Smith suggests that Marco Polo's records of 1275 show that the country had,

> perhaps, even long before his time, acquired that full complement of riches which the nature of its laws and institutions permits it to acquire.
>
> (*WN* I.viii.24)

Carrying capacity, then, was, ultimately, dependent not simply on a fixed ratio between individuals and land area but on prevailing socio-political institutions.

This brings us to our final point—the role of politics and policy. Whilst the stadial theory was presented as an account of the 'natural' path of societal development, Smith was very clear on the crucial role of politics and policy. Indeed, having set up his account 'Of the Natural Progress of Opulence' in chapter one of Book III, nearly the entirety of the rest of Books III and IV were dedicated to explaining how and why, in fact, European societies since the fall of Rome had developed in an 'unnatural and retrograde order' (*WN* III.i.9). The focus of this discussion is how various factors since Rome's decline had contributed to holding back the development of agriculture across the continent, thus slowing the progress of wealth, in general. Whilst the initial explanation relating to the lack of security in the times of 'feudal anarchy' (*WN* III.ii.7) could be written off as a historical accident, Smith was clear that, since the development of modern states, this had been a systematic failure brought about by the wrong thinking and political capture of the 'mercantile system'.

Clearly, then, for Smith, it was not a given that advanced societies should follow the natural path of societal development. His own policy recommendations revolved around removing many of the measures that had served to artificially favour certain kinds of industry over others, on the basis that only such a 'system of natural liberty' would allow the proper division of societal labour to be established. But the extent to which Smith believed that the monopolies that beset existing commercial societies—both old, in the form of the great landed estates (*WN* III.ii.7), and new, in the form of the joint stock companies that controlled much colonial commerce (*WN* V.iii.91)—could be overcome remains unclear. Furthermore, to align the interests of producers and the public would require a perfected legal framing of production—one to which *The Wealth of Nations* offered a guide. Smith's theory implied, then, that a natural balance between societies and the earth would only be realised when these political barriers had been overcome.

6. Conclusion: Smith as ecological thinker

This chapter has put forward a set of claims both about the history of ecological economics and about the ecological content of Smith's thought. I hope, here, to have gone some way to making, even if only in an initial form, a case for

Smith's place in the canon of ecological economics. As I have tried to show, contrary to what some of his environmentalist critics have claimed, Smith's political economy was, in fact, deeply opposed to a myopic focus on money, which was, in his view, the great theoretical failure of the mercantilist system. Instead, Smith founded his political economic theory on a much broader view of wealth as individuals' access to goods and the annual produce of the land and labour. In doing so, he made a case for the foundational role of agriculture in all economic processes, apparently grasping the material and energetic foundations of the pre-industrial organic economy, even whilst he lacked the conceptual vocabulary to articulate this explicitly. His account of modern commerce dovetailed with an account of human societal evolution from hunter-gatherer groups to modern market societies, which paid careful attention to the shifting human-environment relations that this entailed.

These features of his work, I suggest, amply warrant his inclusion within the history of ecological economics. Doing so, however, does somewhat complicate what might be oversimplistic narratives about the progressive discovery of ecological issues in economic thought. Though there was not space here to develop these thoughts in detail, I hope to have indicated, to some extent, the distance of Smith from the 'classical' economics of the early 19th century. Future work could expand further on his relation to these thinkers as well as the connections between Smith and Marx, whose reliance on stadial history and increasingly acknowledged ecological concern make him an obvious point of comparison. Moreover, whilst Smith's focus on the pre-industrial organic economy and failure to recognise the negative environmental externalities associated with economic development might seem to limit his usefulness, his holistic approach which ties in environmental, economic and socio-political analysis (amongst the many other areas that the broader scope of his work touches on) might remain instructive in today's intellectual landscape of disciplinary fragmentation, and thus, repay the attention of ecological economists.

Notes

1 References to *The Wealth of Nations* follow the established referencing format which allows for the use of differing editions. They take the following format: [book].[chapter]. [section (if applicable)].[paragraph].
2 The account of the origins of money in the inefficiency of a barter economy has been accepted by many economists, though it has largely been rejected by economic anthropologists (Nelms and Maurer, 2014).
3 References to Smith's *Lectures on Jurisprudence* again follow the established referencing format: [section].[paragraph].
4 The exact phrase 'mode of subsistence' does not appear directly within *The Wealth of Nations*, or indeed, within the *Lectures*, though Smith regularly uses the word 'subsistence' alone. It was, nevertheless, the term in currency amongst the thinkers of the Scottish Enlightenment (see Berry, 1997, chap. 5).
5 On Smith as an evolutionary thinker, see Maria Pia Paganelli (2018), though the emphasis here is more on socio-political environment, rather than the nonhuman environment, which is my focus.

Bibliography

Berry, C. (1997) *The Social Theory of the Scottish Enlightenment. The Social Theory of the Scottish Enlightenment.* Edinburgh: Edinburgh University Press.

Drayton, R. H. (2000) *Nature's Government: Science, Imperial Britain, and the 'Improvement' of the World.* New Haven, CT: Yale University Press.

Foster, J. B. (2007) 'Earth', *Historical Materialism*, 15 (3): 255–262.

Fragio, A. (2022) *Historical Epistemology of Ecological Economics: Essays on the Styles of Economic Reasoning.* Contributions to Economics. Cham: Springer International Publishing.

Grigg, D. (1979) 'Sir James Steuart and Land Use Theory: A Note', *Scottish Geographical Magazine*, 95 (2): 108–110.

Heilbroner, R. L. (2000) *The Worldly Philosophers: The Lives, Times, and Ideas of the Great Economics Thinkers.* London: Penguin Books.

Hicks, J. (1974) 'Capital Controversies: Ancient and Modern', *The American Economic Review*, 64 (2): 307–316.

Hollander, S. (2016 [1992]) *Classical Economics.* Toronto: University of Toronto Press.

Jonsson, F. A. (2010) 'Rival Ecologies of Global Commerce: Adam Smith and the Natural Historians', *The American Historical Review*, 115 (5): 1342–1363.

Jonsson, F. A. (2014) 'Adam Smith in the Forest', in S. B. Hecht, K. D. Morrison and C. Padoch (eds.), *The Social Lives of Forests: Past, Present, and Future of Woodland Resurgence*, pp. 45–54. Chicago: University of Chicago Press.

Klein, N. (2014) *This Changes Everything: Capitalism vs. the Climate.* Toronto, Canada: Random House.

Linklater, A. (2014) *Owning the Earth: The Transforming History of Land Ownership.* London: Bloomsbury.

Martínez-Alier, J., and Schlüpmann, K. (1987) *Ecological Economics: Energy, Environment and Society.* Oxford: Basil Blackwell.

Meek, R L. (1971) 'Smith, Turgot, and the "Four Stages" Theory', *History of Political Economy*, 3 (1): 9–27.

Meek, R. L., Raphael, D. D., and Stein, P. (eds.) (2014 [1978]) *The Glasgow Edition of the Works and Correspondence of Adam Smith. Vol. 5: Lectures on Jurisprudence.* Oxford: Oxford University Press.

Mirowski, P., and Plehwe, D. (2009) *The Road from Mont Pelerin: The Making of the Neoliberal Thought Collective.* Cambridge, MA: Harvard University Press.

Negishi, T. (1985) *Economic Theories in a Non-Walrasian Tradition.* 1st ed. Cambridge: Cambridge University Press.

Nelms, T. C., and Maurer, B. (2014) 'Materiality, Symbol, and Complexity in the Anthropology of Money', in E. Bijleveld and H. Aarts (eds.), *The Psychological Science of Money*, pp. 37–70. New York: Springer.

Paganelli, M. P. (2018) 'Adam Smith on the Future of Experimental Evolution and Economics', *Journal of Bioeconomics*, 20 (1): 23–28.

Paganelli, M. P. (2022) 'Adam Smith and Economic Development in Theory and Practice: A Rejection of the Stadial Model?', *Journal of the History of Economic Thought*, 44 (1): 95–104.

Pauchant, T. C. (2017) 'Adam Smith's Four-Stages Theory of Socio-Cultural Evolution', in F. Forman (ed.), *The Adam Smith Review*. Vol. 9, pp. 49–74. London: Routledge.

Ricardo, D. (2004 [1817]) *The Works and Correspondence of David Ricardo, Vol. 1: On the Principles of Political Economy and Taxation.* Edited by Piero Sraffa and Maurice Dobb. Indianapolis, IN: Liberty Fund.

Salter, J. (1992) 'Adam Smith on Feudalism, Commerce and Slavery', *History of Political Thought*, 13 (2): 219–241.

Schabas, M. (2005) *The Natural Origins of Economics.* Chicago: University of Chicago Press.

Smith, A. (2014 [1776]) *The Glasgow Edition of the Works and Correspondence of Adam Smith. Vol. 2: An Inquiry into the Nature and Causes of the Wealth of Nations*. Edited by William B. Todd. Oxford: Oxford University Press.

Smith, C. (2020) *Adam Smith*. Cambridge: Polity.

Smith, R. A. (2007) 'The Eco-Suicidal Economics of Adam Smith', *Capitalism Nature Socialism*, 18 (2): 22–43.

Steeds, L. (2022) 'The Social Ecology of Adam Smith: Reconsidering the Intellectual Foundations of Political Economy', *New Political Economy*, 27 (1): 132–145.

Steeds, L. (2023) 'On Land, Life, and Labour: Abundance and Scarcity in Locke, Smith, and Ricardo', *Constellations*: 1–15.

Thomas, K. (1984) *Man and the Natural World: Changing Attitudes in England 1500–1800*. Harmondsworth: Penguin Books.

Thompson, E. P. (1982 [1963]) *The Making of the English Working Class*. Harmondsworth: Penguin Books.

Tribe, K. (2015) *The Economy of the Word: Language, History, and Economics*. New York: Oxford University Press.

Watson, J. W. (1976) 'Land Use and Adam Smith: A Bicentennial Note', *Scottish Geographical Magazine*, 92 (2): 129–134.

Wolloch, N. (2020) 'Adam Smith and the Concept of Natural Capital', *Ecosystem Services*, 43 (June): 101097.

Worster, D. (1994) *Nature's Economy: A History of Ecological Ideas*. 2nd ed. Cambridge: Cambridge University Press.

Wrigley, E. A. (2016) *The Path to Sustained Growth: England's Transition from an Organic Economy to an Industrial Revolution*. Cambridge: Cambridge University Press.

3 On the accommodation of the ecological question in the Sraffian tradition

Chandni Dwarkasing

1. Introduction

The Physiocrats and, in particular, Francois Quesnay's *tableau économique* are often designated as common sources of influence for the classical economist Pierro Sraffa and Ecological Economics. This is particularly apparent in earlier contributions in the field of Ecological Economics which argued that Piero Sraffa's physical and reproductive characterisation of the economy represent a suitable foundation for the joint analyses of the economic surplus, ecological and biophysical processes. Over the years, this assumed compatibility has resulted in various contributions that build on Sraffa's seminal microeconomic framework based on relative prices, the exogenous determination of one or more distributional variables and long-period positions. This chapter presents a brief discussion of the Physiocrats and their impact on both the Sraffian tradition and ecological economics. This is followed by a discussion of intensive and extensive land-rents in which we argue that the standard Sraffian framework already incorporates a narrow treatment of agro-ecological processes. The main aim of this chapter is to present the reader with a practical review of scholarly works that have extended the scope of Sraffa's framework from an ecological perspective. It should be noted that this review is limited to *microeconomic* analyses in the Sraffian tradition and that comprehensive algebraic and technical details are disregarded. Instead, the focus lies with an exposition of each contribution's originality with respect to the relation between ecological issues and surplus distribution.

2. The Physiocrats as a common denominator in Sraffa and Ecological Economics

Physiocracy is a school of economic thought spearheaded by François Quesnay and his peers in mid-18th century France (Vaggi and Groenewegen, 2002). At that time, the bulk of French agriculture was feudally organised and characterised by regular famines and population declines (Serrano and Mazat, 2017, p. 82; Vaggi and Groenewegen, 2002, p. 58). Against the backdrop of an under-performing economy, the inquiries of Quesnay sought to understand the determinants of a nation's wealth in terms of capital accumulation and economic growth (Schachter, 1991). This outlook stood in stark contrast to the mercantilist treatment of wealth

DOI: 10.4324/9781003375425-4

in terms of coinage or precious metals acquired through trade (Magnusson, 2015, pp. 2–3).

Quesnay's analytical treatment of economic growth was demonstrated in *Tableau Économique*, which was first published in 1758 (Quesnay, 2014). The economic model presented in the first version of *Tableau Économique* can be summarised as follows (Eltis, 2000; Kurz, 1980, 1998; Vaggi, 1987, p. 21):

- Production is treated as a circular flow where the surplus represents the difference between the amount of goods produced and the amount of goods used up in production (inputs).
- Agricultural techniques vary according to their effectiveness in the production of a surplus (*produit net*).
- The inputs for agricultural production are seed and farmer's subsistence in terms of the agricultural product. This allows for the measurement of both inputs and surplus in physical terms which are translated to monetary values using fixed and constant prices.
- The effective demand for output in the economy depends on the expenditure of the aforementioned surplus by landlords, where the distribution of demand across sectors determines their relative size.
- The surplus of an economy strictly arises from the agricultural sector, which translates to the dependency of economic growth on agricultural growth.

Quesnay's analytical description of the economy in physical terms and the accentuation of agriculture as a fundamental sector in *Tableau Économique* is often highlighted by ecological economists as a predecessor of the biophysical approach outlined by Nicholas Georgescu-Roegen (Christensen, 1989, p. 19). Readers familiar with field of Ecological Economics will know that the discipline was founded in the late 1980s and out of discontent with the neglect of biophysical constraints by orthodox economists (Beder, 2011; Van den Bergh, 2001; Gowdy and Erickson, 2005; Venkatachalam, 2007). The consideration of biophysical constraints by ecological economists had been largely inspired by Georgescu-Roegen's treatment of economic production as the transformation of low-entropy into high-entropy thermodynamic quantities (Georgescu-Roegen, 1971, 1976).

As such, physiocratic theory and the classical production theories it inspired represent 'a body of theory that provides a framework for an explicit development of the interdependence between materials and energy and the technologies of material and energy conversion' (Christensen, 2001, p. 29). Physiocrats were, arguably, the first biophysical economists in the modern era, since Quesnay's *Tableau Économique* is one of the first analytical representations of an economy that relies on natural resources (Cleveland, 1999; Melgar-Melgar and Hall, 2020; Sherwood, Carbajales-Dale and Haney, 2020). This argument is reiterated by Dale (2021), who highlights how various scholars treat Physiocrats as the ancestors of today's ecological economists.

This importance of nature is apparent in Quesnay's writings on *natural laws*, which determined crucial parameters in the agricultural sector—e.g., rainfall and soil fertility. Following Stokes (1993), Physiocrats were of the conviction that an accurate deduction of economic behaviour dictated by these *natural laws* would safeguard social welfare through the reproduction of the natural environment that guaranteed the circulation of wealth (Stokes, 1993, pp. 17–24). By contrast, the introduction of positive laws that went against *natural laws* would serve to corrupt the circular flow of a nation's wealth (Stokes, 1993, p. 19). In a certain sense, Physiocrats treated the economy as an integral part of nature, which is similar to the treatment of the economy as an open system that is embedded within a closed-system biosphere (Common and Stagl, 2005, p. 2; Daly and Farley, 2011, p. 15).

Prior to this reappraisal by ecological economists, however, Quesnay's *Tableau Économique* influenced the works of Smith, Ricardo and Marx. Even if the resulting contributions differed, the assumption on the agricultural sector being the sole sector capable of producing a surplus was, equally, abandoned (Vaggi, 1987, p. 16). Unlike Smith, Ricardo and Marx, who discarded the analytical treatment of an economy in physical terms (Gehrke and Kurz, 1995), Sraffa retained this treatment along with the concept of surplus product.

According to Kurz (1998), Sraffa contended that physiocratic costs represented physical and real costs, which, in turn, served as 'an appropriate starting point of a probing into the problem of value and distribution' (Kurz, 1998, p. 442). Part of Sraffa's critique of marginalism regarded the latter's treatment of wages as an instrument that incentivises workers to perform labour. Instead, Sraffa drew on the physiocratic treatment of wages as the necessary and advanced subsistence that enables workers to perform labour in the first place (Kurz and Salvadori, 2005). In addition, Sraffa's treatment of the surplus product reflected altered socio-economic circumstances. This meant the introduction of a capitalist class alongside landowners and the subsequent division of the surplus product amongst each (Kurz, 1998, p. 444). Ultimately, Kurz contends that Sraffa's initial intuition on the formulation of a consistent solution to value and distribution relied on data which was exclusively found in the approach of Physiocrats; namely, the system of production in use and the real wage rate in physical terms. This intuition allowed Sraffa to further study the impact of an increase or decrease of the real wage on the profit rate and relative prices (Kurz, 1998, p. 445).

Alongside the economic surplus and assessment of an economy in terms of physical quantities, Sraffa's treatment of the economic system as a circular flow of production and consumption is also said to originate in Quesnay's *Tableau Économique*. Hence, Sraffa's circular treatment of economic reproduction, where the output from one production period is considered as an input in the following production period, stood in contrast to the marginalist conception of production as a one-directional progression from factors of production to final goods via numerous intermediate goods (Bortis, 2002; Kurz and Salvadori, 2005).

The aim of this section was to accentuate the physiocratic school of thought, and Quesnay's contribution in particular, as a common denominator in both Ecological Economics and the Sraffa's analytical method. Broadly speaking, Ecological Economics lauds the physiocratic approach to economics for the centrality of agriculture, and therefore, the economy's material and biophysical basis, which is regenerated as economic production takes place. Instead, Sraffa's approach to production theory builds upon the physiocratic conception of an economic surplus, production as a circular flow, the assessment of costs in terms of physical quantities and wages as labour-enabling subsistence for workers. Given this shared predilection, successive integrations of ecological and biophysical processes in Sraffian frameworks comes as no surprise. Much like the Physiocrats, however, Sraffa's consideration of ecological processes in the *Production of Commodities by Means of Commodities* is limited to the sphere of agriculture and the distribution of a physical surplus across wages, profits and land-rents. A brief exposition of Sraffa's agro-ecological considerations is presented in the following section.

3.   Sraffa and the agro-ecological question: theories of intensive and extensive rent

In his theory of rent, Sraffa treats land as a special type of non-basic commodity[1] that enters the production process of agricultural commodities. While he argued that the scarcity of land enabled land owners to acquire a rent (Sraffa, 1960, p. 88), scarcity is not a given characteristic but strictly related to increases in the demand for the commodity land produces (Kurz and Salvadori, 1995, p. 277). As such, the discussion of agricultural cultivation in Chapter 11 of *Production of Commodities by Means of Commodities* concerns the impact of increased demand on the utilisation of land and the subsequent distribution of the economic surplus across wages, profits and land-rents. In the same chapter, Sraffa discusses two types of land-rent in the presence of land scarcity: extensive and intensive rent, and each of them represent a reinterpretation of David Ricardo's classical theory of rent found in *On the Principles of Political Economy and Taxation* (Gibson, 1984, p. 131; Kurz and Salvadori, 1995, pp. 305–311).

Extensive rent assumes the production of a single agricultural commodity on a fixed quantity of land plots which vary in quality—i.e., due to soil fertility levels. Because of this variation, each plot of land is subject to a different production technique (Sraffa, 1960, p. 88). Hence, assuming that the production of corn requires capital (corn seed), labour and land as inputs, the variation in quality implies a different set of technical coefficients for each plot of land. Plots of the highest quality (most productive or cheapest in terms of input costs) are cultivated first while lower quality plots will only be cultivated as the demand for corn increases.[2] Plots which are not fully cultivated, but nevertheless in use, are referred to as marginal lands while fully cultivated plots are referred to as intra-marginal (Kurz, 1978; Kurz and Salvadori, 1995, p. 284). Finally, competition amongst landlords ensures that only intra-marginal lands yield a positive rent for land owners (Kurz and Salvadori, 1995, p. 279). In other words, extensive rent arises as marginal lands become fully cultivated and therefore intra-marginal.

Intensive rent assumes the production of a single agricultural commodity on a fixed quantity *and* quality of land plots. In this case, different production techniques can co-exist side by side on different parts of the same plot of land (Sraffa, 1960, p. 90). Here, the crucial assumption is that the technique which is subject to the highest yield per acre of land is simultaneously the most cost-intensive where costs include the means of production, profits and wages (Kurz, 1978, pp. 27–28). In this case, competition ensures that the least costly and least productive technique, in terms of yield per acre of land, is utilised first. As long as the demand for corn can be satisfied through the application of the cost-minimising technique, rent is absent. Hence, intensive rent only appears when the cost-minimising technique can no longer meet demand and a secondary, more costly and productive technique is introduced alongside the first.

According to Kurz (1978), Sraffa's rent theory distinguishes itself from other classical rent theories in two important ways. When it comes to extensive rent, both Ricardo and Marx assumed that the order of fertility coincided with the order of profitability, whereas Sraffa argued that the order of profitability depends on the reigning relation between wages and profits. Put differently, the correspondence between fertility and profitability may hold for a wage-rate equal to w but can seize to hold for a wage-rate equal to $w \neq w^*$. This is because Sraffa assumed that different fertility levels not only implied different technical coefficients for land but also for capital and labour. As a result, the wage-profit curves related to each plot of land may intersect one or more times—reflecting Sraffa's renowned proposition on the *reswitching of techniques*. A similar logic holds for Sraffa's conclusion on the discrepancy (or non-monotonicity) between the fertility of land and the rent it yields for landowners. This meant that, unlike Ricardo's contention, a fall in the real wage could be compatible with an increase in the rent per acre *and* decrease in the profit rate (Kurz, 1978, pp. 31–35).

It is possible to argue that Sraffa's approach to land-rents faintly touches upon agro-ecological systems through the consideration of land as a scarce, non-producible and non-basic commodity input. When it comes to extensive rent, the framework acknowledges the reality of variable land qualities in terms of fertility, which, in turn, governs the technical coefficients related to land, capital and labour inputs. At the same time, however, Sraffa neglects the fact that agricultural production alters agro-ecological systems with subsequent impacts on the biological and chemical composition of soil. In other words, Sraffa's integration of agro-ecological issues is limited in its treatment of land quality or land fertility as a static and fixed given. Furthermore, Sraffa's consideration on homogeneous land and intensive rent essentially translates to the idea that agricultural productivity (yield per acre) is a positive function of agricultural intensification. This assumption ignores the reality that agricultural intensification can also bear negative implications for soil fertility (see, e.g., Lehman et al., 2015).

In spite of these shortcomings, a number of ecological economists have argued that the physicalist and circular representation of economic production constitutes a suitable bedrock for the incorporation of more complex ecological and biophysical processes including exhaustible natural resources (see, e.g., Judson, 1989; Martinez-Alier, 1995). In addition, unlike approaches that rely on assumptions belonging to the marginalist tradition, a more accurate integration in the Sraffian framework allows for the joint analysis of ecological issues and surplus distribution. The following section reviews *microeconomic* contributions that have accommodated ecological issues that extend beyond Sraffa's approach to agricultural land-rents. From now on, we will refer to this literature as 'Eco-Sraffian'.

4.   From exhaustible resources to luxury emissions: surplus distribution at the forefront of analysis

This section reviews seminal works that have integrated ecological considerations into the Sraffian analytical framework. This is, by no means, an exhaustive review of the literature, since the purpose of this chapter is to provide readers with an introduction to and not an encyclopaedia of the 'Eco-Sraffian' literature in economics. The contributions cover a wide range of ecological issues, and the following review only offers a general discussion of the analytical frameworks and their related assumptions. This is to say that our review avoids detailed accounts of algebraic technicalities and solutions and instead focuses on the relation between the ecological issue at hand and surplus distribution.

4.1.   *Exhaustible and renewable natural resources*

To the best of our knowledge, the greater part of 'Eco-Sraffian' literature is concerned with the accommodation of exhaustible resources. Both Kurz and Salvadori (2014) and Bidard and Erreygers (2020) provide extensive reviews of the debate on the accommodation of exhaustible resources in the Sraffian tradition. The crux of this debate is whether the inclusion of exhaustible resources allows for the establishment of long-period prices. It is generally argued that *Exhaustible Natural Resources and the Classical Method of Long-Period Equilibrium*, by Parrinello (1983), kick-started the flow of literature contributing to the aforementioned question. In the following subsection, we will only address a 'representative' sample of the literature mentioned in Kurz and Salvadori (2014) and Bidard and Erreygers (2020) with the aim to disclose major differences in the way each contribution relates ecological issues to surplus distribution.

Starting with Parrinello (1983), two distinct analytical treatments are introduced, where the first regards exhaustible resources as two distinct non-basic commodities: *uniform quality resource deposits* used by an extractive industry and *extracted resources* used by a transformative industry. This 'inventory treatment' of exhaustible resources accounts for the conservation of resource deposits by resource owners through the incorporation of Hotelling's Rule. This rule states that free competition among the owners of exhaustible resources translates to a price for resource deposits, which increases at a rate determined by the uniform rate of profit reigning in the economy (Kurz and Salvadori, 2014, p. 313). In terms of distribution, the treatment of exhaustible resources as inventories translates to the absence of a distinction between industrial capitalists and resources. In other words, the standard negative relation between the uniform rate of profit and wage rate continues to hold. In addition, the 'inventory treatment' does not allow one to draw conclusions on how the status of a specific resource deposit influences the choice of technique in the given economy.

As a result of these shortcomings, Parrinello (1983) introduces a second analytical treatment that considers exhaustible resources as *mines* and introduces a single equation related to capture an 'extraction-conservation' production process where the *extracted resource* and *resource deposits* are considered as *joint products*.[3] Resource owners, in this case, are treated differently from industrial capitalists in that they are distributed an amount of value which consists of royalties *and* quasi-rents[1].[4] For a given rate of extraction, each of these components will vary according to the quantity of resources left in the deposits at the end of each period. As long as resource deposits are greater than zero, the system is able to reproduce itself. Evidently, this process of economic reproduction cannot continue indefinitely and, like the 'inventory treatment', it is difficult to assume that the choice of technique is independent from the level of resource deposits. In terms of distribution, the value distributed to resource owners bears no consequences for the determination of relative commodity prices and the wage rate.

The open questions posed by each of Parrinello's analytical treatments have led to contributions that introduce a back-stop technique/technology that is invoked when resource deposits are fully exhausted (Kurz and Salvadori, 1995, 2003a, 2003b; Bidard and Erreygers, 2001; Huang, 2018). Characteristic of these contributions is the assumption of perfect foresight with respect to the exhaustion date of resource deposits and a conclusion on whether Hotelling's Rule is compatible with the derivation of constant long-period prices.

For example, Bidard and Erreygers (2001, 2020) argue that the accommodation of exhaustible resources through Hotelling's Rule requires an abandonment of constant long-period prices in favour of dynamic prices. The authors introduce a *corn-guano model*, where guano is used as a fertiliser input in the production process of corn. The price of guano follows Hotelling's Rule and reflects the royalty rate received by the owners of guano deposits for the *in-situ* preservation thereof. In the period that guano is exhausted, an equally profitable back-stop technique is used alongside the guano technique. The authors find that, for an exogenous profit rate, it is possible to derive a maximum royalty and minimum wage rate, which are gradually arrived at before guano becomes exhausted. In terms of distribution, a dynamic, negative relation establishes itself between a) the exhaustion of a resource and increase in royalties and b) the wage rate. This alongside the standard static negative relation between an exogenous uniform rate of profit and the wage rate.

The conclusion on the incompatibility between constant long-period prices and exhaustible resources that are priced according to Hotelling's Rule has been disputed by Kurz and Salvadori (2003a, 2003b, 2014) and Huang (2018).[5] Absent of technical details, one can conclude that each of the previously mentioned contributions showcase the existence of constant long-period prices under various 'well-defined circumstances' pertaining to a) capacity constraints,[6] b) perfect foresight and the use of back-stop technologies and c) the sum of royalties and rents accrued to resource owners. In terms of distribution and for an exogenous wage, the standard assumption on an inverse relation between profits and rents holds. In addition, constant long-period prices are said to exist when the value accrued to resource owners remains constant due to the inverse relation between rents and royalties.

The assumptions on perfect foresight and the deployment of back-stop technologies are classified by Ravagnani (2008) as far too strong. Interestingly, the author draws on later contributions by Parrinello to present alternative methods to account for exhaustible resources in long-period analyses. The first alternative is a *corn-oil model*, which assumes that there exists a single production period where two distinct corn production processes co-exist while the remaining production periods only deploy the cheapest production process (Parrinello, 2001). In this case, wages and royalties (developing according to Hotelling's Rule) are determined by the techniques and the ruling rate of profit for each given period. This alternative actually coincides with the *corn-guano model* if the single production period with two co-existing processes corresponds with the time of resource exhaustion (Bidard and Erreygers, 2020, p. 434).

The second alternative is an *effectual supply model* in which Parrinello (2004) retains the assumption of two co-existing techniques but also introduces a modification of exhaustible resources and their form in Sraffian price equations. This is said to accommodate the assumption that an exhaustible resource deposit should be subject to a non-zero price, regardless of whether it is left in the ground or consumed in a given period of production. This is done by regarding the *flow* and not the *stock* of an exhaustible resource, which results in the derivation of long-period prices and the endogenous distributive variable akin to an intensive rent on land of uniform quality (discussed in section 3). Rather than perfect foresight, the effectual supply model assumes that resource owners observe exhaustibility and rationally distribute the stock of natural resources between a flow used up in production and an amount left in the ground. With respect to the latter, the analytical framework leaves its price indeterminate rather than equal to zero.

According to Ravagnani (2008), neither backward induction models nor effectual supply models reflect historical evidence on the determination of royalties earned by resource owners. Empirical evidence for the United States suggests that institutional arrangements entitle resource owners to a pre-established share of the oil extracted by the extraction companies through a lease contract. This means that royalties are only subject to change arising out of new leases and the termination of old ones. Ravagnani (2008) concludes that the royalties on exhaustible resources should be considered as separately determined and independent variables in the logical structure of classical theory. If the profit rate is taken as given, then the fixed share of the resource price attributed to resource owners can easily be accommodated in the Sraffian price equations.

As far as we are aware, the only 'Eco-Sraffian' contributions that incorporate renewable natural resources are those by Kurz and Salvadori (1995, pp. 351–357), Erreygers (2015) and Hahnel (2017). The first considers salmon as a renewable resource and treats it as a non-basic commodity. The authors find that, for a given demand for salmon, a) both stable and unstable equilibria exist and b) the population of wild salmon may go extinct, in some cases. In terms of distribution, the standard assumptions on the inverse relation between the uniform rate of profit accrued by capitalists operating salmon fisheries and the wage rate hold.

Erreygers (2015) introduces a *corn-tuna model*, based on the aforementioned corn-guano and salmon models, that assumes two distinct tuna production processes: wild and farmed tuna. When it comes to wild tuna, the model assumes a natural growth and catch function that each depend on wild tuna population dynamics. In turn, farmed tuna production processes resemble any other industrial activity. Consumers in the economic system are assumed to be indifferent between wild and farmed tuna. The five processes that characterise economic reproduction in the presence of renewable tuna are: 1) corn production, 2) wild tuna production, 3) boat production (for wild tuna), 4) farmed tuna production, 5) pond production (for farmed tuna). Erreygers (2015) introduces a sea-rent (akin to a royalty) accrued by boat owners and representative of the advantage earned through the use of sea as a productive agent. Through the algebraic and numerical analysis of a mixed tuna system, Erreygers (2015) concludes that, in the presence of positive sea-rents, there exists an unstable equilibrium that is characterised by a relatively small tuna population. In this case, there's an incentive for boat-owners to increase their fleet and overfish tuna. To combat overfishing, the author suggests two policy recommendations that target boat owners and their sea-rent: a limit on the fleet size or a tax per boat. In terms of distribution, the crucial implication here is that the overexploitation of renewable resources can be prevented through a policy intervention that addresses the boat-owning class that captures a sea-rent. For an exogenous and uniform profit rate, the corn-tuna model illustrates that the prevention of overexploitation does not impact the wage rate.

In *Environmental Sustainability in a Sraffian Framework*, Hahnel (2017) addresses the relationship between *throughput efficiency* and *labour productivity gains*, where throughput is defined as the amount of nature embodied in each of the commodities produced in a given economy. In turn, nature is treated as a homogenous, basic commodity deemed necessary for agricultural, extraction and waste purposes. In a formal setup which considers an economy that reproduces itself by means of labour measured in hours and renewable nature in acres, Hahnel (2017) introduces three conditions for environmental sustainability over an arbitrary period of time—e.g., per year. The first is a simplified iteration of maximum yields discussed in Kurz and Salvadori (1995) and Erreygers (2015): yearly throughput must not exceed the regenerated amount of nature in that same year. The second condition assumes that employment and the total number of hours worked in the economy remain constant. Hence, labour productivity gains necessarily imply higher outputs and therefore throughput. As such, environmental sustainability requires that labour productivity gains are matched with throughput efficiency gains as soon as yearly throughput becomes equal to the regenerated amount of nature. Until that time, labour productivity gains can exceed throughput efficiency gains. Instead, and if yearly throughput exceeds regeneration, throughput efficiency gains must exceed throughput efficiency gains. The implications of this exercise for economic growth are straightforward: for a situation where environmental sustainability is breached—e.g., the current situation regarding carbon emissions—throughput must necessarily decrease.[7] In the same breadth, Hahnel (2017) showcases that labour productivity gains can also translate to a decrease in the total number of hours worked in the economy. In this way, Hahnel (2017) demonstrates that labour productivity gains which lead to an increase in leisure capture growth in terms of well-being and need not jeopardise environmental sustainability. Interestingly, this contribution therefore highlights an ecological aspect of distribution which is not *physical*.

At this point, it is worth mentioning the unique contribution by Kemp-Benedict (2014) which formalises Herman Daly's metaphor of the economy as an 'inverted pyramid' where the total value-added in a given economy is driven by the value-added in the extractive sector (Daly, 1995). The three-sector model introduced by Kemp-Benedict (2014) follows a representation of the economy as 'vertically integrated'.[8] The three sectors are a raw-material sector which accounts for extracted exhaustible and renewable resources (e.g., mineral deposits and carbon fixed in crops), a bulk commodity sector that transforms raw materials into the building blocks of an economy (e.g., steel, agricultural products) and circulating goods and services sector. This last sector produces final goods and services that are used as inputs for all sectors, including the sector itself. The prices for each of the goods is set as a mark-up on costs which include a) the price on raw materials, bulk materials and circulating goods and services, b) resource rents paid to exhaustible and renewable resource owners and c) the wage-bill. While a uniform markup reigns at the sectoral level, the economy-wide markup on resources and wages depends on the structure of production or the aggregate intensity of demand for intermediate inputs (raw and bulk materials). Since raw materials are only used in the bulk material sector, while labour is used in all sectors, the opportunity to compound markups on raw material costs is higher than that for labour. As such, the economy-wide markup on raw materials (exhaustible and renewable resources) is higher than that for labour. This result has implications for the analysis of a resource tax: Kemp-Benedict (2014) shows that the introduction of a resource tax typically results in a slight decrease of the wage-share or a shift in income distribution from wages towards profits.

4.2.   *Waste generation and disposal processes*

The exhaustion of resource deposits and overexploitation of renewable resources represents but one interlinkage between economic reproduction and the state of ecological processes. Another equally relevant interlinkage regards the generation and disposal of waste. This subject has been considered by Perrings (1986), O'Connor (1993) and Hosoda (2001). The reader will notice that some of these contributions study the issue of waste disposal alongside exhaustible and renewable resources, while others recast waste as a special type of exhaustible resource.

The contribution by Perrings (1986) draws on the characterisation of the economy as a thermodynamically closed system which is subject to a *conservation of mass condition*. This implies that economic growth in the global system or any of its subsystems carry with it concrete economic and environmental *transformations*. Put differently, economic processes either 'exact' and 'inert' into nature or the environment. Embedding the conservation of mass condition in a classical dynamic general equilibrium model implies three separate dynamic effects: 1) an equality between the mass of inputs and the mass of outputs, 2) the inability to eject waste material from a closed system and 3) the eventual zero-growth rate of a closed physical system, where expansion without limit is impossible. The second effect implies the treatment of waste material as everlasting residuals resulting in an economic system which is time-variant due to the uncertainty surrounding the nature of change embodied in the disposal of these residuals. Perrings (1986), therefore, contends that a price-vector is unable to act as an instrument of control that can ensure a positive economic growth rate. Hence, the zero-growth rate implied by this uncertainty means that growth in an arbitrary subsystem of the whole economy necessarily implies the contraction of another subsystem. In other words, the pursuit for positive economic growth in an economy characterised as a closed system bears distributive consequences across different subsystems and their respective agents (workers and capitalists).

O'Connor (1993) explicitly builds on the previous analysis of waste disposal and adds a *conflict lens* that treats the sustainability of economic growth in terms of access to natural resources and the impact on *environmental commons*. In all of this, O'Connor's main novelty pertains to the introduction of ecological capital, which covers the stock of natural resources, what is now understood as ecosystem services and, most innovatively, non-industrial economies/para-economies that are rendered vulnerable by expanding modern economies. Ultimately, the model incorporates conflicts of interests concerning the appropriation and use of ecological capital. This is done through the introduction of four related processes: a) the economic production process, b) the economic waste-disposal process operated by proprietors of the economic production-process, c) the ecological production-process and d) the ecological waste-disposal processes operated by proprietors of the ecological production process. The economic waste-disposal process b) requires ecological capital to dispose of the waste associated with process a). A balanced growth path solution renders three distinct cases, of which the last one represents the main novelty of O'Connor's contribution. This is a situation where the growth rate of ecological capital is equal to the growth rate of economic capital. As a result, economic production is a luxury dependent on ecological production, while ecological production can sustain itself in absence of economic production. If these two processes are operated by separate owners, there exists an incentive for economic capital owners to either appropriate ecological capital from the para-economic society or to alienate the para-economic society and impose the 'sale' of ecological capital to economic capital owners. The issue is that such a scheme would divert ecological capital away from self-reproduction until ecological capital is exhausted. In this way, the contribution by O'Connor (1993) incorporates real-world processes that reflect accumulation by dispossession (Harvey, 2005), often exemplified by land-grabbing for the purpose of securing natural resources.

In essence, the contribution by Hosoda (2001) addresses the issue of waste and waste treatment through the specification of landfills as exhaustible resources subject to a price/royalty that abides by Hotelling's Rule. The author's theoretical framework assumes the following production processes a) a normal good with waste residuals as a joint product, b) an exhaustible landfilling process and c) a recycling process which uses waste residuals, alongside labour and the normal good, to transform waste residuals back into the normal good. Recycling is assumed to be more expensive but also more efficient compared to landfilling: for an equal amount of the normal good, recycling is able to treat more waste residuals. Since it is assumed that landfilling is cheaper but exhaustible, the coexistence of landfilling and recycling only manifests itself once the landfill is exhausted. This coincides with the idea of a back-stop technology in the corn-guano model introduced by Bidard and Erreygers (2001). In other words, the landfilling process will be the dominant technique as long as its 'exhaustion state' translates to costs which are cheaper than the recycling technology. As with the corn-guano model, the wage decreases alongside the increasing price/royalty of landfilling. Here, Hosoda (2001) is explicit in mentioning the distributive impact of their dynamic modelling exercise: unless the decrease in the wage rate is compensated for with the increase in the price of landfilling, workers are negatively affected.

4.3.   *Climate change and carbon emissions*

The final subsection in this chapter addresses 'Eco-Sraffian' contributions that explicitly consider the issue of climate change and carbon emissions. It seems that Gehrke and Lager (1995) were the first to investigate the impact of energy taxes on relative prices and the choice of technique in a Sraffian analytical framework. The authors introduce a model which incorporates dated labour and dated energy to understand a) the difference between the methods of production, before and after an energy tax, and b) whether an energy tax increases the relative price of energy-intensive products. The latter aspect is important to understand whether taxation is able to incentivise both consumers and producers to decrease their reliance on energy-intensive goods.

When it comes to methods of production, two alternatives are considered: a labour-saving (energy-intensive) and energy-saving (labour-intensive) technique. Results based on the analysis of profit-tax indicate that the choice of an energy-saving over a labour-saving technique depends on the combination between an exogenous wage rate and the tax level. In fact, the authors illustrate that taxation can actually lead to perverse switches from energy-saving to labour-saving techniques. In addition, there exists a wage rate interval for which the profit-tax curves exhibit re-switching between labour- and energy-saving techniques. For an exogenous profit rate, the authors show that there exists a range of profit rates that is 'immune' to a change in the choice of techniques as the result of an energy tax. This means that either the labour- or energy-saving technique will dominate across all tax rate values.

When it comes to relative prices, results indicate that an energy tax can reduce the price of a more energy-intensive commodity if its production requires relatively more indirect/dated labour than indirect/dated energy. If a commodity holds a larger total but smaller indirect quantity of energy, an increase in the energy tax rate will always lead to a fall in its price. In this way, the authors showcase that the introduction or increase of an energy tax rate need not result in an incentive to switch to a more energy-saving technique. Similarly, the desired impact of environmental taxes on demand depends on the ratio between indirect energy and indirect labour requirements for a given good.

This brings us to the final 'Eco-Sraffian' contribution discussed in this chapter: *Exploring the link between profitability and luxury emissions* by Di Bucchianico and Cappelli (2021). Closely related to the contribution by Kemp-Benedict (2014), a *vertically-integrated wage-commodity sector* model is introduced to account for the empirical fact that wealthier households disproportionately contribute to greenhouse gas emissions through the channel of luxury consumption. Interestingly, the model is able to represent the Marxian surplus value rate (or labour exploitation rate) in a Sraffian set-up following the seminal contributions by Pierangelo Garegnani.[9] A distinction is made between production processes that produce goods and services that directly or indirectly worker's wage-baskets (food, clothing, shelter, etc.) and luxury goods (yachts, swimming pools, high-end watches, etc.). While direct and indirect 'wage-basket' goods are necessary for the system's reproduction, luxury goods are not. For a given wage rate, the surplus value in this economy is equal to the wage-bill paid to all workers *minus* the wage-bill paid to workers in the wage-commodity sector. The long-period rate of profit for the entire economy is then calculated through a reduction of price equations to dated quantities of labour. Solving for the long-period rate of profit ultimately establishes the rate of surplus value as a monotonically increasing function of the long-period rate of profit. The point of this specific set-up is to illustrate an economy where the economic surplus is not solely determined by an excess of wage-basket goods but also by luxury goods.

In light of the general desire 'to live in an economy that respects social and ecological boundaries' (Di Bucchianico and Cappelli, 2021, p. 14), the authors explore three scenarios. The first is coined as a *green-growth scenario*, where ecological boundaries are respected through a progressive elimination of carbon-intensive luxury goods. In this scenario, however, social boundaries, or the equitable and sufficient access to resources that ensure personal well-being, are violated. This is because the economic surplus would only change in form and not in quantity—e.g., the surplus now only consists of low-carbon goods. As such, a positive rate of surplus value—and therefore, labour exploitation—still exists.

The second scenario is a *reformist scenario*, which inverts the assumptions of the green-growth scenario. The idea is that strong unions, low unemployment and a pro-labour state result in the gradual inclusion of luxury goods in the wage-basket. This results in a falling surplus value and lower rate of exploitation, since a higher percentage of the labour force is engaged in producing their own wage-basket goods. At the same time, such a scenario violates ecological boundaries, since carbon-intensive luxury goods are not dealt with.

A situation in which both social and ecological boundaries are respected is referred to as the *just-transition scenario*. Rather than eliminating carbon-intensive goods or driving down the rate of exploitation to zero, the focus of a just-transition scenario rests on the introduction of a 'decent-living' wage commodity bundle that excludes carbon-intensive luxury goods per definition. In this case, profits entirely disappear, since the economy is only meant to provide workers with decent-living wage-baskets. An economic surplus may still manifest itself, but strictly for the purpose of upgrading capital goods or to expand production processes in order accommodate for population growth. Since the decent-living wage-basket excludes carbon-intensive luxury goods, they are not produced, and wasteful consumption is therefore eliminated.

5.   Concluding remarks

This chapter has reviewed a number of seminal contributions that can be classified as 'Eco-Sraffian' through an accommodation of one ecological question or the other. A couple of things are apparent from this review exercise. The first is that the majority of contributions consider either exhaustible or renewable resources and illustrate how the dynamics of each (exhaustion or regeneration) can be accounted for in the Sraffian long-period method of analysis. In addition, and with particular reference to exhaustible resources, there seems to be an explicit focus on theoretical and methodological rigour. A significant part of these contributions (but not all) mainly aims to disclose whether Hotelling's Rule is compatible with constant long-period prices and under which specific conditions. In all of this, the presence of an exhaustible resource speaks to the division of capitalist society in three separate classes: capitalists, resource owners and workers, where the inverse relation between the surplus distributed to each class is not necessarily present and depends on the specific analytical framework.

This review exercise also illustrates how some of the 'Eco-Sraffian' literature integrates policy interventions that aim to limit exhaustion or over-exploitation. Interestingly but not surprisingly, conclusions on the distributional impact of taxation vary due to different analytical setups and assumptions. For example, taxing the 'harvest-tool owning' prevents over-exploitation of a renewable resource without an impact on the wage rate while taxing a resource-owning class in a vertically integrated economy shifts income distribution from wages towards profits. At the same time, 'Eco-Sraffian' literature highlights how the neoclassical internalisation of externalities through taxation is far from a silver bullet policy and may actually increase the emission-intensity in a given economy.

Finally, this chapter showcases the versatility of Sraffa's analytical approach in terms of its ability to accommodate ecological questions *in conjunction with* other considerations such as well-being and leisure, the appropriation of ecological capital pertaining to non-industrial economies, labour exploitation and emissions arising out of luxury consumption. This is particularly important for scholars in the field of Ecological Economics that wish to retain, strengthen and develop analyses that are based on classical theories of production.

Notes

1 A commodity which either directly or indirectly enters the production process of all commodities in a given system is said to be a basic commodity; otherwise, it is a non-basic commodity (Sraffa, 1960, p. 8).

2 Ranking according to fertility is determined by treating each plot of land as if it were marginal and therefore subject to a land-rent equal to zero. This allows one to determine, for each quality of land, the maximum rate of profit for a given wage-rate (Kurz, 1978, p. 20).

3 This means that the single production process produces more than one commodity as an output. Joint production is often invoked when fixed capital—in this case, mines—are included as an input in production processes (see Sraffa, 1960, pp. 43–46; Kurz and Salvadori, 1995, pp. 219–249).

4 Quasi-rents refers to the rent received by 'out-of-date' fixed capital/machinery which are subject to exhaustion (Sraffa, 1960).

5 The contribution by Huang (2018) is unique in that it incorporates a production process which accounts for the 'search for new resource deposits'.

6 Capacity constraints represent a limit to the amount of resources that can be extracted from a resource deposit in a given period of time.

7 Unlike other contributions, Hahnel (2017) does not proceed with a treatment of how a minimisation in throughput should be achieved. How should investment in throughput efficiency gains be incentivised?

8 Vertically integrated models account for the flow of goods between sectors and firms through the introduction of coefficients that multiply the costs of labour inputs (see Pasinetti, 1980).

9 See Value and Distribution in the Classical Economists and Marx (Garegnani, 1984).

References

Beder, S. (2011) 'Environmental Economics and Ecological Economics: The Contribution of Interdisciplinarity to Understanding, Influence and Effectiveness', *Environmental Conservation*, 38 (2): 140–150.

Bidard, C., and Erreygers, G. (2001) 'The Corn—Guano Model', *Metroeconomica*, 52 (3): 243–253.

Bidard, C., and Erreygers, G. (2020) 'Exhaustible Resources and Classical Theory', *Œconomia. History, Methodology, Philosophy*, 10–3: 419–446.

Bortis, H. (2002) 'Piero Sraffa and the Revival of Classical Political Economy', *Journal of Economic Studies*, 29 (1): 74–89.

Bucchianico, S. D., and Cappelli, F. (2021) 'Exploring the Theoretical Link Between Profitability and Luxury Emissions (2114)', *Post Keynesian Economics Society*. Available at: www.postkeynesian.net/working-papers/2114/

Christensen, P. P. (1989) 'Historical Roots for Ecological Economics—Biophysical Versus Allocative Approaches', *Ecological Economics*, 1 (1): 17–36.

Christensen, P. P. (2001) 'Early Links Between Sciences of Nature and Economics: Historical Perspectives for Ecological and Social Economics', in C. J. Cleveland, D. I. Stern and R. Costanza (eds.), *The Economics of Nature and the Nature of Economics*, pp. 15–33. Cheltenham: Edward Elgar Publishing.

Cleveland, C. J. (1999) 'Biophysical Economics: From Physiocracy to Ecological Economics and Industrial Ecology', in N. Georgescu-Roegen, K. Mayumi and J. M. Gowdy (eds.), *Bioeconomics and Sustainability: Essays in Honor of Nicholas Georgescu-Roegen*, pp. 125–154. Cheltenham: Edward Elgar.

Common, M. S., and Stagl, S. (2005) *Ecological Economics: An Introduction*. Cambridge: Cambridge University Press.

Dale, G. (2021) 'Rule of Nature or Rule of Capital? Physiocracy, Ecological Economics, and Ideology', *Globalizations*, 18 (7): 1230–1247.

Daly, H. E. (1995) 'Consumption and Welfare: Two Views of Value Added', *Review of Social Economy*, 53 (4): 451–473.

Daly, H. E., and Farley, J. (2011) 'Part I: An Introduction to Ecological Economics', in H. Daly and J. Farley (eds.), *Ecological Economics: Principles and Applications*. Washington, DC: Island Press.

Eltis, W. (2000) 'François Quesnay's Tableau Économique', in W. Eltis (ed.), *The Classical Theory of Economic Growth*, pp. 1–38. London: Palgrave Macmillan.

Erreygers, G. (2015) 'Renewable Resources in a Long-Term Perspective: The Corn-Tuna Model', *Cahiers d'economie Politique*, 69 (2): 97–130.

Garegnani, P. (1984) 'Value and Distribution in the Classical Economists and Marx', *Oxford Economic Papers*, 36 (2): 291–325.

Gehrke, C., and Kurz, H. D. (1995) 'Karl Marx on Physiocracy', *The European Journal of the History of Economic Thought*, 2 (1): 53–90.

Gehrke, C., and Lager, C. (1995) 'Environmental Taxes, Relative Prices and Choice of Technique in a Linear Model of Production', *Metroeconomica*, 46 (2): 127–145.

Georgescu-Roegen, N. (1971) *The Entropy Law and the Economic Process*. Cambridge, MA: Harvard University Press.

Georgescu-Roegen, N. (1976) *Energy and Economic Myths: Institutional and Analytical Economic Essays*. Oxford: Pergamon Press.

Gibson, B. (1984) 'Profit and Rent in a Classical Theory of Exhaustible and Renewable Resources', *Zeitschrift Für Nationalökonomie*, 44 (2): 131–149.

Gowdy, J., and Erickson, J. D. (2005) 'The Approach of Ecological Economics', *Cambridge Journal of Economics*, 29 (2): 207–222.

Hahnel, R. (2017) 'Environmental Sustainability in a Sraffian Framework', *Review of Radical Political Economics*, 49 (3): 477–488.

Harvey, D. (2005) *Spaces of Neoliberalization: Towards a Theory of Uneven Geographical Development*. Stuttgart: Franz Steiner Verlag.

Hosoda, E. (2001) 'Recycling and Landfilling in a Dynamic Sraffian Model: Application of the Corn—Guano Model to a Waste Treatment Problem', *Metroeconomica*, 52 (3): 268–281.

Huang, B. (2018) 'An Exhaustible Resources Model in a Dynamic Input—Output Framework: A Possible Reconciliation Between Ricardo and Hotelling', *Journal of Economic Structures*, 7 (1): 8.

Judson, D. H. (1989) 'The Convergence of Neo-Ricardian and Embodied Energy Theories of Value and Price', *Ecological Economics*, 1 (3): 261–281.

Kemp-Benedict, E. (2014) 'The Inverted Pyramid: A Neo-Ricardian View on the Economy—Environment Relationship', *Ecological Economics*, 107: 230–241.

Kurz, H. D. (1978) 'Rent Theory in a Multisectoral Model', *Oxford Economic Papers*, 30 (1): 16–37.

Kurz, H. D. (1980) 'Smithian Themes in Piero Sraffa's Theory', *Journal of Post Keynesian Economics*, 3 (2): 271–280.

Kurz, H. D. (1998) 'Against the Current: Sraffa's Unpublished Manuscripts and the History of Economic Thought', *The European Journal of the History of Economic Thought*, 5 (3): 437–451.

Kurz, H. D., and Salvadori, N. (1995) *Theory of Production: A Long-Period Analysis*. Cambridge: Cambridge University Press.

Kurz, H. D., and Salvadori, N. (2003a) 'Classical Economics and the Problem of Exhaustible Resources', in H. Kurz and N. Salvadori (eds.), *Classical Economics and Modern Theory*. London: Routledge.

Kurz, H. D., and Salvadori, N. (2003b) 'Economic Dynamics in a Simple Model with Exhaustible Resources and a Given Real Wage Rate', in H. Kurz and N. Salvadori (eds.), *Classical Economics and Modern Theory*. London: Routledge.

Kurz, H. D., and Salvadori, N. (2005) 'Representing the Production and Circulation of Commodities in Material Terms: On Sraffa's Objectivism', *Review of Political Economy*, 17 (3): 413–441.

Kurz, H. D., and Salvadori, N. (2014) 'The "Classical" Approach to Exhaustible Resources: Parrinello and the Others', in H. Kurz and N. Salvadori (eds.), *Revisiting Classical Economics*. London: Routledge.

Lehman, R. M., Cambardella, C. A., Stott, D. E., Acosta-Martinez, V., Manter, D. K., Buyer, J. S., Maul, J. E., Smith, J. L., Collins, H. P., Halvorson, J. J., Kremer, R. J., Lundgren, J. G., Ducey, T. F., Jin, V. L., and Karlen, D. L. (2015) 'Understanding and Enhancing Soil Biological Health: The Solution for Reversing Soil Degradation', *Sustainability*, 7 (1): 988–1027.

Magnusson, L. (2015) *The Political Economy of Mercantilism*. London: Routledge.

Martinez-Alier, J. (1995) 'Distributional Issues in Ecological Economics', *Review of Social Economy*, 53 (4): 511–528.

Melgar-Melgar, R. E., & Hall, C. A. S. (2020) 'Why Ecological Economics Needs to Return to Its Roots: The Biophysical Foundation of Socio-Economic Systems', *Ecological Economics*, 169.

O'Connor, M. (1993) 'Value System Contests and the Appropriation of Ecological Capital', *The Manchester School of Economic & Social Studies*, 61 (4): 398–424.

Parrinello, S. (1983) 'Exhaustible Natural Resources and the Classical Method of Long-Period Equilibrium', J. Kregel (ed.), *Distribution, Effective Demand and International Economic Relations: Proceedings of a Conference Held by the Centro di Studi Economici Avanzati, Trieste, at Villa Manin di Passariano, Udine*, pp. 186–199. London: Palgrave Macmillan.

Parrinello, S. (2001) 'The Price of Exhaustible Resources', *Metroeconomica*, 52 (3): 301–315.

Parrinello, S. (2004) 'The Notion of Effectual Supply and the Theory of Normal Prices with Exhaustible Natural Resources', *Economic Systems Research*, 16 (3): 311–322.

Pasinetti, L. L. (1980) 'The Notion of Vertical Integration in Economic Analysis', L. Pasinetti (ed.), *Essays on the Theory of Joint Production*, pp. 16–43. London: Palgrave Macmillan UK.

Perrings, C. (1986) 'Conservation of Mass and Instability in a Dynamic Economy-Environment System', *Journal of Environmental Economics and Management*, 13 (3): 199–211.

Quesnay, F. (2014) *Quesnay's Tableau Économique*. Edited by M. Kuczynski and R. L. Meek. London: Palgrave Macmillan.

Ravagnani, F. (2008) 'Classical Theory and Exhaustible Natural Resources: Notes on the Current Debate', *Review of Political Economy*, 20 (1): 79–93.

Schachter, G. (1991) 'Francois Quesnay: Interpreters and Critics Revisited', *The American Journal of Economics and Sociology*, 50 (3): 313–322.

Serrano, F., and Mazat, N. (2017) 'Quesnay and the Analysis of Surplus in the Capitalist Agriculture', *Contributions to Political Economy*, 36 (1): 81–102.

Sherwood, J., Carbajales-Dale, M., and Haney, B. R. (2020) 'Putting the Biophysical (Back) in Economics: A Taxonomic Review of Modelling the Earth-Bound Economy', *Biophysical Economics and Sustainability*, 5 (1): 1–20.

Sraffa, P. (1960) *Production of Commodities by Means of Commodities: Prelude to a Critique of Economic History*. Cambridge: Cambridge University Press.

Stokes, K. M. (1993) *Man and the Biosphere: Toward a Coevolutionary Political Economy*. London: Routledge.

Vaggi, G. (1987) *The Economics of François Quesnay*. London: Palgrave Macmillan.

Vaggi, G., and Groenewegen, P. (2002) *A Concise History of Economic Thought: From Mercantilism to Monetarism*. London: Palgrave Macmillan UK.

Van den Bergh, J. C. M. (2001) 'Ecological Economics: Themes, Approaches, and Differences with Environmental Economics', *Regional Environmental Change*, 2 (1): 13–23.

Venkatachalam, L. (2007) 'Environmental Economics and Ecological Economics: Where They Can Converge?', *Ecological Economics*, 61 (2): 550–558.

Part II
Institutional and post-Keynesian economics

4 Ecology and environment in home economics

David Philippy and Marco P. Vianna Franco

1. Introduction

On 29 March 2009, during the proclamation of Women's History Month with the theme 'Women Taking the Lead to Save our Planet', US President Barack Obama praised the contributions of distinguished female figures to environmental protection. The first mention went to Ellen H. Richards (born Swallow, 1842–1911) as a chemist who was 'the first woman in the United States to be accepted at a scientific school' and whose studies on water quality led to the 'Nation's first state water-quality standards'.[1] Recognised as the founder of the American home economics movement, Richards's life and work have been acknowledged in different strands of historiography, both of the natural and social sciences (Clarke, 1973; Dyball and Carlsson, 2017; Egan, 2011; Sutherland, 2017; Stage, 1997; Swallow, 2014; Weigley, 1974). However, there is still a significant gap in the literature concerning the history of economic thought, despite recent efforts to change this state of affairs (Becchio, 2020; Blayac, 2023; Le Tollec, 2020; Missemer and Vianna Franco, 2024; Philippy, 2021; Soudan, Philippy and Maas, 2021). This acknowledgment concerns not only Richards but the broader field, movement, and eventually, academic discipline of home economics as it emerged in the USA at the turn of the 20th century, and even more so, in the context of their contributions to the interplay between, on the one hand, social and economic factors and, on the other, ecological thinking and environmental issues.

The marginalisation of home economics, both in relation to the mainstream of economic science at its time and as a subject of the history of economics, conjoins unequal intellectual disputes, disciplinary divides and gender issues. Nevertheless, it has, in fact, grappled with issues which still, today, pose controversial theoretical challenges and policy-driven debates, which suggests a renewed appraisal of its intellectual and political relevance. Hence, it will be attempted, here, to redeem not only the work of Richards but home economics as a whole in the sense of its economic thought as applied to ecological and environmental questions.

There are at least two plausible interpretations hinting towards the breadth of the legacy of home economists in relation to ecological and environmental matters. First, the acknowledgement and strengthening of the interconnections between ecology and economics as scientific fields, setting out from the embeddedness of

DOI: 10.4324/9781003375425-6

the economy in the social and ultimately biophysical realms, and thus, imparting a strong type of interdisciplinarity into joint knowledge claims pertaining to what is, today, understood as environmental sustainability. In this respect, there is an intellectual thread linking human ecology to home economics before the turn of the 20th century, which has then resurfaced in contemporary ecological economics, constituting a broad history of ecological economic thought (Martinez-Alier, 1987; Røpke, 2004, 2005; Spash, 1999; Vianna Franco and Missemer, 2023).

Second, as environmental issues became increasingly noticeable as a consequence of rapid industrialisation, they also gained more attention as a phenomenon of relevance within some trends of economic science itself, with a gradual and outspoken interest in conservation and the rational use of natural resources and amenities, justified not least by the perceived role of nature in human welfare (both as a source of energy/materials and as a sink of waste/pollution). This was certainly the case in home economics and its characteristic science-based political discourse, which argued for the need for a healthy environment, as well as in other academic circles that would eventually be described as pioneers of natural resource and environmental economics, from W. Stanley Jevons and Arthur C. Pigou to Harold Hotelling and Ronald Coase (see Banzhaf, 2019; Brown et al., 2016; Kula, 1998; Missemer, 2012; Pearce, 2002; Sandmo, 2015). From the 1960s onwards, with the aggravation of environmental problems at the local and global levels, efforts dedicated to such issues would become widespread, and different ways of approaching nature from an economic perspective would emerge and engage more intensively with national governments and international bodies devising policies for sustainable development. Nevertheless, this has not taken place without a high level of contention and protracted disagreements between and within different academic communities, such as those of environmental, ecological and energy economists (e.g., Daly, 1997; Georgescu-Roegen, 1971; Spash, 2011).

Bearing in mind the objective of elucidating how home economists have grappled with ecological science and environmental questions, this chapter assesses some of their contributions, from Ellen Richards's take on human-nature relations to Hazel Kyrk's, Elizabeth Hoyt's and other second-generation home economists' views on consumption, well-being and sobriety.

2.   Ellen Richards: from human ecology to home economics

Richards introduced the term 'ecology' (originally spelled *oekology*) in American scientific circles, having brought it from Germany in 1876, where she had, very likely, picked it up during a visit to Ernst Haeckel's laboratory in Jena.[2] The meaning assigned by her to the concept, however, lay closer to the current notion of human ecology—i.e., 'universal house/household of nature' (Clarke, 1973, p. 40; Swallow, 2014, p. 93). However, the term would soon adopt a much narrower understanding in the scientific community, excluding human beings as an object of investigation in favour of a focus on plant and animal life. Lacking influence and power within academic circles as a female scientist in a non-traditional field of knowledge, the battle was seemingly lost from the start, with Richards eventually opting for 'euthenics' as her term of choice and, eventually, home economics (Clarke, 1973; Dyball and Carlsson, 2017; Sutherland, 2017; Weigley, 1974).[3] In this respect, it is noteworthy that the Home Economics Department at Cornell University—back then, a hotspot for the advancement of the field—would be renamed to Department of Human Ecology in 1969. By contrast, the same department in Chicago would soon be overtaken by its well-known Department of Economics.[4]

As the founder and leading figure of the American home economics movement at the turn of the 20th century, Richards envisioned a morally-laden but above-all scientific approach to solve the most pressing social issues of the time by putting American households and housewives at the very centre. An expert in sanitary chemistry and heir of a long line of practitioners of the so-called 'domestic science', which goes back as far as the mid-1800s (Leavitt, 2002; Weigley, 1974), she saw her intellectual interests shifting towards a broad notion of what constitutes the 'art of right living' (Richards, 1904). Her understanding of human progress, grounded on efficiency, on the one hand, and on social ethics, on the other, resulted in a type of economic reasoning that was deeply associated with an underlying ecological stance—i.e., how humans are embedded in and interact with their surrounding environment. An emphasis on physiological aspects, including holistic or systemic perspectives which, at the time, were in vogue within scholarly groups, informed her definition and practice of human ecology as

> the study of the surroundings of human beings in the effects they produce on the lives of men. The features of the environment are natural, as climate, and artificial, produced by human activity, such as noise, dust, poisonous vapors, vitiated air, dirty water and unclean food.
>
> (Richards, 1907, p. v)

Richards's work as a human ecologist and its policy-oriented focus on the impacts of poor environmental health over living standards have been fairly documented (e.g. Clarke, 1973; Dyball and Carlsson, 2017; Thompson, 1994; Walsh, 2018). The same applies to her use of the term euthenics (e.g., Richardson, 2000; Weigley, 1974; Philippy, 2021), which would derive from a combination of her notions of human ecology, the 'art of right living', home ecology and home economics and be defined as 'the science of the controllable environment' or, more enlighteningly, 'the betterment of living conditions, through conscious endeavour, for the purpose of securing efficient human beings' (Richards, 1910, p. vii). The recurrent mentions to the efficiency of human beings by means of education and sanitary regulations, which would lead to the formation of the 'right' kind of habits, especially those promoting not only well-being but also higher productive capacity and ultimately increasing local and national wealth, bear traces of the conservatism of most women's movements during the Progressive Era. They strove for the establishment of a specific kind of urban, middle-class American identity. According to Hoy (1995, p. 73), even if such movements encompassed female groups with different backgrounds, they were usually represented by 'white, upper-middle-class, educated, and native-born Protestants of Anglo-Saxon ancestry' whose progressive agendas also encompassed questions such as suffrage, immigration, economic power and community life. Furthermore, the emphasis of Richards's euthenics on efficient and productive human beings lay dangerously close to Francis Galton's eugenics (Cooke, 1998; Egan, 2011).

Independently of the moniker used by Richards to label her efforts to study and devise ways of acting upon human habits, controlling environmental factors and steering their impacts over living standards, the role played by human-nature relations in home economics stands out.[5] The household—or the *oikos* at the root of both ecology and economics (respectively *oikologia* and *oikonomia*)—took centre stage as the level of analysis upon which such relations hinged and a starting point to assessing the individual as well as the community levels. It contrasted with the focus on pristine nature, wilderness and the rational use of resources at national and regional scales given by representatives of the American conservation movement, although, at times, their objects of interest would overlap, especially at the municipal level, as in the case of the construction of dams for the purpose of water supply (Missemer and Vianna Franco, 2024).

According to Benson (2020), there was a difference between the notion of nature and its intrinsic value for preservationists and that of the surrounding environment, particularly urban landscapes, as a useful category for promoting human progress in the eyes of proponents of different kinds of social reform. Amongst the latter, there is the perception according to which, even if the surrounding environment is seen as part of a natural world to be conquered, humans are deeply embedded in and consequently depend on it. In this perspective, one could mention not only home economists but also a plethora of either social or more scholarly movements keen on improving living conditions in municipalities as a result of unbridled industrialisation, such as Municipal Housekeeping, City Beautiful, Municipal Government and the settlement movement (Hoy, 1995; Spain, 2001; Swanson, 2013).

Richards's ecological worldview was based on the interconnections between natural and built environments. The fact that air, water and food are the 'three essentials of human existence' would provide the grounding for her physiological approach to improving living standards and securing more productive lives (Richards and Woodman, 1904, p. 1), with an immediate and clear connection to 'clean' homes as well as cities, towns and villages as surrounding environments. Human-made and natural factors play decisive roles in the intertwining of bodies, homes, cities and nature, as will be further discussed in the next section. In this context, the influence of Richards's works over the American conservation movement and, since then, environmental science and the rise of the modern environmental movement has not gone unnoticed (Ewert, Mitten and Overholt, 2014; Hynes, 1985; Kwallek, 2012; Walsh, 2018).

While home economists have heavily drawn from the natural sciences, they have also integrated other realms of science into their toolkit. From pragmatist philosophy and related currents of psychology and sociology to Thorstein Veblen's institutionalism, Richards mobilised different fields into her theoretical framework and practice of home economics. More specifically, her contributions to economic thinking included early arguments pertaining to women's unpaid labour and its function within marginalising capitalist structures which are, today, associated with ecofeminist strands of thought (Richardson, 2002). More generally, home economists and, above all, Richards have added significantly, even if from an unorthodox standpoint that was and remains marginalised by the mainstream of economic science, to public economics—or, at least, to the early days of a so-called economics of the urban environment (Missemer and Vianna Franco, 2024).

Richards's economic thinking comes as a reaction to the harm caused by industrialisation to environmental and thus human health, which she sees as motivated by a blatant political dominance of private interests over public or collective concerns. Economic efficiency could only be achieved once all costs incurred by a given activity were taken into account. The effects of pollution, for example, were not included in economic calculations and therefore favoured businesses which were, in fact, prejudicial in terms of the social and economic development of the country. Good health for workers meant a more productive economy, and she figured that it would be very unlikely for a polluting activity to compensate for the costs of sickness and death of productive individuals. Reducing the economic value of workers would certainly detract from national wealth. This was deemed as a much more powerful political argument for enforcing more strict sanitary regulations and, in some cases, having the state take over sectors which were liable for public health issues. Serious and encompassing cost-benefit analyses were called for, with the aid from different fields of knowledge, in order to make sure that not only air, water and food complied with certain quality standards but also that all spheres of human welfare were quantitatively and qualitatively satisfied, such as proper leisure options or the ability to enjoy a beautiful natural landscape (Richards, 1911).

Water supply was a case in which Richards argued for state ownership, serving as a perfect example of the need for a public management of the urban environment. It allowed for long-term planning of resource use and focus on the maintenance of high water-purity standards, which were not possible if designed as part of a profit-led business model. Again, one of the arguments put forth by Richards, taken to be scientifically sound, economically rational and politically persuasive, was that higher levels of water quality meant lower overall costs for society over time, as they prevented the spread of diseases. She was confident that any serious risk-based assessment could prove her assertions and tried, herself, to perform the necessary calculations, despite the lack of data and difficulty of assessing the risks involved. Extending this logic to air and food, which encompasses different issues such as adulteration of foodstuffs, dietary habits, biological and chemical contamination, dirty homes and cities and so on, would call for further and different types of preventive state intervention, including an emphasis on public education. Benefits were surely dispersed over long, possibly inter-generational, time horizons, while costs incurred at the present, which certainly did not contribute to the political appeal of the argument.

Richards's ideas and proposals show how far she came in her journey from chemistry and human ecology to euthenics, and finally, home economics. They portray the role of economic thinking in how human and environmental health can be and have been jointly addressed at least since the beginning of the 20th century. In this sense, there is a clear intellectual link between Richards's home economics and later approaches to environmental issues in different schools of economic thought, from the application of cost-benefit analysis to the use of standards of environmental quality in the Pigouvian tradition (Banzhaf, 2009; Berta, 2020). Even more so and as already mentioned, there is a strong connection between home economics and modern ecological economics in the sense of how both seek to integrate the natural and social sciences in their quest to understand the complexities involved in building social provisioning systems and to foster healthier human-nature relations (Franco, 2018; Martinez-Alier, 1987; Vianna Franco and Missemer, 2023).

3.   The home as an allegory for social change and environmental care

In the 1910s, Richards's movement took off across the country, making research and teaching in home economics a central component of the emergence of a new role for women in American society. By the end of the Lake Placid Conferences cycle (1899–1909), followed by Richards's death in 1911, the principles of home economics were increasingly disseminated in schools, universities and federal bureaus. In 1915, almost every land-grant college offered courses on home economics at bachelor's or master's levels (Craig, 1944, p. 29). In the meantime, the great war also proved to be a great opportunity for the professionalisation of home economists by allowing them to demonstrate their expertise in food conservation and canning. Herbert Hoover's *Food Administration*, which was created in 1917 and relied on home economists' knowledge to secure the supply of provisions, is a good example (see Goldstein, 2012, pp. 46–61; Stage and Vincenti, 1997).

Therefore, in the early 20th century, American home economists had gained a reputation as home experts, well-versed in the science and art of managing every single aspect of the household, from cooking to budgeting. Under Richards's influence, the movement established itself as an academic field, producing cutting-edge scientific knowledge, conducting surveys and disseminating its approach across the country. Already by the end of the 19th century, home economists had been key actors in setting new health standards for the general public. As historian Nancy Tomes (1997, p. 36) argues, '[i]n 1899, the year of the first Lake Placid conference on home economics, the United States was in the midst of a national crusade to control the spread of infectious diseases'. Tuberculosis was the deadliest disease at the time, along with typhoid, diphtheria and other pathogens that thrived in closed and dirty spaces. This proved to be a great opportunity for home economists to demonstrate their usefulness in improving living conditions in American households. Backing their advice for domestic cleanliness with new scientific knowledge about the 'invisible germ life' that was taking place inside homes, their expertise played a significant role in decreasing the spread of infectious diseases (Tomes, 1997, 1999). Home economics cannot, however, be reduced to a sort of women-led hygienist movement. As Richards's work demonstrates, their agenda consisted in a wide social vision connecting these new roles occupied by women (in both society and academia) with science and progress. Bringing sanitary and nutrition sciences into American homes was deemed as a powerful way of improving people's living conditions by placing women at the centre of the march of human progress.

More specifically, home economists' vision encompassed a systemic representation of human life, with the surrounding environment serving as a concept to reflect on the different levels of human existence. Swanson (2013) distinguishes four distinct levels: bodies, homes, cities and nature. For home economists, each of these levels requires a specific form of examination but are, at the same time, deeply connected with one another. It could be argued that the manner in which home economists have conceived these relationships can be understood as allegorical and that such a stance reflects a deep-seated ethical approach grounded on the precepts of human ecology. By 'allegorical', we do not imply that such relationships have no substance, but rather, that the notion of a home can be applied to each level described by Swanson. Ideas such as cleanliness, waste or resources are used as cross-level features reinforcing the representation of an integrated existence hinging around the concept of the home.

Although Richards initiated the home economics movement at the end of the 19th century, her views were shared by later home economists. As Mildred Chadsey (1915, p. 54) argued, '[s]uch a home implies not independence, but interdependence. It establishes new bonds of human relationship, coordinated endeavour and community interests'. Human life could not be reduced to its individual traits, and 'human progress', as Richards put it, required such an integral conception. Taking care of the home also meant taking care of nature. This was also made clear in several other publications in the *Journal of Home Economics*. As Lucy Griscom argued in the same journal:

> Conservation of our resources should be understood to apply to housekeeping, as well as to mines and forests. We need to be interested in civic and national affairs, for only when these are rightly conducted can homes be ideal; unless street cleaning is properly done, house cleaning cannot be very effective. If the vacuum cleaner is allowed to dump the dirt cleaned from the rugs of a house on the street in front of the house, the dirt will find its way back to the same rugs from which it had just been so scientifically extracted.
>
> (Griscom, 1910, p. 292)

There is a strong relationship between the home and collective life beyond the home. Having a clean house without clean surroundings is perceived as ecological nonsense. People live in an integrated environment in which their actions reflect on larger scales—the largest being nature. Thus, the concept of environment played a somewhat particular role in establishing the vocabulary of social change. Because home economists were essentially addressing women, it seemed relevant to start from the home and to use it as an allegory to foster the ethics of a productive life, with special attention to the need for 'wise consumption'. Using resources and minimising waste apply equally to the home and nature. Of course, avoiding waste was self-evident: in a context of resource scarcity, one should always look for the most efficient uses and beware of resource depletion:

> Many persons are, from ignorance, unable to realize the value of commodities which they are accustomed to seeing in quantity, and forget how valuable a little of it might be to some less fortunate person. Such persons are careless at large, in the destruction of forests, and the pollution of rivers; and, at home, in wasting water, and taking on their plates more food than they eat. All these short-sighted persons must be taught. Let us see that economy at home and abroad are closely related, and let women learn to apply the laws of economics to the household.
>
> (Ibid.)

To address the general problem of waste and scarce resources, education was thought to be the most efficient lever. Teaching wise use, frugality and thriftiness was only one aspect among a wider agenda ranging from consumer education to public policy at each and every level. Home economists witnessed what they perceived as a significant transformation of the role of women in the household at the turn of the century, making it the starting point of their analysis. As Richards herself argues: 'The home has ceased to be the glowing centre of production from which radiate all desirable goods, and has become but a pool toward which products made in other places flow—a place of *consumption*, not of *production*' (Richards, 1899, p. 25, italics in original). From being hitherto a domestic producer, women were progressively turning into modern consumers and should adjust to it. As Chadsey argued:

> Under modern conditions the homemaker does right to buy the household necessities, the furniture, the food, the clothes from the factory because they are made more cheaply and better there than she can have them made at home. She would be a social and economic failure if she did not adjust herself to the new industrial order of the factory system.
>
> (Chadsey, 1915, p. 53)

This changing role of women entailed a sense of adaptation to modernity, and home economists viewed their role as one of guidance in a rapidly evolving world. For them, the modern consumer society was neither something to accept or reject as a whole, but rather, an opportunity to improve people's living conditions by making women the central character of this process. Besides, this transformation also affected home economists' positioning as a group of experts and professionals, since their knowledge could help them carve a new academic niche (Goldstein, 2012; Stage and Vincenti, 1997). Making use of chemistry, sanitary sciences and the social sciences, they managed to move away from the old-fashioned domestic art of housekeeping.

4.   Elizabeth Hoyt's *The Consumption of Wealth* and the depletion of natural resources

During the first two decades of the 20th century, consumption studies became an increasingly hot topic in the home economics community. Curricula in high schools and universities offered 'consumption economics' courses, reflecting the higher demand for consumption expertise and, more generally, the prevalence of consumption studies within the profession (see Folbre, 1998; Goldstein, 2012; Stage and Vincenti, 1997). By the end of the 1910s, the significant transformation in hygiene habits and public sanitation reforms, which were also spurred by home economists, had paid off and made the 'germ war' threat less pressing (Tomes, 1997). This new expertise proved helpful for developing new career paths for women, leading, in the 1920s, to the emergence of a new generation of home economists, who secured more academic positions in universities and federal bureaus such as the US Department of Agriculture's Bureau of Home Economics and the Bureau of Labor Statistics, primarily conducting cost-of-living studies.[6]

Although the study of consumption was already taking larger spaces in curricula at the time, Hazel Kyrk's *Theory of Consumption* (1923) gave a strong boost to the establishment of a new field called 'the economics of consumption' (see Pietrykowski, 2009; Philippy, 2021). In the early 1920s, Kyrk focused on building a theoretical account of consumer behaviour from an institutional perspective (van Velzen, 2003). To our knowledge, Kyrk did not concern herself with issues of ecology and environment, as first-generation home economists did. In the 1930s and 1940s, when she abandoned her theoretical approach in favour of empirical work, these subjects remained out of her scope (Alberti and Asso, forthcoming).

Elizabeth E. Hoyt (1893–1980) was part of the second-generation of women who developed and constituted the field of the 'economics of consumption' initiated by Kyrk in the early 1920s (see Parsons, 2013; Bankovsky, 2020). Although Hoyt defended a more socio-anthropological approach, she explicitly drew inspiration from Kyrk's 1923 *Theory of Consumption*, noting that 'Miss Kyrk broke ground with *A Theory of Consumption*' (Hoyt, 1928, p. vi). Hoyt's 1928 book *The Consumption of Wealth* was an important piece of work in the field of the economics of consumption at the time. Joan Robinson published a review of the book in the *American Economic Review* (Robinson, 1929) and Hazel Kyrk published another one in the *Journal of Political Economy* (Kyrk, 1930b). Both reviews were rather positive, although Robinson lamented that some parts were too superficial (see p. 514). Kyrk's review highlighted the novelty of Hoyt's interdisciplinary perspective and its potential importance for the study of consumption. Just like Kyrk, Hoyt considered marginalism to be a fair theoretical starting point but one that would never be sufficient for building a proper theory of consumption. Her interest in anthropological studies reflects this need for anchoring her work in real practices rather than abstract analyses. As she argued: 'Arbitrary and analytical study of marginal utility, which may be excellent as far as it goes, is but the point of departure for the study of consumption. In consumption we must be realistic and concrete' (Ibid.). In line with the institutionalist framework, she pointed out the limits of confining the study of consumption to the mere marginalist abstraction and went on to develop her own approach to the subject, which, as Parsons (2013, p. 341) argues, led her to focus her attention on 'large scale theory of the relationships between culture, consumption and the use of economic resources'.

In the chapter titled 'Ecology: Man's interests and the geographic environment', Hoyt (1928) explained the different relations between geography, climate and the development of culture, emphasising the close connection between the availability of resources and the development of industrial modernity. Because of the direct relationship between humans and their surrounding environment, consumption is shaped by available resources as much as by the effect nature may have on people's minds. She pointed out the view according to which 'the general aspects of nature, whether monotonous or noble and awe-inspiring . . . and so influence the type of thought of a people' (Ibid.). According to her, the climate affects human life in different ways:

> The relationship of climate to our consumption. It is clear that the climate reacts on us in three ways: it affects the flora and fauna available for our choices; it affects our physical needs; and it affects our energy, just how subtly we cannot tell.
>
> (Hoyt, 1928, p. 59)

In a later section called 'The Economic Value of Natural Resources', she attempts to examine the historical trajectory of the modern industrial order. She posed the question whether modernity is 'ultimately explained by the presence of certain mineral deposits [coal and iron] which make factory manufacturing possible' (Ibid.)—a sort of geographical determinism which was then in vogue. Despite the controversies lying behind such historical narratives, Hoyt further explored the implications of resource exploitation resulting from modern industrial modes of production. Quoting C.K. Leith's 'Exploitation and World Progress' (1927), she alerted that '[t]he acceleration of the rate of mineral exploitation may be realised from the fact that the world has exploited more of its resources in the last twenty years than in all preceding history' (Hoyt, 1928, p. 60). Given the focus on consumption, it was the implication of such a trend that interested her the most. Acknowledging the sharp increase in resource exploitation was an invitation to recognise that the production of most people's daily products now relied on their availability. 'This exploitation of mineral resources lies back of [sic] every one of the factory-made products entering into our consumption. Our daily food, our clothing, our homes and their furnishings, most of our recreation: all these things are dependent upon it' (Ibid.). By pointing out that individual consumption is deeply connected to the exploitation of natural resources that most people did not even know about, Hoyt sought to reflect on the global implications of the rapidly increasing level of goods production:

> Our conservationists, of course, are warning us that at our present rate of exploitation our own mineral resources will presently be exhausted, and we shall be in the same boat with those peoples who never had any. This raises two new questions: the question of making substitutions for the present approved industrial minerals; and the greater question of making a substitution for the industrial civilization itself.
>
> (Hoyt, 1928, p. 61)

Beyond the consequences of resource exhaustion and the effects of consumption levels, Hoyt thus took the opportunity to ask whether the depletion of natural resources should lead to questioning the present industrial order itself. She certainly was critical of the global distribution of power between countries and focused her work on development economics after the Second World War (see e.g. Hoyt, 1951, 1969). However, like most second-generation home economists, she did not reject modern consumer society as a whole, but rather, aimed at displaying its shortcomings, which education could help overcome. According to Kyrk (1923), progress was attainable by raising standards of living, which indirectly meant raising standards of consumption. Hoyt, too, believed that a materialist society was a sign of human progress if it implied new products with higher quality and lower prices improving human welfare and comfort for all: 'The specific bearing of all this on the evaluation of consumption is that material progress brings into existence the conditions under which men's powers can be most fully awakened' (Hoyt, 1928, p. 320). However, such a progress came with renewed challenges that home economists believed they were capable of addressing. It meant guiding consumers through a maze of new goods by means of consumer education. Yet, carrying out such an agenda entailed a unified vision of its means and ends: What exactly should be taught? Should consumer education be confined to schools or be disseminated throughout the general public? What constitutes wise consumption? These questions became crucial for the success of their research programme.

5.   Modernity and sobriety in the age of consumerism

As we argued in the previous section, home economists progressively abandoned environmental health issues in the 1920s and focused more on market selection and consumption studies in general. Although such subjects were generally not the most represented in home economics curricula in high schools and universities, it became clear that home economists were regarded as America's 'consumer experts'. The federal Bureau of Home Economics, created in 1923 within the US Department of Agriculture, would become known in the 1930s as the 'consumers' bureau' (Goldstein, 2012, p. 107). This progressive shift made environmental health issues less prominent in home economists' works, especially after the First World War and the Great Depression, when the 'high cost-of-living problem' became the most pressing issue of the time (Rauchway, 2001; Jacobs, 2005; Stapleford, 2009).

Most second-generation home economists did not focus explicitly on environmental issues. The case of Elizabeth Hoyt explored in the previous section is representative of how the matter was basically perceived as a by-product within broader considerations about the factors affecting consumption. To address the high-cost-of-living problem, home economists made use of their earned expertise and reputation to tackle it from the perspective of the household. Although the high cost of living had complex and intricate causes (Rauchway, 2001; Aldrich, 2013), home economists chose to address it from the consumer's perspective—i.e., helping consumers get the best products for the cheapest price while avoiding the subject of wage increase. Moving away from conservationist and environmental health arguments which were firmly present in the agenda of first-generation home economists, the second generation adapted the ecological home allegory to the market environment. The theoretical accounts of consumption developed in the 1920s and 1930s raised, instead, important questions about the meaning of choice in a time that witnessed the emergence of the modern consumer society. Most home economists positioned themselves as experts guiding consumers' choices and helping them navigate through a new world of goods. At the core of this endeavour was the idea of 'wise' or 'rational' consumption as a result of improved choices.

In contemporary market economies, consumption is regarded as a key aggregate pertaining to environmental issues—a means to reduce ecological footprints. Today, the term 'responsible consumption' can mean both reducing one's absolute levels of consumption—associated with the idea of sobriety, sufficiency or voluntary simplicity—or choosing brands or products that have lower environmental impacts. We argue, in this section, that second-generation home economists' theories of consumption have particular relevance for contemporary environmental challenges. As suggested by Bankovsky (2024), home economists' expertise on thriftiness as a tool to fight the high-cost-of-living problem during wars or recessions has a particular resonance with our current ecological predicament. Despite very dissimilar contexts, home economists sought to address the issue of making rational use of resources in a time of actual or expected situation of depletion. Home economists' views during the emergence of modern consumer society unveil the very core of what lies behind the act of consumption as an individual and social practice.

Right in the middle of the Great Depression, Hazel Kyrk further developed her theoretical account of consumption to devise a normative agenda which aimed at improving people's consumption choices, understood as an individual act having both social origins and social consequences and taking place in what she called a 'total environment' (Kyrk, 1923, p. 104). More specifically, she argued, in an article titled 'Education and Rational Consumption' (1930a), that consumption must not be thought of as a science but as an art, which can teach consumers 'rational consumption'. Kyrk distinguished three meanings of the term: first, it could mean 'rational use'—i.e., using the good appropriately to make it last the longest—'it means brushing and repairing one's clothes' (p. 15). This definition relates to the owner's utilisation of the product after the act of buying, and essentially, means avoiding waste and maximising the product's longevity. Secondly, it could also mean 'market selection' in the sense of helping consumers 'secure the good that will best serve [their] purpose with a minimum expenditure of time, energy, and money' (Ibid.). Finally, rational consumption could also mean changing one's wants: 'an attempt to shape the desires, interests, and values that are behind choice' (p. 16). By distinguishing these three meanings, Kyrk sought to challenge the view according to which consumption could be reduced to the act of buying, ultimately calling into question the very idea of consumer sovereignty. According to her, the ability of consumers to enforce their tastes through market selection could vary depending on people. A key task for home economists was to help them assess these inner desires by questioning their origins and making sure that they fit the product they are buying.

For most second-generation home economists, consumer education was generally thought of as a vague set of educational policies that could be implemented, among other places, at schools and universities, in addition to their dissemination through the work of federal bureaus, extension offices, professional associations, consumer's associations and women's leagues. Kyrk also joined this broad consumer education agenda and suggested the creation of a 'bureau of markets and a bureau of standards' to 'undertake the education of the consumer' (Kyrk, 1923, p. 125). In addition to these general propositions, she developed a comprehensive framework to better account for consumers' concrete needs. She was quite critical of the attempts of producers at shaping demand by means of advertising and believed that making information available would not suffice to provide consumers with adequate defences against such influences.

To remedy the situation, Kyrk (1930a, pp. 17–19) went on to develop a framework built on three different axes: (i) information—i.e., providing as much information as possible about a product and its quality; (ii) awareness, to make consumers aware of the origin and motives of their choices; and (iii) autonomy, to foster choice autonomy by allowing the consumer to 'form his own judgments, to desire for himself' (p. 19). These three axes aimed at emancipating consumers from producers as much as from their own socially embedded drives—the ultimate goal being to give them understanding about and power over their own desires rather than just pointing them to the best standardised option to select. Learning rational consumption meant not only choosing wisely but being able to recognise the selling techniques producers use. Teaching marketing was, therefore, part of the curriculum as a means to encourage reflexivity and initiate a dialogue with one's own desires.

Kyrk's normative agenda regarding modern consumerism can be characterised as a prudent one, seemingly adequate to a time when new marketing techniques were booming and consumers had few legal protection (Diamond, 2002; Jacobs, 2005). In the 1920s and 1930s, Kyrk embodied the home economists' desire to defend women and consumers in general against the rapid development of forces leading to the modern consumer society. It is, for that matter, not incidental that her work became, at the same time, the flagship of the economics of consumption and a central text for consumer movements (Finch, 1985, p. 25; see also Cohen, 2003).

Yet, home economists' yearning to carve themselves a professional niche led to a divide in the profession, as an increasing number of them started working for private companies and acting as an intermediary between producers and consumers (Goldstein, 2012, see esp. Chaps. 4–6). Although this divide emerged gradually, it led to a serious questioning of the very nature of home economists' positioning *vis-à-vis* businesses and consumers and regarding their place in modern consumerism.

The case of Christine Frederick (1883–1970, born McGaffey) certainly is the most eloquent example of the spat among second-generation home economists.[7] An early enthusiast of 'domestic taylorism'—i.e., applying scientific management to the household (see Frederick, 1913, 1919, 1928)—she made a career for herself as a business consultant, helping them to better understand consumers and improve sales.[8] For Frederick, advertising and 'progressive obsolescence' were considered as important drivers of economic growth.[9] Like Kyrk, she sought to address the question of how to cope with the emergence of modern consumer society. However, she offered a radically different perspective regarding consumer protection and the 'sobriety ethos' that home economists had been advocating since the mid-19th century.

In 1912, Frederick co-founded, with her husband J. George Frederick, the *League of Advertizing Women of New York*, a project she quickly abandoned to create the *Applecroft Home Experiment Station*, which conducted product testing and displayed models of efficient kitchens (Rutherford, 2003, pp. 51–56). In 1929, she published *Selling Mrs. Consumer*—a handbook written for 'X-Raying the Consumer' (p. 89)—and addressed it to salespeople who wished to better understand 'what and how women buy'. Frederick sought to convince women to replace their kitchen appliances for newer ones, arguing that the advent of the modern household will contribute to reducing women's workload and fatigue in the house as well as promoting an idea of 'creative waste', which was beneficial for national economic growth (Frederick, 1929, p. 79). Her husband had just conceptualised the idea of 'progressive obsolescence' in a paper published in 1928, titled 'Is Progressive Obsolescence the Path toward Increased Consumption?' (Frederick, 1928). Although producers had already been relying on this idea in their practices, the concept in itself had never been put into words before. Christine Frederick took the idea and made it a key element of her consumerist agenda, which would come to prominence in the aftermath of the Great Depression (Slade, 2007, pp. 58–64).[10]

However, Frederick's business perspective contradicted home economists' long tradition of thriftiness and sobriety. Day Monroe, a PhD student of Kyrk at Chicago, wrote a review of Frederick's book for the *Journal of Home Economics* criticising her approach and lamenting that she offered and encouraged such an unflattering depiction of women as consumers:

> Mrs. Frederick also urges that consumers subscribe to an 'obsolence [sic] psychology' which she defines as a 'readiness to 'scrap' or lay aside an article before its natural life of usefulness is completed in order to make way for the newer and better things [. . .] Goods should not be consumed up to their last ounce of usability. This doctrine may please the manufacturer whose goods are to be replaced but is it sound advice for the housewife of limited income?
> (Monroe, 1929, p. 857)

Frederick (1929, p. 201) argued that 'the great mass of American women demand *mass* fashions', which went hand in hand with the idea of standardised production that would benefit businesses (italics in the original). Of course, mass production was already a reality before Frederick, and one could argue that she merely offered an adequate depiction of the changing nature of American mass-consumption lifestyles. Nevertheless, while home economists like Kyrk or Hoyt advocated avoiding

waste at all costs and making consumer protection a priority, Frederick emphasised the economic potential—which, according to her, would ultimately lead to
an income increase at a macro level—accompanying waste generation spurred by
progressive obsolescence. Frederick's work was, understandably, much more appreciated in the business and advertising world. Textbooks on advertising from the
1900s in the US (see, e.g., Scott, 1908) had already welcomed Frederick's gospel
of consumerism, as Kenneth M. Goode's *Manual of Modern Advertising* (1932,
p. 79) indicates: *'Selling Mrs. Consumer*, by Mrs. Christine Frederick, an excellent
book of the Business Bourse, which despite its feminine title, is more valuable to
most advertising men than their more pretentious tones'.

Frederick's take did not become so popular among home economists, who
remained, for a large part, faithful to their original thrift-inspired proposals. The
same cannot be said about the path taken by American society and its characteristic way of life. In the post-war period, the early insights of home economists on
consumption and sobriety would gradually lose influence over public discourse,
not to mention Richards's concern for environmental health and intellectual roots
in human ecology. Programmed obsolescence, arguably the epitome of a productivist and wasteful worldview captured by corporate interests and underlying the
consolidation of an ecologically impaired economic system, became a widespread
practice during the Golden Age. The legacy of home economists remains, nevertheless, as the struggle for improving living standards and reducing the cost of
living, which aligned itself with ecological tenets and environmental concerns by
means of concepts such as the home and sobriety. Their vision of a productive
but healthy society still echoes today in economic arguments about the limits of
growth, the relations between happiness and consumption and, voluntary simplicity
as a means to face current social and environmental crises.

Notes

1 See https://www.govinfo.gov/content/pkg/CFR-2010-title3-vol1/pdf/CFR-2010-title3-
  vol1-proc8351.pdf
2 Swallow (2014, p. 93) indicates that Richards wrote a letter to Haeckel to ask him per-
  mission to use the term, which he accepted. See also the article published in the front
  page of the *Boston Daily Globe*: 'New Science. Mrs. Richards Names It Oekology'
  (Ibid.).
3 The term 'home economics' was established during the Lake Placid Conferences, with
  Richards taking centre stage in the discussions about the field. In 1909, already at the
  end of the 10-year series of meetings at Lake Placid, the American Home Economics
  Association (AHEA) was founded. In 1994, it would be renamed to American Association of Family and Consumer Sciences (McGregor, 2020, p. 28).
4 See www.human.cornell.edu/about/history. On the history of the transition from home
  economics to human ecology at the University of Wisconsin-Madison, see Apple et al.
  (2003).
5 For a more thorough assessment of Richards's different names for her field of knowledge, see McGregor (2020).
6 Nevertheless, there are several examples that remind us of the difficulties at the time
  of obtaining a full professorship at the expected department. The case of Hazel Kyrk,
  another key figure in the field, is quite representative: when she arrived at the University

of Chicago in 1925, she asked to be affiliated with the Department of Economics but would remain at the Home Economics Department until 1929 and would not be granted full professorship until 1941 (see Folbre, 1998, pp. 47–48).

7   Other figures as famous as Christine Frederick at the time are rare. On the subject of home economists who worked in the private sector, see Goldstein (2012) and Chatriot, Chessel and Hilton (2006).

8   Harrington Emerson, one of the two leading figures of the 'efficiency movement' alongside with Frederick W. Taylor, was Christine Frederick's mentor (Rutherford, 2003, p. 56). Emerson was well known for his 1912 book *The Twelve Principles of Efficiency*, which spurred Frederick's ambition to apply them to the household (Rutherford, 2003, pp. 46–47).

9   According to Slade (2007, pp. 72–73), the term 'programmed obsolescence' was popularised by Bernard London in his 1932 essay 'Ending the Depression through Planned Obsolescence', although the term may have already been 'circulating in New York's business community' (Ibid.).

10 Here is how Christine Frederick defined Progressive Obsolescence: 'What is "progressive obsolescence?" It is a somewhat pompous phrase, let us take it apart. These are its characteristics: (1) A state of mind which is highly suggestible and open; eager and willing to take hold of anything new either in the shape of a new invention or new designs or styles or ways of living. (2) A readiness to "scrap" or lay aside an article *before its natural life of usefulness is complete*, in order to make way for the newer and better thing. (3) A willingness to apply a very large share of one's income, even if it pinches savings, to the acquisition of the new goods or services or way of living' (Frederick, 1929, p. 246, our emphasis).

References

Alberti, M., and Asso, P. F. (forthcoming) 'Hazel Kyrk and the Rise of Empirical Research in Interwar America', *Journal of the History of Economic Thought*.

Aldrich, M. (2013) 'Tariffs and Trusts, Profiteers and Middlemen: Popular Explanations for the High Cost of Living, 1897–1920', *History of Political Economy*, 45 (4): 693–746.

Apple, R. D., et al. (2003) *The Challenge of Constantly Changing Times: From Home Economics to Human Ecology at the University of Wisconsin—Madison, 1903–2003*. Madison: Parallel Press, University of Wisconsin-Madison Libraries.

Bankovsky, M. (2020) 'A History of Early Household Economics: Improving the Family's Contribution to Industrial Production and Rationalizing Family Consumption', *Oxford Economic Papers*, 72 (4): 985–1005.

Bankovsky, M. (2024) 'What Should Families Want? From Hazel Kyrk to Margaret Reid and Beyond', in Rebeca Gomez Betancourt (ed.), *Research in the History of Economic Thought and Methodology: Including a Symposium on Hazel Kyrk's: A Theory of Consumption 100 Years after Publication. Research in the History of Economic Thought and Methodology*, pp. 95–116. Bingley, UK: Emerald Publishing Limited.

Banzhaf, H. S. (2009) 'Objective or Multi-Objective? Two Historically Competing Visions for Benefit-Cost Analysis', *Land Economics*, 85 (1): 3–23.

Banzhaf, H. S. (2019) 'The Environmental Turn in Natural Resource Economics: John Krutilla and "Conservation Reconsidered"', *Journal of the History of Economic Thought*, 41 (1): 27–46.

Becchio, G. (2020) *A History of Feminist and Gender Economics*. New York: Routledge.

Benson, E. S. (2020) *Surroundings: A History of Environments and Environmentalisms*. Chicago and London: University of Chicago Press.

Berta, N. (2020) 'Efficiency Without Optimality: Environmental Policies and Pollution Pricing in the Late 1960s', *Journal of the History of Economic Thought*, 42 (4): 539–562.

Blayac, J. (2023) 'Jessica Peixotto, a Home Economist Not Thrilled by the Thrift Culture', *The European Journal of the History of Economic Thought*: 1–20.

Brown, G. M., Smith, V. K., Munro, G. R., & Bishop, R. (2016) 'Early Pioneers in Natural Resource Economics', *Annual Review of Resource Economics*, 8: 25–42.

Chadsey, M. (1915) 'Municipal Housekeeping', *The Journal of Home Economics*, 7 (2): 53–59.

Chatriot, A., Chessel, M.-E., and Hilton, M. (eds.) (2006) *The Expert Consumer: Associations and Professionals in Consumer Society*. Gateshead: Ashgate Publishing.

Clarke, R. (1973) *Ellen Swallow: The Woman Who Founded Ecology*. Chicago: Follett Publishing.

Cohen, L. (2003) *A Consumers' Republic: The Politics of Mass Consumption in Postwar America*. New York: Knopf.

Cooke, K. J. (1998) 'The Limits of Heredity: Nature and Nurture in American Eugenics Before 1915', *Journal of the History of Biology*, 31 (2): 263–278.

Craig, H. T. (1944, June–October) *The History of Home Economics* (Parts 1–4). New York: Detached from Practical Home Economics. Available at: https://catalog.hathitrust.org/Record/009425834

Daly, H. E. (ed.) (1997) 'Forum: Georgescu-Roegen Versus Solow/Stiglitz', *Ecological Economics*, 22: 261–306.

Diamond, J. (2002) 'Who Shall Meet the Foe If Not She? Women's Participation in the Movement Leading Up to the Federal Food and Drug Act of 1906, as Seen Through the Pages of Good Housekeeping', *Harvard Library Office for Scholarly Communication*, Students Student Papers Collection. Available at: https://dash.harvard.edu/handle/1/8889492 [retrieved on 5 March 2024].

Dyball, R., & Carlsson, L. (2017) 'Ellen Swallow Richards: Mother of Human Ecology?', *Human Ecology Review*, 23 (2): 17–28.

Egan, K. R. (2011) 'Conservation and Cleanliness: Racial and Environmental Purity in Ellen Richards and Charlotte Perkins Gilman', *WSQ: Women's Studies Quarterly*, 39 (3–4): 77–92.

Ewert, A. W., Mitten, D. S., and Overholt, J. R. (2014) *Natural Environments and Human Health*. Boston: CABI.

Finch, J. E. (1985) 'A History of the Consumer Movement in the United States: Its Literature and Legislation', *Journal of Consumer Studies & Home Economics*, 9 (1): 23–33.

Folbre, N. (1998) 'The "Sphere of Women" in Early-Twentieth-Century Economics', in H. Silverberg (ed.), *Gender and American Social Science: The Formative Years*, pp. 35–60. Princeton: Princeton University Press.

Franco, M. P. V. (2018) 'Searching for a Scientific Paradigm in Ecological Economics: The History of Ecological Economic Thought, 1880s–1930s', *Ecological Economics*, 153: 195–203.

Frederick, C. M. (1913) *The New Housekeeping; Efficiency Studies in Home Management*. Garden City: Doubleday, Page & Co.

Frederick, C. M. (1919) *Household Engineering: Scientific Management in the Home*. Chicago: American School of Home Economics.

Frederick, C. M. (1929) *Selling Mrs. Consumer*. New York: The Business Bourse.

Frederick, J. G. (1928) 'Is Progressive Obsolescence the Path Toward Increased Consumption?', *Advertizing and Selling*, 5 September.

Georgescu-Roegen, N. (1971) *The Entropy Law and the Economic Process*. Cambridge, MA: Harvard University Press.

Goldstein, C. M. (2012) *Creating Consumers: Home Economists in Twentieth-Century America*. Chapel Hill: University of North Carolina Press.

Goode, K. M. (1932) *Manual of Modern Advertising*. New York: Greenberg.

Griscom, L. M. (1910) 'The Elimination of Waste in the Household', *The Journal of Home Economics*, 2 (3): 292–297.

Hoy, S. M. (1995) *Chasing Dirt: The American Pursuit of Cleanliness*. New York: Oxford University Press.

Hoyt, E. E. (1928) *The Consumption of Wealth*. New York: Macmillan.

Hoyt, E. E. (1951) 'Want Development in Undeveloped Areas', *Journal of Political Economy*, 59 (3): 194–202.

Hoyt, E. E. (1969) *Choice and the Destiny of Nations*. New York: Philosophical Library.

Hynes, H. P. (1985) 'Ellen Swallow, Lois Gibbs and Rachel Carson: Catalysts of the American Environmental Movement', *Women's Studies International Forum*, 8 (4): 291–298.

Jacobs, M. (2005) *Pocketbook Politics: Economic Citizenship in Twentieth-Century America*. Princeton: Princeton University Press.

Kula, E. (1998) *History of Environmental Economic Thought*. London: Routledge.

Kwallek, N. (2012) 'Ellen Swallow Richards: Visionary on Home and Sustainability', *Phi Kappa Phi Forum*, 92 (2): 9–11.

Kyrk, H. (1923) *A Theory of Consumption*. Boston and New York: Houghton Mifflin Company.

Kyrk, H. (1930a) 'Education and Rational Consumption', *The Journal of Educational Sociology*, 4 (1): 14–19.

Kyrk, H. (1930b) 'The Consumption of Wealth by Elizabeth Ellis Hoyt', *Journal of Political Economy*, 38 (1): 112.

Leavitt, S. A. (2002) *From Catharine Beecher to Martha Stewart: A Cultural History of Domestic Advice*. New ed. Chapel Hill: The University of North Carolina Press.

Le Tollec, A. (2020) *Finding a New Home (Economics): Towards a Science of the Rational Family, 1924–1981*. PhD Thesis, Université Paris-Saclay.

Martinez-Alier, J. (1987) *Ecological Economics: Energy, Environment and Society*. Oxford: Basil Blackwell.

McGregor, S. L. T. (2020) 'Home Ecology to Home Economics and Beyond: Ellen Swallow Richards' Disciplinary Contributions', *Journal of Family & Consumer Sciences*, 112 (2): 28–39.

Missemer, A. (2012) 'William Stanley Jevons' The Coal Question (1865), Beyond the Rebound Effect', *Ecological Economics*, 82: 97–103.

Missemer, A., and Vianna Franco, M. P. (2024) 'Municipal Housekeeping and the Origins of the Economics of the Urban Environment (1900s–1920s)', *Review of Political Economy*, 36 (1): 97–115.

Monroe, D. (1929) '"Selling Mrs. Consumer" by Mrs. Christine Frederick (Review)', *Journal of Home Economics*, 21 (11): 856–857.

Parsons, E. (2013) 'Pioneering Consumer Economist: Elizabeth Ellis Hoyt (1893–1980)', *Journal of Historical Research in Marketing*, 5 (3): 334–350.

Pearce, D. (2002) 'An Intellectual History of Environmental Economics', *Annual Review of Energy and the Environment*, 27: 57–81.

Philippy, D. (2021) 'Ellen Richards's Home Economics Movement and the Birth of the Economics of Consumption', *Journal of the History of Economic Thought*, 43 (3): 378–400.

Pietrykowski, B. (2009) *The Political Economy of Consumer Behavior: Contesting Consumption*. New York: Routledge.

Rauchway, E. (2001) 'The High Cost of Living in the Progressives' Economy', *Journal of American History*, 88 (3): 898–924.

Richards, E. H. (1899) *The Cost of Living as Modified by Sanitary Science*. New York: John Wiley & Sons.

Richards, E. H. (1904) *The Art of Right Living*. Boston: Whitcomb & Barrows.

Richards, E. H. (1907) *Sanitation in Daily Life*. Boston: Whitcomb & Barrows

Richards, E. H. (1910) *Euthenics: The Science of the Controllable Environment*. Boston: Whitcomb & Barrows.

Richards, E. H. (1911) *Conservation by Sanitation: Air and Water Supply, Disposal of Waste (Including a Laboratory Guide for Sanitary Engineers)*. New York and London: John Wiley & Sons and Chapman & Hall.

Richards, E. H., and Woodman, A. G. (1904) *Air, Water, and Food from a Sanitary Standpoint*. Second Edition. New York and London: John Wiley & Sons and Chapman & Hall.

Richardson, B. (2000) 'Ellen Swallow Richards: Advocate for "Oekology", Euthenics and Women's Leadership in Using Science to Control the Environment', *Michigan Sociological Review*, 14: 94–114.

Richardson, B. (2002) 'Ellen Swallow Richards: "Humanistic Oekologist," "Applied Sociologist," and the Founding of Sociology', *The American Sociologist*, 33: 21–57.

Robinson, J. S. (1929) 'Review of the Consumption of Wealth', *The American Economic Review*, 19 (3): 513–515.

Røpke, I. (2004) 'The Early History of Modern Ecological Economics', *Ecological Economics*, 50: 293–314.

Røpke, I. (2005) 'Trends in the Development of Ecological Economics from the Late 1980s to the Early 2000s', *Ecological Economics*, 55: 262–290.

Rutherford, J. W. (2003) *Selling Mrs. Consumer: Christine Frederick and the Rise of Household Efficiency*. Athens: University of Georgia Press.

Sandmo, A. (2015) 'The Early History of Environmental Economics', *Review of Environmental Economics and Policy*, 9 (1): 43–63.

Scott, W. D. (1908) *The Psychology of Advertising in Theory and Practice: A Simple Exposition of the Principles of Psychology in Their Relation to Successful Advertising*. Boston: Small, Maynard & Co.

Slade, G. (2007) *Made to Break: Technology and Obsolescence in America*. Cambridge, MA: Harvard University Press.

Soudan, G., Philippy, D., and Maas, H. (2021) 'Crossing the Doorsteps for Social Reform: The Social Crusades of Florence Kelley and Ellen Richards', *Science in Context* 34 (4): 501–525.

Spain, D. (2001) *How Women Saved the City*. Minneapolis: University of Minnesota Press.

Spash, C. L. (1999) 'The Development of Environmental Thinking in Economics', *Environmental Values*, 8 (4): 413–435.

Spash, C. L. (2011) 'Social Ecological Economics: Understanding the Past to See the Future', *American Journal of Economics and Sociology*, 70 (2): 340–375.

Stage, S. (1997) 'Ellen Richards and the Social Significance of the Home Economics Movement', in S. Stage and V. Vincenti (eds.), *Rethinking Home Economics: Women and the History of a Profession*, pp. 17–33. Ithaca: Cornell University Press.

Stage, S., and Vincenti, V. B. (1997) *Rethinking Home Economics: Women and the History of a Profession*. Ithaca: Cornell University Press.

Stapleford, T. A. (2009) *The Cost of Living in America: A Political History of Economic Statistics, 1880–2000*. Cambridge: Cambridge University Press.

Sutherland, S. (2017) *Discovering Science for Women: The Life of Ellen Swallow Richards, 1842–1911*. PhD Thesis, University of Rochester.

Swallow, P. C. (2014) *The Remarkable Life and Career of Ellen Swallow Richards: Pioneer in Science and Technology*. Hoboken: TMS & Wiley.

Swanson, R. L. (2013) *Clean Up Our Home: Ellen Swallow Richards' Human Ecology and Emerging Environmental Ideologies, 1890–1915*. Honors Program Theses, 50, University of Northern Iowa.

Thompson, P. J. (1994) *Ellen Swallow Richards (1842–1911): Ecological Foremother*. ERIC Report ED374014. Available at: https://eric.ed.gov/?id=ED374014 [retrieved on 5 March 2024].

Tomes, N. (1997) 'Spreading the Germ Theory: Sanitary Science and Home Economics, 1880–1930', in S. Stage and V. Vincenti (eds.), *Rethinking Home Economics*, pp. 34–54. Ithaca: Cornell University Press.

Tomes, N. (1999) *The Gospel of Germs: Men, Women, and the Microbe in American Life*. Cambridge, MA: Harvard University Press.

Van Velzen, S. (2003) 'Hazel Kyrk and the Ethics of Consumption', in D. K. Barker and E. Kuiper (eds.), *Toward a Feminist Philosophy of Economics*, pp. 38–55. New York: Routledge.

Vianna Franco, M. P., and Missemer, A. (2023) *A History of Ecological Economic Thought.* London: Routledge.

Walsh, E. A. (2018) 'Ellen Swallow Richards and the "Science of Right Living": 19th Century Foundations for Practice Research Supporting Individual, Social and Ecological Resilience and Environmental Justice', *Journal of Urban Management*, 7: 131–140.

Weigley, E. S. (1974) 'It Might Have Been Euthenics: The Lake Placid Conferences and the Home Economics Movement', *American Quarterly*, 26 (1): 79–96.

5 Nature, exploitation and institutions

On the political ecology of Thorstein Veblen and Karl Polanyi

Manuel Ramon Souza Luz[1] and Ramon Vicente Garcia Fernandez

1. Introduction: exploitation, expropriation and the institutionalist dialogue

The continuous expropriation of the environment is a self-evident characteristic of the incessant process of capitalist valorisation. The seizure of natural resources, whether forests, mines, water or energy resources, presents itself as the frontier for the advancement of capital in the world. However, this process of appropriation and expropriation of resources is something that is not justified by the institutionalisation of salaried work and its exploitation. The expropriation of natural resources is located in another field, its justification occurring in terms external to the exploitative logic of work. In this sense, access to these resources is sustained simply by the right to expropriate—the granted and institutionally structured right that allows the taking of community resources.

It is important to emphasise that the analysis of the relationship between expropriation and capitalism appears clearly in Karl Marx's *Capital* under the name 'primitive accumulation', being later integrated into the very logic of advancement of the capitalist mode of production in Luxemburg (1913). In more recent works in the Marxist field, David Harvey (2003) sought to expand this argument through the concept of 'accumulation through dispossession', something that is followed and complemented by Nancy Fraser and Rahel Jaeggi (2018) and which presents a dialogue with the arguments by Lazzarato (2019) on the role of debt in globalisation and with the post-colonial perspective proposed by Mbembe (2018). These studies, by highlighting expropriation as an inherent to the capitalist mode of production, address the central issue of this process of capture; that is, the function of institutions as enablers of expropriation processes.

In the terms presented, the institutionalisation of expropriation stands as a fundamental object of study for understanding capitalist sociability. In this sense, the present work seeks to present two perspectives from the field of Original Institutionalist Economics (OIE) regarding this phenomenon. The first perspective to be presented is that of the Austro-Hungarian thinker Karl Polanyi (1886–1964), who shows the active processes of implementing fictitious commodities in Western society aiming at the institutionalisation of the self-regulated market. Among these commodities, we highlight the primacy of the 'natural environment' commodity.

DOI: 10.4324/9781003375425-7

The second approach to be verified is that of the pioneer of North American institutionalism, Thorstein Veblen (1857–1929), who tried to identify the barbaric origins of capitalist institutions, which include the 'absentee ownership' of the large industrial company in relation to the natural environment. The institutionalisation of 'absentee ownership' presents itself as the cornerstone of the 'sabotage' of the captains of industry in relation to the common well-being.

This article seeks to bring together the Polanyian and Veblenian diagnoses regarding the expropriative face of the capitalist mode of production and its institutional foundation, placing these perspectives in dialogue with contemporary approaches to the frontier of the capital valorisation process in the world and its relationship with the natural world. In this sense, in the first item, we will present how exploitation is presented in the critical literature with a Marxist background, taking as a point of reference Marx's concept of 'primitive accumulation' and its subsequent developments. Next, we will describe how Polanyi and Veblen identify the institutional foundations of expropriation based on the reference to the natural world and its incorporation into capitalist sociability. Finally, we will seek to present differences and common aspects in order to promote a dialogue between the institutionalist approach and the Marxist literature on the subject.

2.   From primitive accumulation to dispossession: expropriation as the foundation of the capital valorisation process

As rightly pointed out by Luxemburg (2003) [1913], chapter XXIV of Marx's *Capital* (1990) appears as a type of anomaly within the theoretical body of his work. If the process of capital appreciation within the expanded reproduction scheme was based on the institutionalisation of wage labour and the control of the means of production by the bourgeoisie, then we would have a self-fuelled 'vicious circle' of production of surplus value and consequently surplus capital. Rosa Luxemburg's critique (1913) points out that in this description of the valorisation process, based on the institutionalised exploitation of work, the incorporation of capital through theft and expropriation is considered as something external to the logic of the system itself. In this aspect, interestingly, that chapter, called 'The So-Called Primitive Accumulation', appears not only as evidence of the exteriority of expropriation in the author's work but also as a reference for understanding the logic of expropriation as a fundamental aspect of the capitalist mode of production. In this chapter, Marx deals with what he called 'primitive accumulation'; that is, the 'starting point' that enabled the capitalist mode of production; it would be 'the historical process of separation between producer and means of production'. It appears as 'primitive' because it constitutes the prehistory of capital—'the moment when the capital is born' (Luxemburg, 2003, p. 314).

For Marx (1990), expropriation is 'inscribed in the annals of humanity with traces of iron and fire'; it would be present in the process of 'usurpation of communal lands' from rural producers and peasants, creating a mass of dispossessed workers who would be exploited as salaried workers. However, the genesis of industrial capital would have an even more violent origin, linked to primitive capital originating from the conquests and expropriations of the colonial system; in this sense '[t]he discovery of gold and silver in America, the extermination, enslavement and imprisonment of the native population in mines, the beginning of the conquest and plunder of the East Indies, the transformation of Africa into a hunting enclosure to trade black skins, mark the dawn of the era of capitalist production' (Marx, 1990, p. 285).[2]

Primitive capital as a starting point for capitalist accumulation is harshly criticised by Luxemburg (2003) [1913)]. For her, capitalist accumulation is expropriating and violent not only in its primitive phase, but this constitutes a permanent characteristic of imperialism that constantly eliminates any barriers to capitalist expansion. Luxemburg understands, therefore, that there is no exteriority of expropriation in relation to exploitation, but that capitalist accumulation always requires the encapsulation of what escapes it.[3] Like Marx (1990) [1867], Luxemburg points to this expropriation in a broad way—something that includes the environment and the communities in a 'primitive communist state'—that is, formations called 'natural economies'—which present themselves as not assimilable to capitalist accumulation. Thus, for the author '[c]apital knows no other solution than violence, a constant method of capitalist accumulation in the historical process, not only at its genesis, but even today' (Marx, 1990, p. 37).

Considerations about expropriation as an inherent character of the capitalist mode of production were taken up by numerous contemporary authors inside and outside the Marxist perspective. One of the most relevant contributions is that of Harvey (2003), who, advancing the vision of Luxemburg (2003) [1913], presents the process of expropriation as a general characteristic of contemporary capitalism, called by the author 'accumulation by dispossession'. Harvey points out that capitalism tends to seek geographic expansion and temporal displacement to resolve crises of overaccumulation; the logic is simple: 'If there are surpluses of capital and labour power within a determined territory (as for example a national state) that cannot be absorbed internally (by means of geographical adjustments or social expenses), they must be sent elsewhere in order to find a new terrain for its profitable realization so as not to be devalued' (2003, p. 103). In this aspect, what is outside the orbit of accumulation through exploitation would end up, sooner or later, being taken over through the same violent procedures highlighted by Marx and Luxemburg.

Nancy Fraser and Rahel Jaeggi, in their *Capitalism: A Conversation in Critical Theory* (2018), point to the necessary articulation between the concepts of exploitation and expropriation to understand contemporary social processes. The exploitation-expropriation key is presented by the authors as a characteristic element of this system that reproduces itself at its bases, but at the same time, needs to continually appropriate what exists outside its exploratory sphere—something classified by the authors as 'brute confiscation'.

Just like Luxemburg (2003) [1913], Fraser and Jaeggi (2018) understand that expropriation is a continuous phenomenon and that it is therefore the basis of capitalist development, here and now. The distinction between the concepts of exploitation and expropriation is clear: 'In the case of exploitation, capital pays for the socially necessary cost of the worker's reproduction in the form of wages, while appropriating the surplus created by their work. In expropriation, on the contrary, he simply takes labour, people, and land for itself without paying for their reproduction costs' (2018, p. 58).[4] In this sense, the two concepts have a fundamental difference that the authors present as essentially institutional and political. For them, this becomes very evident when comparing humanities forged at institutionally distinct based on the exploration-expropriation key. Institutionally, there would be a rule that separates those human beings subject to exploitation—that is, those considered free workers, bearers of rights—from human beings subject to expropriation—that is, helpless subjects, fundamentally racialized, not free, who do not have political protection in the capitalist society.[5] In addition to the different humanities, the authors point out that the relationship with the natural world would also be based on the institutionalisation of a set of expropriation rules that would allow the confiscation of the natural world and of human beings themselves. It is evident, therefore, that institutions would be the central element that determines what will be exploited or expropriated in our sociability.

The natural world is therefore positioned as the boundary between what is exploited and what is expropriated.[6] In this sense, it is important to point out that the border is not objective; it is an institutional construction that is established based on how relations of power and submission are constituted. It is clear that the natural world requires a set of institutions that qualify it as the thing to be expropriated. The institutionalisation of confiscation and expropriation therefore emerges as an object of study on the border of capitalism and nature itself.

The study of the institutionalisation of the expropriation of the natural world is the object of this chapter. In this aspect, we will seek to articulate and complement the discussion of this topic with the diagnoses and considerations of two central contributions to what constitutes the tradition of the Original Institutionalist Economics school. In this sense, we will seek to present a guided reading from the perspective of two fundamental institutionalist works; namely, Karl Polanyi's classic *The Great Transformation* and Thorstein Veblen's latest work *Absentee Ownership and Business Enterprise in Recent Times*. The description presented will seek to articulate the ideas of these two authors based on the exploration-expropriation conceptual key, highlighting common elements, relevant differences and, mainly, showing the current reading of Polanyi and Veblen on the issue of capitalist sociability and the institutionalisation of the destruction of the natural world.

3.   Karl Polanyi: fictitious commodities and the environment

The Great Transformation (2001) [1944], Karl Polanyi's masterpiece, presents us with a precise diagnosis of the conditions of the relationship between human beings and their environment in a society organized by markets. For Polanyi, the self-regulated market does not constitute an order resulting from nature or human rationality, but rather, it would be an ideological and practical construction carried forward by a historically identifiable institutionalisation process. This process, encompassed by the active action of the State, would have deliberately reconstructed the bases of what it would mean to be human, also defining the boundaries and possible relationships between human beings and the natural world.

For Polanyi (2001 [1944], 1977), the 'real' (or substantive) economy is defined as the process of transformation of nature by human beings, who, through work, seek to satisfy their needs; in the words of the institutionalist thinker: 'The substantive meaning points to the elemental fact that human beings, like all other living things, cannot exist for any length of time without a physical environment that sustains them' (Polanyi, 1977, p. 19). As a cultural entity, humanity mediates its needs and its action in nature through an institutionalised process (Polanyi, 1977, p. 31). Thus, Polanyi escapes from the idea of the economy as a univocal manifestation of human natural proclivities (generally understood from the notion of human as bargainers) and presents a conception where the environment and culture establish a myriad of possibilities for integration with varied institutional patterns and which could constitute different forms of economic organisation. In this aspect, the economy, in a substantive sense—that is, in its general sense, as the common denominator of human societies—would be an institutionalised process of interaction whose function is to supply society with material resources (Polanyi, 1977).

Polanyi (2001 [1944], 1977) points out that the possibilities of economic organisation could be quite varied, and curiously, societies organised by market means would be a great exception in terms of the historical and ethnographic record. In reality, the market itself (as a place of bargain) would appear incidentally as an anthropological reference, always on the margins of kinship, religious, status or command relationships. Contrary to the view of economic orthodoxy, which has as its premise that the only form of economic organization of societies is based on commercial exchange, Polanyi (2001 [1944], 1977) highlights that there are other forms of organisation that are much more recurrent and general in human societies. These forms of organisation could be classified into three distinct types of integration, from which their respective institutional models would be defined. They would be: (i) reciprocity, a form of integration in which a symmetric institutional model allows groups or subgroups to establish relationships of reciprocal mutuality with their symmetrically identified peers; this form allows, for example, exchanges of gifts established in a system of benefits and considerations, far from any concept of equivalence[7]; (ii) redistribution, a form of integration that starts from an institutional model based on centrality, in which some centralising entity collects, stores and redistributes resources to the rest of the community's members in accordance with established rules of a traditional nature;[8] and (iii) domesticity, a form of integration built from an institutional model based on the principle of autarky, which comprises production and storage aimed at satisfying the needs of the person or group itself.[9] In this way, Polanyi (2001 [1944], 1977) highlights that commercial exchange, for most societies, was not the main form of integration, being less important than redistribution, reciprocity and domesticity. In this case, the integration of communities through markets would be a major exception in terms of economic organisation.

Polanyi (2001) [1944] points out that, in most human communities, commercial relations, when existing, are embedded in social relations. Thus, in all types of economic integration presented, the market, if it existed, would appear as a foreign element and necessarily rooted in principles that would not allow its autonomy. If it existed, the market would be limited and regulated by traditional forms of integration common to all mankind. There was only one exception to this rule: modern market society.[10] It is emphasised here, therefore, that Polanyi identifies all existing forms of social integration as being based on institutional models that consider commercial exchange as an element external to what is controllable. A society organised through markets would be, in this sense, a form of integration that subverts and reframes humanity and nature in innovative terms.

Polanyi (2001) [1944] emphasises that 'a market economy can only exist in a market society'; thus, for the Hungarian thinker, the economy ordered by markets resulted from a deliberate effort to create its specific human and social bases in the sense of this order. In this new world, the market would have been artificially uprooted (disembedded) from other social relations so that they now become 'an accessory to the economic system' (Polanyi, 2001, p. 81). If the market was normally a marginal institution, subject to other existing forms of integration, in a society organised by the form of market integration, submission occurs in the opposite direction; that is, the fields of life that were traditionally not organised by commercial exchange would become marginalised and subjected to these relationships.

The process of implementing a society organised by markets was based on the deliberate reconstruction of what human nature would be and on the reframing of the environment in which human beings are inserted. Avoiding dwelling too much on Polanyi's (2001) [1944] argument, it is necessary to point out that the process of institutionalisation of the capitalist order is presented by the author based on a historical study of the institutions of the country that led the industrial revolution: England. In this sense, Polanyi explains that the widespread introduction of machinery—a fundamental characteristic of mass industrial production—would have been the origin of the process that culminated in market society. The need for a continuous flow of labour, raw materials and markets would be the major requirements of this new industry, which, to guarantee its expansion, required a complete modification of the institutions that founded the traditionally existing society.

To meet the aforementioned demands of the expanding industry, the English State between 1834 and 1846 deliberately built formal institutions unprecedented in the history of humanity,[11] which created the three fictitious commodities necessary for the implementation of the self-regulated market: Land, Labour and Money. According to Polanyi (2001) [1944], the fiction lies in the fact that, despite being essential elements for the support of an organised society with a certain level of complexity, land, labour and money had never been considered commodities, since 'none of them are produced for sale' (Polanyi, 2001, p. 78). Thus, the fact that labour, land and money began to act as commodities is entirely fictitious—an institutional necessity of capitalist industrial society to enable the institutionalisation of the self-regulated market. In this sense, it is worth noting that the tragic nature of the implementation of the self-regulated market would be linked to the human and natural consequences of the institutionalisation of these fictions.

The institutionalisation of the fictitious commodities land, labour and money provided all the necessary elements for the flow of industrial production. These elements were reconfigured in an innovative way to be accessed according to the pricing system. Thus, according to the vision that emerges from this process, workers, forced by the threat of hunger, would be willing to sell their work for a salary; in turn, business people, motivated by profit, could find on the market the labour force necessary for their industries, in addition to the commodity land, required to implement their factory production as well as to provide them with the raw materials necessary to be transformed. Finally, the realisation of this social relationship would be based on the fiction of money, which would allow the purchase of all these 'goods' necessary for the implementation of industrial activities, which also earn profits on the market through the sale of what was produced. In this sense, all elements of economic activity would have been institutionally reconfigured, aiming at the integration made possible by the self-regulated market, thus establishing a market society.

Contrary to the view of the market as a natural or spontaneous order, commonly found in laissez-faire rhetoric, Polanyi points out that the society integrated by markets was made possible by the active intervention of the State. This intervention would not have occurred only when the self-regulated market and its fictitious goods were implemented but would have been permanent in nature. According to the author:

[T]he introduction of free markets, far from abolishing the need for control, regulation and intervention, has enormously increased their reach. Administrators had to always be alert to ensure the system ran smoothly. Thus, even those who ardently desire to free the state from all unnecessary duties, and whose global philosophy demanded the restriction of the state's activities, had no alternative but to entrust to that same state the new powers, organs and instruments required for the establishment of the laissez-faire.

(Polanyi, 2001, p. 157)

If the reality of the market society was an intervention, curiously its ideological content is in the opposite direction. Polanyi pointed out that, *pari passu* with the institutionalisation of a society organised by markets, a type of interpretation of its reality has emerged: liberalism. For Polanyi (2001) [1944], liberalism would be 'a true faith in the secular salvation of man through a self-regulating market' (Polanyi, 2001, p. 151). In this sense, liberal non-economic institutions used the concept of laissez-faire, which can be translated as the idea that exchange relationships between human beings should not suffer external interference, especially from the State. From this perspective, these relationships always represent a virtuous natural order, as they are based on human nature itself. According to liberalism, human beings would have a natural tendency to exchange, to trade, and, therefore, the only way to organise society would be to let human nature manifest itself, for which it would be essential for society to intervene in the State as to remove all external influences, thus ensuring that markets function freely. In other words, the motivations created by the society and the illusion of laissez-faire justified that the economic system came to fully represent the society and, therefore, the dynamics of functioning of this society would be subordinated to the logic of the self-regulated market.

For Polanyi (2001) [1944], the fictional triad of land, labour and money was responsible for shaping a new society, ideally organised only by markets.[12] Human beings, who, in any other type of economy, had their work linked to a set of instrumental and ceremonial institutions of diverse origins, now depended exclusively on the sale of their labour power to receive a wage and guarantee their existence. In this aspect, it is worth noting that not only the fear of hunger was understood as the great driver of human action; it was also necessary to institutionalise the business counterpart—the institutionalisation of an insatiable hunger for profit.

The anthropology of the market society points out that the relationship with the external world should be guided by bargaining.[13] The environment, 'which in the recent past would be linked to relationships of kinship, creed, such as the tribe and the temple, the village, the guild and the church' (Polanyi, 2001, p. 199) now starts to be treated as a movable and alienable asset, which should be subjected to the demands of the self-regulated market. In this sense, it is necessary to emphasise the centrality of the natural environment for Polanyi and the fictionalisation of its existence. Here, it is important to return to the author's concept of 'substantive economy', since he places nature itself, as well as labour, as the elements that form the common denominator of a human economy. The specificity consists of the institutional form of the relationship between labour and nature. A society integrated by principles of centrality, reciprocity or domesticity presents institutional forms of the relationship between humans and the natural world that consider broad factors of sociability in that world. In integration via the market, nature appears only as a commodity—a somewhat fake commodity.

Polanyi (2001) [1944] offers us a fundamental element to understand the relationship between the natural world and its expropriation within capitalist society.[14] He presents us the non-human nature as one which is taken, dispossessed, appropriated from a relationship of violence—a reality based on the institutionalisation of a lie. In this sense, fraud would consist of the established understanding that the natural world in itself is a commodity. The fiction of the commodity land highlights the structural need of the capitalist world to expropriate the natural world and, at the same time, the need to conceal such action, framing it in terms of fair exchange. Polanyi (2001) [1944] addresses what is most important in the implementation of liberal economic ideology: the ideological-institutional conversion of labour exploitation and the expropriation of nature into commodities. Such a conversion, due precisely to the lack of real foundations, would necessarily be false. In this sense, the fiction that Polanyi points to is the very impossibility of so much labour, land or even money being regulated by the market. The institutionalisation and implementation of this belief in market societies would be, for the author, the reason for the economic and social crises that have accompanied Western societies in the last three centuries.

The destruction of the natural world, of the social ties and of the common wellbeing are essentially due to the institutionalisation of the self-regulated market and its fictions. The institutional transformations brought about by the introduction of machinery guaranteed the foundations for the insatiable advance of capitalism on a finite planet. Thus, for Polanyi (2001) [1944], it was possible that the market form of economic integration went from being an exception within the forms of integration existing in humanity to becoming hegemonic in human societies—a domain that ended up allowing it to be understood as if that this type of economy would be the only possible type.

4. Thorstein Veblen: vested interests, absentee ownership and the confiscation of nature

The institutionalist pioneer, Thorstein Veblen (1857–1929), has a complex work that sought to provide the fundamental elements for understanding the logic of contemporary capitalist sociability. The Veblenian perspective had a strong impact on economics and, together with the contributions of another institutionalist, John Commons (1862–1945), founded what became known as Original Institutionalist Economics, which was part of the economic mainstream, especially in the United States, between the beginning of the 20th century and the end of the Second World War (Morgan and Rutherford, 1998)

Born in the Midwest of the United States to immigrant Norwegian farmers, Veblen witnessed significant transformations in the natural world and rural life throughout his life. These transformations, derived from the advancement of capitalist relations in the countryside, in addition to having impacted the author's life at different times, ended up being incorporated into his economic perspective (Mitchell, 2007, p. 10).[15] With the aim of making this Veblenian political ecology evident, we will present here a descriptive path that initially seeks to return to Veblen's historical-anthropological understanding regarding the relationship between human beings and the natural world, and later, specifically address the author's ideas regarding the relationship between contemporary industrial society and the environment.

At first glance, Veblen's anthropological perspective has clear influences from the evolutionism of Lewis Henry Morgan (1818–1881) and Edward Tylor (1832–1917) because, like the pioneers of social anthropology, Veblen understood that humanity could be classified historically at different stages of development. However, this similarity is debatable. According to Anne Mayhew (1998, p. 240), these influences would only be of form because, in relation to the content of his perspective, Veblen's anthropological ideas would be in line with Franz Boas (1858–1942)— interestingly, one of the greatest opponents of evolutionism in anthropology. Mayhew points out that Veblen, like Boas, understood that social change was not teleological, with some tendency to improve. The two thinkers converged on the understanding that all human beings had common instincts and that the differences between the diverse human communities would only be of a cultural and institutional nature.[16] Thus, we must point out that Veblen's view (1899, 1914), contrary to the evolutionary perspective, does not understand that everything that remained in the past in the history of humanity is necessarily inferior when compared to the present moment. On the contrary, despite speaking about different stages, Veblen's anthropological argument presents the history of the institutional transformations of humanity as a process of degradation, and in this negative process, the relationship between humans and the natural environment has absolute centrality.

Veblen's (1899, 1914) historical-anthropological perspective focuses on the description of four historical periods that transform and succeed each other, based on identifiable processes of institutional change. The first one, which comprises the Neolithic period, is called by the author the Era of Peaceful Savagery; the second, fundamentally marked by the institutionalisation of property and class distinctions, is called the Barbarian Era; the third one, characterised by the introduction of money and the advancement of mercantile exchange, is called the Era of Handcrafts or the Peaceful Pecuniary Era; and finally, industrial capitalism constitutes a distinct period, which Veblen called the Machine Age (Veblen, 1899, 1914).

For Veblen (1899, 1914), the history that permeates and connects all these eras presents a rupture in a fundamental institutional content that led humanity towards a fundamentally predatory type of sociability. This central transformation would be located in the transition between the era of Peaceful Savagery and the Barbarian Era. In Veblen's view (1899), it was during the Barbarian Era that the institutions that supported the prevalence of 'vested interests' in human societies were created, including the institutionalisation of private property and the leisure class. For Veblen, the institutions inaugurated by the barbaric world founded the general institutional conditions of our contemporary life, since, as Diggins (1977, p. 123) points out, we would be living in continuity with: 'the barbaric past, with the modern captain of industry carrying the role of the archaic chieftain of combat'.

Veblen's description of the age of peaceful savagery points to important aspects that, as emphasised earlier, would be displaced in later ages. According to Veblen (1899, 1914), these first human communities were characterised by being small and peaceful groups, without command, without classes or hierarchies. They were societies founded on cooperation and centred on the survival and well-being of the community as a whole (Hall and Kirdina-Chandler, 2017, p. 561). Work in these communities was carried out as an industry; that is, as the act of transforming nature by creating something that has a new useful purpose for that community.[17] These characteristics presented, which several authors describe as fundamental anarchist elements,[18] lead us to a principle that is central to our present investigation: the impossibility for these communities to generate surpluses. If we understand that surplus would be the property of producing beyond what is socially necessary, then we can say that the traditional and peaceful communities described by Veblen were incapable of producing in excess of what was necessary for their survival.[19]

In the opposite direction to the peaceful principles, a barbaric society is based on the differentiation between its members. Such differences are given according to the type of work performed. In this sense, in addition to activities of a productive or industrial nature, a new type of activities would be added—those of a competitive nature, centred on the demonstration of prowess and called ceremonial activities by Veblen. In this sense, a class of people would have emerged that represents those who carry out some kind of prowess in their activities, essentially made up of warriors, athletes, bishops, chiefs, nobles, aristocrats and, nowadays, the bourgeoisie. All of these would make up a type of class characterised by having the power to command and extract what was produced by others—and, exactly for this reason, Veblen calls this group the Leisure Class.

For Veblen (1899, 1914), the barbarian era would have inaugurated a new type of social order based on status' demonstrations and on the exercise of power. Status would be the honorific element that justifies hierarchies within a society. On the other hand, power would come from the ability of some to impose their will on others, fundamentally given through the command and appropriation of what is produced by others. In the barbaric world, status offers the institutional foundations that guarantee the exercise of power. The institutionalisation of status and power led to its corollary; that is, the introduction of private property. This occurs because, in its most developed stages, a society of barbarian origin is characterised by the institutionalisation of the struggle for the possession of private goods with a view to achieving status and power and, at the same time, by the use of this status and power to obtain a greater accumulation of wealth assets. As highlighted by Mitchell (2007): 'The power to exploit is conferred by wealth or status. It allows one to acquire, trade, sell, use, or even waste property, materials, or anything else to demonstrate one's position of dominance' (Mitchell, 2007, p. 13).

It is important to note here that barbarism has a predatory character that did not exist in the peaceful societies of the previous period. The latter, despite having some status relationship, did not have institutionalised power relations.[20] Barbarism would have inaugurated, in this sense, command as a natural consequence of status—something that altered not only the relationship between human beings but also between them and the natural world—if, among humans, the institutionalisation of status and power allowed an unprecedented command over the work of others through their exploitation.[21] On the other hand, these same institutions enabled the expropriation of the natural world in a broad and continuous way. If, in peaceful communities, their egalitarian nature led to a relationship with the natural world based on satiability, in the barbaric world, surplus would have become the rule because the relationship between status, power and property enables unrestricted predation of the natural world.[22] The institutionalisation of this relationship based on excess is called 'absentee ownership' by Veblen and is one of his major research concerns in his latest works.

Veblen's last major work, *Absentee Ownership and the Business Enterprise in Recent Times* (AO) (1923), is based on a reflection on the relationship between 20th century industrial capitalism and the environment.[23] We argue here that AO provides some elements that can be integrated with the Polanyian diagnosis on the environmental issue, seeking to form the foundations of a joint institutionalist vision. In this sense, like Polanyi, Veblen looked into the anomaly of considering nature as a commodity and sought to unravel the foundations of this strange interpretation. In his book, Veblen emphasises the incompatibility between the concept of 'natural right to property' and what he called 'absentee ownership'. Absentee ownership would be 'the ownership of means in excess of what the owner can make use of, personally and without help' (1923, p. 12). Absentee ownership would be the central concern of the actions of authorities in Western nations who, as a result, would work incessantly to 'safeguard the security and gainfulness of absentee ownership' (1923, p. 4). In this sense, ownership over nature is, for Veblen, the great example of absentee ownership.

Veblen (1923) points out that property over nature is far from what was established as the natural right to property. Following Locke, Veblen points out that this natural right to property would be based on the idea of industry, which comes from the possession of the result of the objective combination of human work with the natural resources used for production.[24] For Veblen, the credit and salary relationship could also be characterised as absentee ownership, as they are based on a relationship of exploitation and expropriation of resources and people aiming to create a surplus for the absentee owner. This type of absentee ownership could still be 'traceable to workmanship', as it was still linked to the appropriation of what was the product of human work; that is, produced for the community.[25] In a different sense to this, Veblen will point to the ownership of nature as an example of distinct and deeper absentee ownership, since

> [the] ownership of natural resources—lands, forests, mineral deposits, water-power, harbor rights, franchises, etc.—rests not on a natural right of workmanship but in the ancient feudalistic ground of privilege and prescriptive tenure, vested interest, which runs back to the right of seizure by force and collusion.
>
> (1923, pp. 50–51)

In this sense, despite its 'feudal' origins, it should be noted that the absentee ownership in the world of Business Enterprises is more than mere ownership over natural resources: it is directed towards the manipulation of this property in function of market control. Absentee ownership would lead to the implementation of a vested interest; that is, the right to sabotage the community production according to the profit interests of the business enterprise.[26] In this sense, in AO, Veblen emphatically points to the absentee ownership of 'key industries', such as iron, gold, coal, wood and real estate. For Veblen (1923), credit, the wage relationship and natural resources are clear evidence of the establishment of absentee ownership which, in the 'last decades' has become 'the prime institutional factor that underlies and governs the established order of society' (1923, p. 4).

Veblen (1923) understands that the taking of the natural world for private gain through 'absentee ownership' is a fundamental characteristic of the capitalist development of his time, especially in the United States. In the world of business enterprises, natural law, coming from an era of handicraft, would be 'playing the role of a dead hand'. For the institutionalist thinker, with the emergence of the large corporation, the fundamental institutions became vested interests and absentee ownership, and this applied in the relationship with the natural world. For Veblen, this relationship occurs through direct expropriation to obtain private gains. Taking the case of the United States as a reference, Veblen points out that, in this country, natural resources 'have progressively been taken over into private ownership on a reasoned plan of legalized seizure' (122). The absentee ownership of natural resources is a source of free income, as it is based on sabotage by those who have ownership over these resources, constituted in the contemporary world under the pecuniary interests of the business enterprise. Being necessary resources for the general production of the community, their value would be directly related to the power of control of their owners over them *vis-à-vis* the productive needs of the community. In this respect, absentee ownership of these resources manifests itself as a simple vested interest, administered through sabotage techniques.

This forced conversion of natural resources into absentee ownership is called the American Plan by Veblen (1923). In this respect, Veblen is clear: '[The] American plan or policy is very simply established practice of converting all public wealth to private gain on a plan of legalized seizure' (1923, p. 168). This procedure would have manifested itself in different ways within American history, including 'the debauchery and manslaughter imposed on the Indian population' and the consequences of the private appropriation of land in the South, leading to production with enslaved black labour.

5. Final remarks

Capitalist sociability is founded on processes of submission sedimented by specific institutions. These processes are recurrently explored by Marxist thinkers interested in the articulations between the principle of exploitation and expropriation. As we have seen, an important effort carried ahead by these thinkers is the search to incorporate expropriation as an endogenous principle of capitalist system, something emphasised by Luxemburg (2003) [1913] and nowadays developed by thinkers such as Harvey (2003) and Fraser and Jaeggi (2018). For us, it is precisely under the aegis of the expropriatory nature of capitalism that we can find the elements that enable us to deal with the socio-political foundations of environmental destruction.

Based on the observation of expropriation as an object of analysis as well as its relationship with the environment, this work sought to provide new elements for the incorporation of an institutionalist political ecology as a contribution to the foregoing debate. Among the various thinkers interested in understanding the nature of institutional processes of capitalist sociability, we selected the contribution of two of its greatest exponents—i.e., the institutionalist point of view of Thorstein Veblen as well as that of Karl Polanyi. The choice of these thinkers is justified because they offer a complementary perspective based on the combination of historical, anthropological and economic references. These references enabled them to provide an innovative vision regarding the institutional changes that have consolidated the predatory relationship between Western society and the natural world.

It was observed here that both Polanyi and Veblen present a critical position in relation to how modern industrial society understands the environment (basically, the land and natural resources). For both thinkers, the idea of the natural world as being considered a commodity would be nothing more than a dangerous lie. In this sense, in Polanyi (1944), we find the identification of a fiction inherent to the institutionalisation of market society; that is, the fiction that nature would be a commodity and as such; would become subject to widespread manipulation based on the (also manufactured) universal motive of profit. Veblen (1923), in turn, places emphasis on absentee ownership—i.e., the principle that guides the appropriation of nature within contemporary capitalism. For Veblen, it is private control, forged by force and fraud, that allows business enterprises to earn profits simply by interposing themselves between natural resources and the productive needs of society. Thus, both the commodity nature described by Polanyi and Veblen's absentee ownership emphasise the same thing: the manufactured and fraudulent institutional foundations that guarantee the right to expropriate the natural world in capitalist society.

In addition to the institutionalist diagnosis regarding the pernicious relationship between industrial society and the environment, Polanyi and Veblen present a common alternative to curb the process of destruction of the natural world. In this sense, we find in the anthropological perspective of thinkers the seed for a proposal that emancipates humans and the nature of the exploitative and expropriative character of capitalist sociability. Thus, it is important to note that Polanyi (1977, 1944), when presenting the different forms of social integration, places the market order as an exception compared to other forms of economic organisation of human societies. Polanyi's anthropological perspective states that, instead of being a general rule of human communities, the self-regulated market represents an anomaly which is incompatible with the dynamics of the existence of human groups as well as their relationship with the natural world. Therefore, Polanyi explicitly points to the need to control and the re-embedding of market within society—something that is not new but a rule of all human communities except ours. The Veblenian perspective also does not shy away from anthropological and ethnographic references to propose an alternative to the pulverisation of the planet by absentee ownership. In Veblen, this alternative is linked to his fundamentally anarchist description of the era of peaceful savagery. As seen here, the compartmentalisation of the history of humanity into eras does not imply that Veblen believed in the existence of a teleological process of improvement of human societies. His anthropology, on the contrary, emphasised the idea of the unity of human beings and the plurality of cultures. Thus, a peaceful, egalitarian and cooperative world without surpluses might no longer be seen as an archaic feature of the beginnings of human communities; on the contrary, this idyllic community must be imagined and built here and now.

Notes

1 The researcher acknowledges the support from the Brazilian National Research Council (CNPq), grant 309984/2021–1.
2 It is important to note that Marx connects the violence of the colonial system with its form of veiled expropriation, which appears under the name of public debt, 'one of the most energetic levers of primitive accumulation' (Marx, 1990 [1867], p. 288).
3 For an anthropological reference on how traditional communities organise themselves as to build a barrier against the expansion of the capitalist mode of sociability, we recommend reading Sahlins (1972) and Clastres (1974, 1989).

4 It is interesting to notice that, in the typical discussions of orthodox economics and New Institutionalism, the concept of expropriation is restricted to the compulsory withdrawal by the State of someone's property—typically, the owners of some asset.

5 This political separation between what would be considered human and what is on its margins is emphasised by Mbembe (2018) in his discussion of the legal aspects of the process of conquest and colonisation, thus pointing out that 'law was a way of legally establishing a certain idea of humanity divided between a race of conquerors and another of slaves. Only the race of conquerors could legitimately attribute human quality to itself' (2018, p. 115).

6 Even in the process of labor exploitation, the natural world enters in the form of raw materials; that is, as an expropriated element, which no longer generates value.

7 The best-known example of this form of integration is found in the ethnographic records of Malinowski (2018 [1922]) and in the analysis of Mauss (2003 [1950]). In this case, the system of exchanging gifts among the Trobrianders, known by the term Kula, shows the web of symmetrical relationships in a system of iterative debts. According to Malinowski: 'The basic principle on which the rules of the transaction itself are based is the fact that Kula consists of the giving of a ceremonial gift in exchange for which, after a certain time, an equivalent gift must be received . . . [t]he equivalence of the counter-gift is decided by its donor and not by imposition or any type of coercion' (2018 [1922], p. 165).

8 Here, the most frequently cited example is the potlatch of the North American Kwakiutl. Before Polanyi, Thorstein Veblen already mentioned the potlatch to present the ostentatious practices of burning wealth of this indigenous group much studied by Franz Boas. The Kwakiutl festivals, in which blankets and whale blubber were burned, can be understood as a form of redistribution in favour of the honor of the tribal leader and consequently of the tribe that promotes the festival, as noted by Mauss: 'The goods are lost in the potlatch as they are lost in war, in gambling, in fighting. In some cases, it is not even about giving and giving back, but about destroying' (2003, p. 239).

9 Sahlins (1972) and Clastres (1974) emphasise the autarchic ideal of indigenous groups who, contrary to the myth of the natural exchanger, seek to produce everything they need to avoid depending on any type of exchange with external groups. Groups, thus, seek to maintain their independence in relation to other groups. In this sense, autarchy would be the rule among indigenous groups and exchange would represent an exception.

10 Note that this society is not just a society in which there are markets but one in which a vast majority of economic activity is organised through them. Much of Polanyi's intellectual effort after the 'Great Transformation' was focused on studying the role of markets in societies in which they existed without being dominant.

11 These laws are: (i) the Poor Law, which removed government protections for poor populations and made available a human army to serve as labor force according to market logics; (ii) the Peel Bank Act, which instituted the gold standard and; (iii) the repeal of the Corn Laws, which removed the protection of local farmer producers and left the unprotected peasantry of continental Europe to the whims of the markets making the unprotected Continental peasant-farmer subject to whims of the market (Polanyi, 1944, p. 113).

12 Polanyi (2001, p. 77) is clear in this sense: 'Labor and land are nothing more than the human beings themselves of which all societies consist, and the natural environment in which they exist. Including them in the market mechanism means subordinating the substance of society itself to the laws of the market.' Therefore '[the] commodity description of labor, land and money is entirely fictitious' (2001, p. 76).

13 Lacher (2007, p. 54) emphasises that 'The great transformation of the early nineteenth century thus put the profit motive at the center of society's interaction with nature [. . .] this emerging centrality of the profit motive was not a mere shift in mentalities. It was the result of a fundamental transformation in the very structure of society that forced people to pursue profitable economic enterprise or earn wages if they wanted to survive and maintain their social position'.

14 As Gregory Baum (1996, p. 19) reminds us, '[l]ong before the public outcry against the devastation of the environment, Karl Polanyi was the prophetic theoretician of the ecological movement'.

15 We point here to the Veblen family's own history as farmers expelled from the country-side in Norway and who managed to continue their activity as immigrants on a plot of land donated by the Minnesota state. It should also be noted that, in addition to his rural origins, Veblen always rema0ined connected to a life close to the natural world, having built a cabin in the mountains of northern California in which he spent long stays. A good description of Veblen's relationship with the natural world can be found in Camic (2020) and Mitchell (2007).

16 As William Dugger (1988, p. 12) teaches us, the anthropological perspectives of both Veblen's and Boas' challenge the notion that humankind is on some kind of progressive and favourable path that differs based upon historically conditioned realities. Mayhew (1998) goes further, stating that Veblen's ideas follow the emergent anthropological paradigm of Boas, and this can be characterised by an orientation towards ethnography and cross-cultural comparisons.

17 This tendency towards industry would be linked to a human instinct called by Veblen (1914) as the 'instinct of workmanship'.

18 As a note, we highlight Dugger (1984) and Plotkin (2007), which points out that in these peaceful communities the 'inclinations to anarchic and quasi-anarchic institutions fol-low from instinctive and spontaneous inclinations toward communally directed and or self directs work' (Plotkin, 2007, p. 50).

19 Plotkin (2007) highlights Veblen's vision of the relationship between humans and the natural world during the period of peaceful savagery: 'For him, we are, at some deeply organic level, sensitive to the fact of our interdependence on each other and nature. We apprehend that the other- whether another person, the community, or some phenomenon in nature—is too vital to the collective destiny of species, to waste or abuse' (p. 33).

20 For a detailed description of the institutional mechanisms that prevent the convergence of status with power in traditional societies, we refer to Clastres (1989, 1994).

21 Here it is important to understand that if, in the era of Peaceful Savagery, work is un-derstood as industry, in later eras, work was understood as exploitation, defined as the ability to convert to its own ends the energies previously directed by another agent for other purposes (Veblen, 1899).

22 As Dugger (1984, p. 978) highlights: 'Barbarism differed economically from earlier savagery in that an economic surplus had arisen'.

23 The institutionalist movement, which would continue Veblen's work, maintained this attitude. According to James Swaney (1987, p. 1748), '[t]he instrumental value criteria of the continuity of human life, the noninvidious re-creation of community, and the corollary of environmental compatibility form the core of institutionalist values'.

24 According to Locke (2010 [1659]), private appropriation would be a result of the hu-man right to self-preservation and would extend to all of nature, which would have been provided by God for man to appropriate. In this aspect, according to natural law, this appropriation should be carried out through work. We therefore see that, from this per-spective, property would be a result of the state of nature and not a social construct; as Macpherson (1983, p. 222) points out, 'Locke established the natural right to individual property, a right prior to civil society and government'.

25 It is important to emphasise the separation that Veblen makes between production and earnings, to understand this mix between workmanship and business. In this aspect, in the author's words: 'Production is a matter of workmanship, whereas earnings is a mat-ter of business' (1923, p. 61).

26 According to Veblen (1919, p. 38), vested interests are 'a marketable right to get some-thing for nothing'. The vested interest does not stem from the productive use of a plant but from the 'ways and means of driving a bargain'. In the first case, wealth derives

from the use of a tangible asset; in the other case, wealth derives from intangible assets, or the 'immaterial relations between owners and the industrial system'. In this sense, the wealth derived from the use of intangible assets is not a result of 'an increase of the equipment or the material resources in hand'.

References

Baum, G. (1996) *Karl Polanyi on Ethics and Economics*. Montreal: McGill-Queen's University Press.

Camic, C. (2020) *Veblen: The Making of an Economist who Unmade Economics*. Cambridge, MA: Harvard University Press.

Clastres, P. (1974) *Archeology of Violence*. Los Angeles: Semiotext(e).

Clastres, P. (1989) *Society Against the State*. New York: Zone Books.

Diggins, J. (1977) 'Animism and the Origins of Alienation: The Anthropologial Perspective of Thorstein Veblen', *History and Theory*, 16 (2): 113–136.

Dugger, W. (1984) 'Veblen and Kropotkin on Human Evolution', *Journal of Economic Issues*, 27 (4): 971–985.

Dugger, W. (1988) 'Radical Institutionalism: Basic Concepts', *Review of Radical Political Economics*, 20 (1): 1–20.

Fraser, N., and Jaeggi, R. (2018) *Capitalism: A Conversation in Critical Theory*. London: Polity Press.

Hall, J., and Kirdina-Chandler, S. (2017) 'Towards an Intellectual History of Evolutionary Economics: Competition and Struggle Versus Cooperation and Mutual Aid', *Brazilian Journal of Political Economy*, 37 (3): 551–564.

Harvey, D. (2003) *The New Imperialism*. Oxford: Oxford University Press.

Lacher, H. (2007) 'The Slight Transformation: Contesting the Legacy of Karl Polanyi', in A. Bugra and A. Kaan (eds.), *Reading Karl Polanyi for the Twenty-First Century*. New York: Palgrave Macmillan.

Lazzarato, M. (2019) *El Capital Odia Todo el Mundo: Fascismo o Revolución*. Buenos Aires: Eterna Cadencia.

Locke, J. (2010 [1659]) *Two Treatises of Government*. London: Everyman.

Luxemburg, R. (2003 [1913]) *The Accumulation of Capital*. New York: Routledge.

Macpherson, C. B. (1983) *The Political Theory of Possessive Individualism*. Oxford: Oxford University Press.

Malinowski, B. (2018 [1922]) *Os Argonautas do Pacífico Ocidental*. São Paulo: Ubu.

Marx, K. (1990 [1867]) *Capital*. Vol. 1. London: Penguin.

Mauss, M. (2003 [1950]) *Sociologia e Antropologia*. São Paulo: Cosac & Naify.

Mayhew, A. (1998) 'Veblen and the Anthropological Perspective', in W. Samuels (ed.), *The Founding of Institutional Economics*. London: Routledge.

Mbembe, A. (2018) *Crítica da Razão Negra*. São Paulo: N-1 Edições.

Mitchell, R. (2007) 'Introduction: Political Ecology and Thorstein Veblen', in R. Mitchell (ed.), *Thorstein Veblen's Contribution to Environmental Sociology: Essays in the Political Ecology of Wasteful Industrialism*. Lewiston: Edwin Mellen.

Morgan, M., and Rutherford, M. (eds.) (1998) *From Interwar Pluralism to Postwar Neoclassicism. History of Political Economy*. Supplement to volume 30. Durham, NC: Duke University Press.

Plotkin, S. (2007) 'Animism and the Roots of a Veblenian Political Ecology', in R. Mitchell (org.), *Thorstein Veblen's Contribution to Environmental Sociology: Essays in the Political Ecology of Wasteful Industrialism*. Lewiston: Edwin Mellen.

Polanyi, K. (1977) *The Livelihood of Man*. Edited by H. Pearson. New York: Academic Press.

Polanyi, K. (2001 [1944]) *The Great Transformation: The Political and Economic Origins of Our Time*. Massachusetts: Beacon Press.

Sahlins, M. (1972) *Stone-Age Economics*. New York: de Gruyter.

Swaney, J. (1987) 'Elements of a Neoinstitutionalist Environmental Economics', *Journal of Economic Issues*, 21 (4): 1739–1779.

Veblen, T. (1899) *The Theory of Leisure Class*. New York: Macmillan.

Veblen, T. (1914) *The Instinct of Workmanship and the State of the Industrial Arts*. New York: Augustus M. Kelley.

Veblen, T. (1919) *Vested Interests and the State of Industrial Arts*. New York: B. W. Huebsch.

Veblen, T. (1923) *Absentee Ownership and Business Enterprise in Recent Times: The Case of America*. London: George Allen & Unwin.

6 Principles for building a post-Keynesian environmental macroeconomics

Revisiting Keynes in times of crises[1]

Marcio Alvarenga Junior and Carlos Eduardo Frickmann Young

1. Introduction

Although heterodox approaches to environmental problems have gained ground in recent years, neoclassical economics remains strongly hegemonic. This predominance of orthodox theory in the environmental economics literature reflects the hegemony of neoclassical thinking in economics itself and the late awakening of heterodox to these issues. Some exceptions, such as ecological economics, criticise the mainstream approach to environmental issues (Lavoie, 2014). However, most of these alternative views base their arguments on the existence of physical limits to economic growth and do not consider the effective demand problem. Therefore, they tend to focus on calls to reduce production and consumption to conserve natural resources and avoid environmental damage without payment equal to the effects of reducing the economic activity level on income generation and unemployment rates.

Post-Keynesian economics can contribute significantly to this debate. Its criticism of neoclassical economics in the ontological field argues that general equilibrium models are not genuinely descriptive because they are built upon 'as if' premises—i.e., they derive their results assuming that agents and markets behave differently to reality (Lavoie, 2014). In the field of sustainability, however, many post-Keynesian scholars still behave 'as if' environmental sustainability does not matter when building their models and their economic policy recommendations do not impact the environment.

In recent years, the Covid-19 economic crisis has exposed the disconnection between mainstream economic theory and the practicalities of society. Orthodoxy's inability to propose a positive agenda to solve the health and economic crises has resulted in adopting policies that go against its recommendations in favour of a Keynesian prescription of countercyclical policies (Carvalho, 2020).

The world seems to be approaching post-pandemic normality. Nevertheless, several social, economic and environmental problems that preceded or were inherited from Covid-19 pandemic remained unsolved. The challenges of improving social inclusion, reducing poverty and inequality in all their forms and manifestations and dealing with environmental crises of unprecedented proportions are very

DOI: 10.4324/9781003375425-8

much alive today, and their solution will require long-lasting commitment from policy makers. For instance, unlike regular economic crises, the climate crisis is not a passing phenomenon, and its resolution will depend on a broad effort in various sectors over the following decades.

In this scenario, it's crucial for post-Keynesians to be capable of proposing a positive agenda concerning environmental issues, especially the climate crisis. The central aspect of this agenda is the understanding that macroeconomic policies have real effects on production levels and agents' wealth accumulation strategies and, therefore, are not neutral to the environment.

Acknowledging the need to promote a greater engagement of PKs in environmental sustainability-related issues, we propose four delimiting principles for a post-Keynesian environmental macroeconomic:

  i. The principle of environmentally extended effective demand.
 ii. The principle of environmental non-neutrality.
iii. The principle of non-convergence towards sustainability.
 iv. The principle of constrained growth.

This chapter has four sections in addition to the introduction and conclusion. The first introduces the neoclassical approach to environmental issues. The second presents post-Keynesian thinking in general terms. The third section introduces the four defining principles of this new approach. The final section shows how Keynesian thinking has influenced the main green recovery proposals over the last decade and a half.

2.   The mainstream view of environmental economics

Neoclassical theory considers natural resources in the same way as any other production factor, so that the price mechanism, once operating correctly, is sufficient to resolve the overuse of these resources. To better understand this fact, suppose a production function based on two factors in which the output is unique and homogeneous (equation 1):

$$Y = f(K, RN) \tag{1}$$

In this function, Y denotes the quantity produced, K is the quantity of capital, RN is the amount of natural resources, and f is the production possibility frontier (the set of techniques that produces the maximum product with factors currently available). By assumption, the production of Y does not require labour (to simplify the model), and the production function is assumed to have constant returns to scale and diminishing marginal returns for each production factor—i.e.:

$$f(\mu.K, \mu.RN) = \mu.f(K, RN) \tag{2}$$
$$fk' > 0 \text{ e } fk'' < 0 \tag{3}$$
$$fRN' > 0 \text{ and } fRN'' < 0 \tag{4}$$

Additionally, the conditions of Inada (1963), given in equations 5 and 6, are assumed to be valid:

$$\text{Lim} k \to 0 \ (fk') = \text{Lim} RN \to 0 \ (fRN') = \infty \tag{5}$$
$$\text{Lim} k \to \infty \ (fk') = \text{Lim} RN \to \infty \ (fRN') = 0 \tag{6}$$

There is a functional form for the production function capable of simultaneously meeting the constant returns to scale, the decreasing marginal productivity of factors and the Inada conditions. The functional form follows the Cobb-Douglas production function, where the sum of the exponents is unitary (equation 7).

$$Y = Ka \ .RN1\text{-}a \tag{7}$$

As specified in (7), the production function has the property of unitary elasticity of substitution, which means that changes in the price of one of the factors imply its substitution in equal proportion. Equation (8) states that the remuneration of production factors equals their marginal productivities, where f_k' and f_{RN}' denote the marginal productivity of capital and natural resources, respectively.

$$Pk = fk' \ (K^*, RN^*); \ PRN = fRN' \ (K^*, RN^*) \tag{8}$$
$$Y^* = fk'(K^*, RN^*).K^* + fRN'(K^*, RN^*).RN \tag{9}$$

Equation 8 provides the conditions for maximising profit in Walrasian general equilibrium. Meanwhile, equation (9) shows the equilibrium output, which is given by the marginal product of each production factor at the optimum level, multiplied by the optimum quantity of these factors. At this point, one can notice that, if natural resource scarcity increases, its price will tend to increase (Hotelling Rule). To ensure profit maximisation under the new relative prices, the current production technique will have to be replaced by less resource-intensive ones.[2] Since production factors have diminishing marginal returns, this reduction in the use of the natural resource will lead to an increase in its marginal productivity. The substitution of the natural resource by other production factors will remain up to the point where its marginal productivity equals its new price.

In this sense, adopting a production function with unitary elasticity of substitution assumes that natural resources can indefinitely substitute for capital (and vice versa), keeping production levels constant. Since price and marginal productivity changes are always compensating for one another, it follows that changes in the relative prices do not have distributive effects—i.e., the contribution of each of these factors to production remains constant.

In the neoclassical framework, the full functioning of the price mechanism is enough to ensure the optimum use of natural resources. However, the constitution of markets depends on well-defined property rights—a characteristic that does not permeate most of these resources. If property rights are not well established, economic agents tend to perceive natural resources price as zero, resulting in their overuse and, consequently, environmental impacts (negative externalities). The solutions advocated by neoclassical theory involve re-establishing the functioning of the price mechanism, either by imposing taxes on the use of these resources or by establishing tradable emission rights (Perman et al., 2003). Once the price mechanism has been re-established, the system returns to the optimal level of natural resource use that maximises social welfare.

Extending the foregoing conclusions to the long term, the possibilities of infinite substitution between capital and natural resources not only reveal that it is possible to produce the same level of output when the natural resource becomes scarcer but also admit that it is possible to circumvent any limits to economic growth imposed by the depletion of these resources. Hartwick (1977) formalised the possibilities of indefinite output expansion, arguing that it is possible to achieve a sustainable growth path if the rents from the current exploitation of non-renewable resources are invested in labour-reproducible capital. This argument has become known as the 'Hartwick Rule' in the literature. Ultimately, this rule admits that it is possible to grow indefinitely if capital accumulation compensates for natural resource depletion so the total stock of capital in the economy is non-decreasing over time. If the economy deviates from the sustainable path, changes in relative prices, and eventually, in consumers' intertemporal preferences would be enough to bring the system back to an optimal point where both sustainability and full employment of factors are in place. In this sense, in the neoclassical tradition, the state's role in the transition to a green or carbon-neutral economy would be very much based on its role in helping markets function fully.

In summary, the environmental economics literature concerning economic growth usually follows the standard neoclassical approach, which does not consider the effective demand problem—i.e., full employment is taken for granted (for example, see Solow, 1986). The emphasis is correcting externalities by fixing market distortions ('putting a price on nature'), usually associated with undefined property rights. Once 'the prices are right', the economy tends to follow its equilibrium trajectory, and there is no concern about unemployment in the formal neoclassical models.

On the other hand, standard Keynesian macroeconomics focuses on the unemployment problem but ignores the sustainability issue. Multiplier-accelerator interaction models analyse the intertemporal linkages between current production and the long-term effects of man-made capital accumulation. Nevertheless, problems concerning changes in the stocks of non-produced assets, such as resource exhaustion or pollution, are not formally addressed (Young, 1997). The objective of the following sections is to discuss principles to combine sustainability issues with the effective demand problem.

3.   Economic dynamics in a monetary economy of production

In his General Theory of Employment, Interest and Money, Keynes (1936) presents the Principle of Effective Demand (PED) as the explanatory element of the level of economic activity. The author develops the PED based on two functions related to the level of employment (N): a Z(N) function, which represents the value of aggregate supply resulting from the employment of N workers and a D(N) function, which represents the value of aggregate demand resulting from this same volume of employment. The Z(N) function relates the level of employment to the revenue that the entrepreneur believes is sufficient to justify employing N workers. The D(N) function represents how much the entrepreneur expects to receive from employing N workers. Therefore, whenever the amount that entrepreneurs expect to receive for a given volume of employment (D(N)) exceeds the amount that justifies this very same level of employment (Z(N)), there will be an incentive for entrepreneurs to increase their production level for what a higher level of N will be required.

In other words, entrepreneurs' decisions regarding the production and employment levels are grounded in their expectations about the size of aggregate demand (D); more precisely, about the level of consumption (D1) and investment (D2). Assuming that D1 + D2 = D(N) = Z(N), where D1 is also a function of N—namely, C(N)—then Z(N) – D1= D2. Therefore, increases in the level of employment result in increases in aggregate income and, given the 'psychology of the community', smaller increases in aggregate consumption. As Keynes points out (1936, p. 40):

> Thus, to justify any given amount of employment there must be an amount of current investment sufficient to absorb the excess of total output over what the community chooses to consume when employment is at the given level. For unless there is this amount of investment, the receipts of the entrepreneurs will be less than is required to induce them to offer the given amount of employment.

Therefore, for Keynes, the level of employment is defined in the output market, reflecting entrepreneurs' expectations about the demand for their production and not in the labour market as in neoclassical theory. In the foregoing equations, the intersection of the D(N) and Z(N) curves determines the level of employment at what is known as the point of effective demand.

In the exposition proposed by Keynes (1936), consumption is a relatively stable function concerning the income level, given that the marginal propensity to consume tends to change slowly over time. That being said, oscillations in investment level are the key element in explaining fluctuations in the levels of activity and employment. In the approach proposed by Davidson (1984) and Carvalho (1992), understanding these oscillations involves money's unique role in capitalist accumulation in a system marked by non-probabilistic uncertainty.

This type of uncertainty, unfamiliar to neoclassical models, results from the temporality of economic processes and their non-ergodic nature. The first of these elements concerns that a non-negligible time interval separates production decisions and their monetary results. The decision to produce happens in the present when the entrepreneur contracts the factors needed to materialise the desired scale of production and for which a certain amount of money is advanced as remuneration for the contracted factors. However, there is no guarantee that the income generated for undergoing the production will be entirely spent on the acquisition of the goods and services produced in that period. In this way, the crucial decisions in a monetary economy are fundamentally based on the entrepreneur's expectation of the monetary yields they hope to obtain from these decisions.

Non-ergodicity, on the other hand, establishes that time runs unidirectionally— meaning that, once a crucial decision is made, it is impossible to re-establish the preexisting conditions of the economy. As Robinson (1969 [1956], p. 180) pointed out, '*a given short-period situation contains within itself a tendency to long-period change*'. In other words, crucial economic decisions are not only based on expectations but they rewrite, at every turn, the trajectory of the economic environment for which such expectations are formulated. This implies that expectation errors do not generate a set of information that enables agents to foresee, in advance, the demand for their products in following periods, in order to make more accurate decisions regarding their respective production levels.

If decisions on how much to produce can be revised at a relatively low cost each period, decisions to invest hardly fit into this reality. Understanding this issue involves the fact that the investment decision represents a change in portfolio composition, in which agents move from a fully accepted asset (money) to specific assets (capital goods). This leap from a general form of wealth representation to a specific form only makes sense if the agents expect to obtain more money at the end of the accumulation process than they initially had. In practice, given the low liquidity of capital goods, their monetary returns will fundamentally depend on the realisation of the income flow generated by the production facilitated by them throughout its lifetime.

Although choosing to retain a portion of the wealth in monetary form does not generate any monetary return by the end of the accumulation process, this remains a very convenient decision to deal with highly uncertain economic environments. The maximum liquidity of money allows agents to readily adjust their accumulation strategies, since money can be immediately convertible into any other form of wealth at any point in time. In this sense, in a monetary economy, money is a *sui generis* asset, capable of competing with other assets in the course of the wealth accumulation process. In a modern economy, liquidity preference is standard defensive behaviour when uncertainty exceeds acceptable limits, beyond which agents have little or no inclination to immobilise their wealth through new investments. As such, the trajectory of accumulation depends heavily on the agents' perception of uncertainty, their expectations regarding the future and their confidence in their prognoses, which will determine how much of their wealth they want to keep in monetary form.

However, the decisions to resort to assets that do not require the use of labour to be produced, as in the case of money, will result in insufficient effective demand, and thus, in involuntary unemployment. It is in this sense that Keynes states that '*the course of events cannot be predicted, either in the long period or in the short, without a knowledge of the behavior of money between the first state and the last*' (Ibid., 1973, pp. 408–409). In other words, the production and employment level depend on the wealth accumulation decisions that will determine which portion of wealth goes towards the formation of new fixed capital (D2) and which goes towards other forms of wealth that cannot be reproduced by labour.

4.   Principles for a post-Keynesian macroeconomics of the environment

One of Keynes' main contributions was to demonstrate that agents decide to keep part of their wealth in the form of money in an environment of non-probabilistic uncertainty and that these decisions have real impacts on the level of activity, employment and income (Keynes, 1936).

It is interesting to note that the concepts of uncertainty and irreversibility, so relevant to post-Keynesian theory, as expressed by Davidson (1984) and Carvalho (1992), are also fundamental principles within ecology. Most ecological processes—the erosion of natural capital that leads to problems such as biodiversity loss and climate change—are deeply uncertain, and from certain thresholds, can become irreversible. In this scenario, projecting the ecological future based on past conditions becomes problematic because decisions on using natural resources and the environmental impacts associated with these decisions alter the conditions of the environment in which life and the system evolve (Mearman, 2009). Therefore, like production and investment decisions, the use of natural capital can also be included in what Davidson (1983, p. 193) called crucial decisions: '*Crucial choice involves, by definition, situations where the very performance of choice destroys the existing [probability] distribution functions*'.

Seeking to increase the engagement of post-Keynesians in the environmental agenda, we propose a theoretical structure for a post-Keynesian Environmental Macroeconomic approach based on four principles:

i The principle of environmentally extended effective demand.
ii The principle of environmental non-neutrality.
iii The principle of non-convergence toward sustainability.
iv The principle of constrained growth.

The first principle states that effective demand not only determines employment, output and income levels but also the degree of utilisation of natural resources, pollutants emissions and other environmental impacts. Since natural resources (renewable or not) serve as production factors, it is reasonable to assume that the degree of utilisation of these resources also stems from spending decisions made by economic agents. There is to say, spending decisions determine the level of economic activity and, thus, the extent in which the natural capital will be used or depleted in the production process (Alvarenga Jr. and Young, 2019)

A post-Keynesian rejects the neoclassical idea that the labour market determines the aggregate level of employment. Similarly, we propose that the natural resource markets do not determine the aggregate level of use of natural resources. Both labour and natural resources levels are determined in the output market, according to entrepreneurs' expectations about the demand for their products. The same is true for pollutant emissions. Although specific markets have emerged in recent years—especially to deal with carbon emission—what these markets do is to price the negative externality.

Economic mechanisms for environmental management such as Pigouvian tax and tradable emission certificates are not 'free market' based solutions but instruments to flexible the targets and restrictions imposed by public environmental policy. Once the social planner (usually the public administration) establishes the price for a given emission level, directly by a tax or indirectly by the number of emission certificates, entrepreneurs internalise this cost in their production function. However, the desired scale of production and the resulting level of emissions will continue to be a function of their expectations about the level of demand for their products.

The second principle is a consequence of the first. Since the decision to keep wealth in the monetary form results in idle capacity, macroeconomic policies have real impacts in the economy. By generating changes in the output, income and employment level, macroeconomic policies also drive changes in the degree of utilisation of the natural capital. Expansionary economic policies will generate positive incentives to increase production, whether by raising the degree of capacity utilisation or by undertaking new investments. In both cases, this will imply greater consumption of natural resources and more emissions, embodied in producing either final goods and services or the inputs needed to produce them.

Unlike the neoclassical approach, the third principle of environmental macroeconomics holds that the economy does not converge towards full employment or sustainability.

Several criticisms have been directed at the way neoclassical theory derives convergence to equilibrium at the level of full employment.[3] Within this theoretical framework, the endowment of production factors is exogenous and it is up to the aggregate demand to adjust to the level of full employment. For achieving such a convenient result, neoclassical theory admits the existence of multiple production techniques capable of producing the same quantity of output, all exhibiting constant returns to scale. The exogenous endowment of factors combined with the multiplicity of production techniques, each with constant returns to scale, implies diminishing marginal returns for each factor (Cesarato and Serrano, 2002). Consequently, it only becomes profitable to expand the utilisation of a production factor if its price decreases hand-in-hand with its marginal productivity. This inverse relationship between the demanded quantity of the factor and its price directly arises from the principle of substitution, which posits that it is possible to unrestrictedly substitute production factors whenever a change in their relative prices occurs.

In this regard, constant returns to scale for productive techniques and diminishing marginal returns are central elements of the neoclassical adjustment mechanism to equilibrium, and '*apparently minor differences in assumptions about F (*) can generate radically different theories of economic growth*' (Barro and Sala-I-Martin, 1995, p. 16). Regarding the underlying hypothesis of the production function, Pitchford (1960) drew attention to the possibility of an absence of a well-behaved steady-state when the assumption of unitary substitution elasticity is relaxed in Solow-based growth models. Few years later, Conlisk (1968) assessed the effects on these same types of models when the assumptions of constant returns to scale and non-unitary substitution elasticity are relaxed. The author demonstrated that, if the substitution elasticity is not unitary, constant returns to scale must exist to ensure a well-behaved steady state.[4]

The absence of endogenous mechanisms for converging towards sustainability can also be addressed in a macroeconomic perspective. In a monetary economy, the level of output is not determined by supply conditions but by the behaviour of aggregate demand. As mentioned earlier, there is no guarantee that, in the aggregate, the sum of entrepreneurs' expectations regarding the demand for their products will result in a level of output compatible with the production factors fully employed or the levels of natural resource utilisation and pollution being optimal.

As a corollary, if the system does not converge to full employment and sustainability, then it needs to be driven to this situation by some exogenous factor; in this case, the active action of the state. The non-convergence to economic and environmental equilibrium redefines the importance of the state's role in achieving sustainability. In the neoclassical approach, the State plays a regulatory role, correcting market failures so that changes in relative prices and eventual changes in consumers' intertemporal preferences can drive the system to sustainability at the level of full employment of factors in the long term.

However, from a post-Keynesian environmental macroeconomics standpoint, sustainability results from a particular process of capital accumulation, which must be pursued as an objective of the economic planning process through consistent economic policies. These policies should be used for greening aggregate demand and creating the institutionality needed for ramping up the transition toward sustainability. Governments can directly influence the environmental quality of economic growth by greening government consumption and public investment (Alvarenga et al., 2024, forthcoming). Therefore, greening fiscal policy by adopting green procurement systems and tools for mainstreaming environmental criteria into public investments projects is a central plank in these sustainability-induced transitions. By increasing the demand for goods and services that comply with the best environmental practices and objectives, green production tends to come along.

Additionally, a wide range of economic and institutional policies could also help to guide entrepreneurs' decisions towards sustainable practices. Public banks could charge lower interest rates from firms that meet desirable environmental criteria, while changes in regulations and the tax system assist in internalising the environmental costs (Alvarenga, Costa and Young, 2022). Government action leading and coordinating research and development (R&D) efforts seems to be even more strategic to induce the transition. This effort should target green innovation capable of reducing the cost of green technologies or increasing the productivity and competitiveness of green sectors.

The most radical innovations, in recent decades, relied on a proactive participation of governments, whether through directly undergoing efforts in basic and applied R&D, mobilising resources or establishing and strengthening links between universities, public research centres and private companies (Mazzucato, 2013). R&D activities involve a significant uncertainty about when and if the technology generated will prosper in the market. Since radical innovations often demand more financial resources and time and result from highly uncertain R&D efforts, the private sector is often reluctant to take the lead in this process. As Mazzucato (2013, p. 166) pointed out:

> The 'green' energy industry is still in its early stages: it is still characterized
> by both technological and market uncertainty. It will not develop 'naturally'

through market forces, in part because of embedded energy infrastructure, but also because of a failure of markets to value sustainability or to punish waste and pollution. In the face of such uncertainty, the business sector will not enter until the riskiest and most capital-intensive investments have been made, or until there are coherent and systematic policy signals in place. As in the early stage of IT, biotech and nanotech industries, there is little indication that the business sector alone would enter the new 'green' sector and drive it forward in the absence of strong and active government policy.

Public investment, if well placed, can reduce costs and increase expected profits of green sectors and technologies, thereby attracting new, private investment to push transitions further. At this point, the dual contribution of greening investment should be stressed. In the short run, increasing green investment will result in higher levels of economic activity, income and employment while helping to redirect aggregate demand to cleaner sectors. To date, there are still few studies that compare the macroeconomic benefits of green spending to spending in traditional sectors. Alvarenga, Costa and Young (2022) found that a green investment package for Brazil would result in higher levels of output, income and more and better jobs (with higher wages and levels of formalisation). On the other hand, in the long-run, green investment creates new productive capacities in strategic sectors to support the transition to sustainability. This dual role played by investment is one of the cornerstones of the green recovery plans presented in the next section.

The fourth principle holds that economic growth depends on the total capital stock (manufactured and natural capital). The depleted portion of the natural resource used for current production purposes cannot be used in the future. If investing creates productive capacities, depleting natural resources works otherwise, destroying it (Young, 1993, 2018).[5] As Keynes (1936, pp. 99–100) pointed out: *'In the case of raw materials the necessity of allowing for user cost is obvious; if a ton of copper is used up today it cannot be used tomorrow, and the value which the copper would have for the purposes of tomorrow must clearly he reckoned as a part of the marginal cost'.*

When it comes to non-renewable, natural capital, it urges us to consider the transition from the current linear economic system to a circular economy (with maximum reuse of natural resources). Economic policies must convert the 'reduce, reuse, recycle' principle into practical measures concerning non-renewable resources. As for renewable resources, economic policies should be in place to guarantee that the production pressure on their stocks remains under the environment's regenerative capacity.

At this point, it is worth recalling, once again, that, unlike the approach presented in section 2, the transformations necessary to either mitigate the depletion of non-renewable natural resources or to keep renewable resource consumption below the regenerative capacity of the environment are not endogenously produced. Moreover, if the unsustainable use of natural capital negatively impacts economic activity in the long-run, it is also possible to turn environmental spending into a vector for economic growth. The following section shows that this idea is at the heart of the green recovery proposals of the last decade and a half.

5.   Crises and the New Keynes

The confluence of social, economic, environmental and health crises has been a hallmark of the recent period. Although Covid-19 is no longer a global health emergency, many problems inherited from or predating it still persist. The persistence of these crises challenges the economic science to produce solutions capable of responding to the practical issues of our time. For example, the environmental agenda has increasingly influenced the debate on post-pandemic economic recovery (Young and Mathias, 2020). In this scenario of multiple crises, governments, multilateral organisations and key stakeholders are reviving proposals that align economic growth with the conservation and restoration of natural capital and the transition to a low-carbon economy. Among these proposals are the Green New Deal (GND GROUP, 2008; UNEP, 2009), the Green Economy (UNEP, 2011) and, more recently, the Environmental Big Push (Gramkow, 2019).

The Green New Deal (GND) was initially designed to articulate solutions to the effects of the 2008 financial crisis, global warming and the historic peak in oil prices (GND GROUP, 2008; UNEP, 2009). The original documents proposed far-reaching changes to international financial regulation, the tax system and an extensive fiscal package to stimulate the economy through 'green investments'. The GND pointed to the importance of regulatory reforms in the financial system to adapt it to the context of climate change, reducing financial risks stemming from a potential deflation of assets in carbon-intensive sectors during the global decarbonisation and due to increased frequency of extreme weather events. Regulatory changes are also vital to stimulating green finance and mobilising resources for investing in mitigation and adaptation. The documents also mentioned the importance of tax reforms capable of promoting the internalisation of the social costs of using fossil fuels, while new public and private investments are made in renewable energy and resilience building.

More recently, the Green New Deal concept has incorporated a broader spectrum of social welfare policies, including programs to expand the coverage of health systems to meet the demand for public health services as well as job guarantee and workforce training programs (Nersisyan and Wray, 2019; Mathias et al., 2021). This last point recognises that, even though the transition creates new jobs,[6] many occupations will be lost in emissions-intensive sectors. In this sense, workforce training and job-guarantee programs aim at minimising the social costs of transitioning to a carbon-neutral economy.

The concept of the green economy was launched in 2011 by UNEP, aiming at conciliated environmental, economic and social outcomes by proposing an economic growth pattern capable of improving *'human well-being and social equality while reducing environmental risks and ecological scarcity'* (UNEP, 2011, p. 1). To achieve these goals, UNEP reiterates the role of the State in promoting and coordinating a set of investments capable of guiding the global economy to a decarbonisation path and efficient use of natural capital while activating economic activity and social inclusion. According to UNEP (2011, pp. 37–38):

> Although the bulk of the investments required for the green transformation will come from the private sector, public policy will also have a leading role to play in overcoming distortions introduced by perverse subsidies and externalized costs. And public investment will be required to jump-start an effective transition to a green economy.

The green economy proposal placed fiscal policy in the centre of the stage, as it highlighted the importance of prioritising public investments in strategic areas to conserving and restoring the natural capital, the need for greening public procurement and reforming tax and subsidy systems.

Finally, the Environmental Big Push for sustainability aims at achieving an economic, social and environmental development pattern in Latin America and the Caribbean, aligned with the 2030 agenda. This proposal stems from a structuralist view of the economic, environmental and social crises in the region, understanding that these crises are interconnected and the roots of their causes lie in the structural backwardness of the region. The outdated productive structure of Latin American countries leads to issues such as structural heterogeneity, low productivity, unemployment, high informality, socioeconomic inequality as well as very particular environmental problems resulting from the international insertion of these countries as exporters of goods highly intensive in natural resources and environmental impacts, such as agricultural and industrial commodities.

To overcome these problems, public policies should mobilise resources for a package of investments capable of promoting a structural change marked by three types of efficiency: (i) Keynesian, approaching sectors with greater economic dynamism; (ii) Schumpeterian, driving growth in sectors that are intensive in technology, knowledge and have a high potential for technological spill-over and innovation; (iii) environmental, redirecting growth towards low-carbon and low-resource intensive sectors (Gramkow, 2019). These investments would be pushed by the action of the State, either directly—through public investment—or indirectly—through public policies capable of inducing private investment in strategic sectors.

Despite the particularities of each proposal, they share several elements. First and foremost, they all represent a departure from microeconomics in favour of a macroeconomic approach to environmental issues. This latter approach recognises the dual importance of public and private green investments for kicking-off the transition. In the short term, green investments result in higher levels of economic activity, employment and income. In the long term, they transform the productive structure, creating the capacities needed for decarbonisation and the ecological transition.

The second element that brings these proposals closer together is the defence of the active participation of the State, using public investment and all sorts of economic policy to signalise where resources should be placed. All of them share a clear understanding that the State must go beyond its regulatory and stabilising functions in order to face the challenges of the green transition. The investments needed to mitigate and adapt to climate change are unprecedented and require decades for implementation. To rise up to the scale needed and make investment consistent with social, environmental and economic needs, it is necessary a long-term coordination and planning to redirect investments, reform incentives and deal with risks and uncertainty arising from transitioning to a low-carbon economy. The State has to resume its other functions as: i) investor, expanding critical social and economic infrastructure for the transition or in cutting-edge technologies and markets in which the uncertainty is still too high for the private sector to jump in; ii) social protector, expanding assistance to the population vulnerable to climate change and workers whose jobs are at risk due to the transition; and iii) service providers, given the need to expand public services, such as the health service, to face the increasing risks of airborne and waterborne diseases and new pandemics that deriving from both climate and biodiversity crises (Nersisyan and Wray, 2019; Alvarenga, Costa and Young, 2022; Mathias et al., 2021).

Finally, the third element that brings these plans closer together is their essentially Keynesian theoretical structure, whether due to their macroeconomic approach, the importance given to investment as a transformative element both in the short and long run or the need for active participation of the state to rekindle and reshape economic growth.

6.   Conclusion

Despite recent advances, the participation of post-Keynesians in the environmental agenda is still at an early stage. Motivated by this fact, this chapter sought to offer a theoretical contribution, based on four delimiting principles of what we call post-Keynesian Environmental Macroeconomics:

(i)   The environmentally extended Principle of Effective Demand: it holds that, by determining the level of production, effective demand also defines the level of use of natural resources and emissions.

(ii)   The principle of the non-neutrality of macroeconomic policies to the environment: if macroeconomic policies are not neutral, whether in the short or long term, then it also impacts the degree of utilisation of natural resources and emissions.

(iii)   The principle of non-convergence towards sustainability: according to this principle, the economic system lacks endogenous mechanisms capable of driving the economy towards full employment and sustainability.

(iv)   The principle of growth constrained by the depletion of natural resources: it states that depletion of natural capital is growth-reducing.

These principles redefine the role played by the State in transitioning towards sustainability. It is acknowledged that, in the absence of endogenous mechanisms for converging towards sustainability, it should be conducted to this point by consistent economic policies. Since entrepreneurs' decisions on how much to produce and invest depend on their expectation regarding the effective demand, economic policy should work on greening it.

Among all sets of policies governments can use, we argue that fiscal policy stands out. Green procurement or public investments directly influence the size of the demand for products that meet desired social and environmental standards. By greening effective demand, production will tend to come along. The role played by investment in this process is critical, since, besides its effect on the level of activity in the short-run, it also creates new productive capacity in the long-run. Therefore, if one is to avoid productive bottlenecks in a green and low-carbon economy, investments need to be planned accordingly. Besides, tax and subsidies also help in redirecting agents' decisions to more sustainable practices.

Interestingly, this vision has largely influenced the green recovery proposals over the last decade and a half, whether in their versions derived from the 2008 financial crisis or those aimed at overcoming the Covid-19 crisis. The political importance of the Green New Deal and other similar proposals show the practical relevance of this debate.

Notes

1 This chapter is a posthumous tribute to Professor Fernando Cardim de Carvalho, who, in his lifetime, contributed to the education of generations of post-Keynesians, including the authors of this chapter.
2 An indirect process of substitution also takes place as relative price changes. In this case, consumers, seeking to maximise their utilities, will tend to change their basket of goods towards products that are less resource-intensive, since these goods have now become more expensive.
3 As mentioned earlier, the convergence towards an environmentally sustainable equilibrium falls under the same adjustment process. Indeed, if market failures are solved, the price mechanism automatically drives the economic system towards an environmentally sustainable situation.
4 If increasing returns ($\varepsilon > 1$) are assumed, then: (i) the share of wages in income will tend towards zero when the substitution elasticity is greater than 1 ($\sigma > 1$); (ii) the share of profits in income will tend towards zero when $\sigma < 1$. Conversely, in the case of $\varepsilon < 1$: (i) the share of wages in income will converge to zero with $\sigma < 1$; (ii) the share of profits in income will converge to zero with $\sigma > 1$.
5 We assume that long-term growth has a 'path dependence' component to the past decisions to use and wear down natural capital.
6 Alvarenga, Costa and Young (2022) estimate the economic benefits of a potential green growth plan (the Green New Deal Brazil) and compare it with a business-as-usual scenario. The authors applied an equally sized demand shock in both scenarios and found that the Green New Deal would generate 9.5 million jobs by 2030—approximately 800,000 more positions than in the business-as-usual scenario, with a greater formalisation of the workforce and an average salary 19.8% higher. Equally important is the fact that the Green New Deal Brazil would result in an emission reduction of 1 GtCO2e every year compared to the business-as-usual scenario.

References

Alvarenga, M. J., Costa, L. A. N., Passoni, P., Costa, K., Eguino, H., and Young, C. E. F. (2024, forthcoming) 'Public Expenditure and GHG Emissions in Brazil: A Structural

Decomposition Analysis for the 2000–2019 Period', Working paper, Institute of Economics, Federal University of Rio de Janeiro.

Alvarenga Jr., M., and Young, C. E. F. (2019) 'Contribuições à construção de uma agenda Pós-Keynesiana do meio ambiente', in *XII Encontro Internacional da Associação Keynesiana Brasileira*. Campinas (Brazil): Associação Keynesiana Brasileira (AKB).

Alvarenga, M. J., Costa, L. A. N., and Young, C. E. F. (2022) *Green New Deal – Brasil: construindo um modelo de crescimento justo, igualitário e sustentável*. São Paulo, SP: GV executivo.

Barro, R., and Sala-I-Martin, X. (1995) *Economic Growth*. New York: McGraw-Hill.

Carvalho, F. J. C. (1992) *Mr Keynes and the Post-Keynesian: Principles of Macroeconomics for a Monetary Production Economy*. Aldershot: Edward Elgar.

Carvalho, L. B. (2020) *Curto Circuito: o vírus e a volta do estado*. São Paulo: Todavia.

Cesarato, S., and Serrano, F. (2002) 'As Leis de Rendimento nas Teorias Neoclássicas do Crescimento: Uma Crítica Sraffiana', *Ensaios FEE*, 23 (2): 701–730.

Conlisk, J. (1968) 'Non-Constant Returns to Scale in a Neoclassical Growth Model', *International Economic Review*, 9 (3): 369–373.

Davidson, P. (1983) 'Rational Expectations: A Fallacious Foundation for Studying Crucial Decision-making Processes', *Journal of Post Keynesian Economics*, 5 (2): 182–198.

Davidson, P. (1984) 'Reviving the Keynes' Revolution', *Journal of Post Keynesian Economics*, 6 (4): 561–575.

GND GROUP – GREEN NEW DEAL GROUP. (2008) *A Green New Deal: Joined-up Policies to Solve the Triple Crunch of the Credit Crisis, Climate Change and High Oil Prices*. London: New Economics Foundation.

Gramkow, C. (2019) 'O Big Push Ambiental no Brasil Investimentos coordenados para um estilo de desenvolvimento sustentável'. *Perspectivas*, 20. Brasília: ECLAC.

Green New Deal Group [GND GROUP]. (2008) *A Green New Deal: Joined-up Policies to Solve the Triple Crunch of the Credit Crisis, Climate Change and High Oil Prices*. First Report. London: New Economic Foundation.

Hartwick, J. M. (1977) 'Intergenerational Equity and the Investing of Rents from Exhaustible Resources', *American Economic Review*, 67: 972–974.

Inada, K. (1963) 'On a Two-Sector Model of Economic Growth: Comments and a Generalization', *The Review of Economic Studies*, 30 (2): 119–127.

Keynes, J. M. (1936) *The General Theory of Employment, Interest and Money*. Cambridge: Macmillan.

Lavoie, M. (2014) *Post-Keynesian Economics: New Foundations*. Cheltenham: Edward Elgar.

Mathias, J. F. C., Young, C. E. F., Couto, L. C., and Alvarenga, M. J. (2021) 'Green New Deal como estratégia de desenvolvimento pós-pandemia: lições aprendidas da experiência internacional', *Revista Tempo do Mundo*, 26: 145–174.

Mazzucato, M. (2013) *The Entrepreneurial State: Debunking Public vs. Private Sector Myths Stirred Up Much-needed Debate about the Role of the State in Fostering Long-run Innovation Led Economic Growth*. London: Anthem Press.

Mearman, A. (2009) 'Recent Developments in Post-Keynesian Methodology and Their Relevance for Understanding Environmental Issues', in R. Holt, S. Pressman and C. Clive (eds.), *Post Keynesian and Ecological Economics: Confronting Environmental Issues*. Cheltenham: Edward Elgar.

Nersisyan, Y., and Wray, L. R. (2019) *How to Pay for the Green New Deal?* Working paper no. 931. New York: Levy Economics Institute.

Perman, R., Yue, M., McGilvray, J., and Common, M. (2003) *Natural Resource and Environmental Economics*. New York: Pearson.

Pitchford, J. D. (1960) 'Growth and the Elasticity of Substitution', *Economic Record*, 36: 491–503.

Robinson, J. (1969 [1956]) *The Accumulation of Capital*. London: MacMillan.

Solow, R. M. (1986) 'On the Intergenerational Allocation of Natural Resources'. *The Scandinavian Journal of Economics*, 88 (1): 141–149.

UNEP (United Nations Environmental Program) (2009) *Annual Report. Seizing the Green Opportunity*. Nairobi, Kenya: United Nations.

UNEP (United Nations Environmental Program) (2011) *Annual Report*. Nairobi, Kenya: United Nations.

Young, C. E. F. (1993) 'Sustainability, Economic Growth and Employment', in A. Gomez-Lobo, K. Hamilton and C. E. F. Young (eds.), *Three Essays on Sustainable Development*. London: CSERGE/University College London and University of East Anglia.

Young, C. E. F. (1997) *Economic Adjustment Policies and the Environment: A Case Study for Brazil*. London: University College London, PhD Dissertation. Available at: CSERGE/University College London and University of East Anglia.

Young, C. E. F. (2018) 'Mr. Keynes and the Environment: Tropical Deforestation and the Concept of User Cost', *Revista de Economia Contemporânea*, 22 (2): 1–22.

Young, C. E. F., and Mathias, J. F. C. (eds.) (2020) *COVID-19, meio ambiente e políticas públicas*. Hucitec: São Paulo.

7 Environment, development and equity in the work of Geoff Harcourt

Shachi Amdekar and Matthew Fright[1],[2]

1. Introduction

In 2014, the late post-Keynesian economist Geoff Harcourt commissioned and edited a special issue edition of the *Economic and Labour Relations Review (ELRR)* on the economics of climate change in response to Marglin's (2013) manifesto paper, 'Climate Change and the Premises for a New Economy', published in *Development*. Long renowned for his analysis of the Cambridge Capital Controversy (1969, 1972) and contributions to the Cambridge Keynesian set such as his investment model (1976) and historical analysis of economic theory, Harcourt's contributions as a pillar of the global economics community are equally significant. As an intellectual figure, Harcourt represents a true stalwart of the post-Keynesian tradition and powerful advocate for pluralism in economic thought. Harcourt's works span a spectrum of progressive and evolutionary political economy, meshing environmental considerations, development and equity in his engaging, collaborative and distinctly narrative style.

Yet, for a subject that evidently engaged him as a monumental—and existential—case study in intergenerational social and economic justice, Harcourt's theoretical writings on ecological economics alone are remarkably few. This chapter considers Harcourt's thought and approach; in particular, his customary blend of post-Keynesian first principles with an evolutionary approach, drawing out parallels and clear consistencies in his conceptual analysis as well as contributing to wider post-Keynesian discussions on environmental economics. While his first-principles thinking on the environment and social justice is peppered across his numerous works, we focus particularly here on the ELLR *Special Issue* in response to Marglin (2013). This, we argue, exemplifies his mature thought on these themes and willingness to contribute to the debate surrounding the ability of theoretical first principles to understand—and indeed, withstand—the existential challenges posed by climate change. We make the case that, while as editor, curator and rapporteur, Harcourt arguably remains in listening mode in his response to Marglin (2013), his advocacy and pluralism is personified in the *Special Issue* in both complement and compliment to Marglin's call to arms.

This chapter is divided into two parts. The first of these identifies and establishes Geoff Harcourt in terms of his intellectual environment. In this section, we

DOI: 10.4324/9781003375425-9

consider Harcourt's approach towards economic discourse—particularly upon the backdrop of the tradition from which he came and propounded and of the escalating global political momentum around climate change outlined by Marglin, each in turn. Upon this backdrop, the second section of the chapter then outlines the development of Harcourt's thought as it materialised in his response to Marglin (2013) and the production of the *Special Issue* in the following year. This section of the chapter illustrates the *Special Issue* as Harcourt's denouement on climate economics and highlights the fruitfulness of Harcourt's approach in building and convening a clear set of critical perspectives. This draws upon the firsthand account of one of the authors of this chapter, who contributed to the *Special Issue* under Harcourt's leadership, together with fellow Cambridge post-Keynesian Ajit Singh and climate scientist and negotiator Sir David King. Here, Harcourt's high-energy approach and emphasis on debate and exchange are contextualised within an analysis of Harcourt's curation of a symposium of voices.

In doing so, we present the *ELRR Special Issue* as embodying Harcourt's method of intellectualisation of the climate crisis—notably, with the objective of plurality rather than necessarily coherence of specialist perspectives and discipline.

2.   Situating Geoff's intellectual environment

2.1   *The eclectic economist*

Greatly celebrated both during his lifetime and following his passing in 2021 for his prolific works, other pens will no doubt more effectively sketch Harcourt's biography and life as a Cambridge post-Keynesian (see for example Vellupillai's chapter in Cord (2017). It is further helpful that, as a deeply self-reflective and engaging individual who valued and invested in the economic community, Harcourt leaves a legacy of interviews, personal reflections and scores of obituaries by peers and students alike (see, for example, Cohen's *Afterword* in Harcourt (2023)). The following, focused on Harcourt's approach to the environmental challenges, is neither and both of these. Drawing upon facets of Harcourt's biography, influences and approach, we focus here on the intellectual context upon which Harcourt approached the climate question and the tenets he applied. We argue that the manner in which the symposium that was to become the *ELRR Special Issue* was developed speaks to the plurality, social advocacy and latent policy-grounded approach that typified the numerous works of Geoff Harcourt. In this section, these different dimensions are identified, and later, explored in section 2.1 to illustrate the way in which Harcourt's eclectic approach to economics opened a space for new economic approaches.

A self-reported 'horses-for-courses person' (Tran-Nam and Harcourt, 2016, p. 502) and cemented more recently in the titular article by Green, Harcourt and Junankar (2023), Harcourt took a practical approach to the application of economic theory. He disagreed with the idea that there was a single economic approach with which to approach policy challenges. Economic theory was, to Harcourt, not a matter of abstraction but grounded in context: 'instead, whatever is suitable for the issue you are looking at, you frame your theory and extract your inferences in order to check them against your data. We call this procedure "horses-for-courses'" (Tran-Nam and Harcourt, 2016, p. 502). By its very definition, this approach necessitated a tolerance, respect, and indeed, necessity for alternative approaches. As Repapis (2014, p. 1530) shows, this emphasis on methodological pluralism could also be seen in his other works, including his book reviews. Harcourt's economic writing was distinguished from the mainstream by downplaying the need for an axiomatic mathematical proof, and instead, emphasising the need for an approach which engaged with the conceptual foundations of a specific problem (Velupillai, 2021, p. 213, Tran-Nam and Harcourt, 2016, pp. 508–509).

In part, this approach was informed by a recognition that theory in the social sciences can be a value-laden process. As reflected in Tran-Nam and Harcourt (2016), Harcourt drew a parallel with Hugh Stretton's assessment of political science in that the separation of analysis and ideology was impossible.

> They are indissoluble and therefore, you have to tell your students what your ideology and values are, and not pretend you are dealing with a value-free, objective social science because you are not.
>
> (2016, p. 497)

The same applied in economics, which Harcourt felt increasingly led to technically competent individuals 'but there is no point in being technically proficient if you don't understand what is the underlying conceptual model that these techniques are meant to take you to the data to illuminate—so I really worry about this' (Tran-Nam and Harcourt, 2016, p. 505).

This empowered an economic approach which Harcourt felt was more practical, grounded and relevant to the real world. As he expressed in an interview to Binh Tran-Nam, he

> tried to develop a structure of thought about the economy which reflected what was actually going on and who tried to seek out why it was going wrong, why it is impacting most on those people least able to defend themselves (that is a tautology) and then designed policies which would make it work better.
>
> (Tran-Nam and Harcourt, 2016, pp. 508–509)

Harcourt's self-acknowledged approach to economics did not see the pursuit of economic knowledge as an end in itself but a means to better the world from which on could then 'try and design realistic and humane policies that make it better, especially for those are most affected by the malfunctions of the system' (Tran-Nam and Harcourt, 2016, p. 493). To that end, economics and economic policy making are embedded in complex social reality which require consideration in any policy design process.

Tran-Nam and Harcourt (2016, p. 496) lay the foundations upon which we can analyse Harcourt's grounded and sometimes activist approach to economic theory, which embedded a complex social reality in policy design. As an active participant in grassroots politics and a socially-minded and ardent anti-Vietnam War protestor, Harcourt was keenly aware of the social inequity and the need for policy to reflect this. As Tim Harcourt argues, 'Geoff thought economics went hand in hand with political activism' (Harcourt, 2021, p. 210). Indeed, Tim Harcourt, in a joint article, portrayed Harcourt as a political and social activist, 'who worked for peace and justice for indigenous people and who supported full-employment with decent wages and good working conditions for working people' (Green, Harcourt and Junankar, 2023, p. 15). Harcourt is shown to be engaged with the Australian Labour movement both as an activist, a Fabian and a close policy adviser in the capacity of his role working on an Australian Labour Party Committee of Inquiry. In this frame, influenced by his Keynesian conviction that full employment could not be guaranteed, Harcourt presented a strong advocate for interventions that improve employment and ensure equity (Green, Harcourt and Junankar, 2023, pp. 16–19).

2.2   The tradition

We can consider Harcourt's broad-minded approach to economics as symptomatic of the Cambridge economic milieu within which Harcourt located himself and that underpinned his post-Keynesian ideas and, crucially, intellectual values. The following attempts to summarise some of the key elements that characterised Harcourt's method in the frame of his own influences and deep knowledge of framework-building upon well-defined first principles. In this short section and respecting Harcourt's own proficiency as a historian of economic theory, we would hardly claim to do justice to this set of influential thinkers per Cord (2017) (and within it, Velupillai (2017)), for example. Rather, we establish some common threads that drew this community together and formed the backdrop for Harcourt's approach—both generally and to the climate question in particular.

Situating Harcourt as one of the last 'true' Cambridge economists of the unambiguously Keynesian lineage provides immediate context. Harcourt's approach enhanced and amplified a distinctively 'Cambridge economics' approach, which distinguished itself from and in contrast to the mainstream economics that typified and continues to typify contemporary teaching. Harcourt's sustained engagement with Cambridge—including being a resident for at least three periods: 1955–1958, 1962–1966, 1982–1998—saw him influence and be influenced by the post-Keynesian school of economists (Velupillai, 2021, p. 213, Tran-Nam and Harcourt, 2016, p. 492, Harcourt, 2021, p. 209). This coterie, focused around the works of scholars such as Joan Robinson, Khan, Kaldor, Sraffa and Kalecki, developed new ways of approaching macroeconomics in the tradition of John Maynard Keynes (Velupillai, 2021, p. 213). In this section of the chapter, we would draw attention to how this set of Cambridge thinkers understood the likes of focus in particular on capital, growth (and growth limitations) and uncertainty.

It would be remiss, in any analysis of Harcourt's work, not to consider the intellectual footprints he left across the piece for which he became most well-known. Harcourt gained notable acclaim for his work analysing and defining a theoretical cleft over the analysis of capital between two broad groupings of economists in Cambridge, Massachusetts and Cambridge in the United Kingdom—the so-called 'Cambridge Capital Controversy' (Harcourt, 1969). Pivotal to that debate—and as Harcourt reflects in Tran-Nam and Harcourt (2016)—was the in-depth analysis of the use of long-run equilibrium as an analytical approach for understanding historical processes and dynamics in their context. In later works, Harcourt argued that, since both Cambridges embroiled in this debate took disparate approaches to evaluation, there was no agreed conclusion to the debate (Cohen and Harcourt, 2003, p. 207). Indeed, revisiting these debates in considering how these forged a methodological pathway for Harcourt opens up a wider analysis of the fundamental explanatory and causal concerns involving, in his own words, 'the return to capital, visions of accumulation, limitations of equilibrium tools' (Cohen and Harcourt, 2003, p. 211).

A significant focus of the post-Keynesian set was on re-energising debates in the post-War period and, in particular, the use of classical influences to the analysis of capital. Harcourt's greatest contribution in his own estimation was his two-sector model concerning the distribution of income and level of short-run employment (Harcourt, 1965; Tran-Nam and Harcourt, 2016). This accompanied a strong momentum around alternative approaches to the more dominant neoclassical models in contemporary textbooks, yet this did not necessarily lead to a more thorough analysis of the environment. Emphasis was upon growth and directing employment to realise growth potential; indeed, this focus on growth may have been to the detriment of environmental analysis, in one sense. Indeed, as Perry (2013) argues within a work incidentally edited by Harcourt, the period up to the 1980s saw a distinct 'paucity' of post-Keynesian contribution to the field of environmental economics. This is echoed in Politt (2019), who bemoans the lack of centrality, and thus, influence of post-Keynesian models in modern environmental economics and policy.

Consideration of resource (and thus) growth limitations across the Keynesian set presents a useful lens through which to approach Harcourt's work, including as an in-road to environmental considerations. Perry, for example, highlights an inherent tension between the mainstream environmental economics literature and post-Keynesianism, in that the latter places priority and emphasis on growth particularly in the manufacturing sector (2013, p. 395). This can be linked back, as does Perry, to the very earliest Keynesian thinkers; for example, Kalecki and Keynes, commenting on the 'little evidence of ecological limits being breached'. We might equally cite the influence of Kaldor's Growth Laws, establishing industrial patterns and resource allocation as a determinant for long-term development in the Global South (Kaldor, 1967). Despite being an early advocate for and participant in this economic debate, as Perry (2013, p. 395) notes, Harcourt was an advocate for a post-Keynesianism concept of capitalism that considered 'the long-term constraint of global warming'.

Yet, as Brown and Shaw (1983) show, the argument on the limitations of neoclassical economics shown in Bird (1982) can be extended further when due consideration is given to the capital controversy. The problems with effective competitive pricing of physical capital are made worse when applied to non-renewable resources or pollution, as 'uncertain user costs and an inherently unknowable future mean the market cannot determining the correct rate of discount, social value of resources or pollution, or the payments to resource owners' (Brown and Shaw, 1983, p. 141). While this 1980s application of post-Keynesian thinking to environmental economics came later than earlier environmental thinking evidenced in the 1970s environmental movements, this does not reduce the potency of their contribution.

As others have argued the post-Keynesian, and specifically, post-Keynesian environmental economics opens the literature environmental economics debate by positing a broader range of real world conditions such as latent uncertainty, income distributional concerns and complex system dynamics (Perry, 2013, pp. 391–304). And, though, as Perry (2013, p. 392) argues, post-Keynesian contributions to the question of environmental economics made limited substantial contributions until the publication of Bird (1982), there have since been post-Keynesian skeins of environmental research seeking to address some of the pressing global environmental challenges including understanding implications of socio-economic inequalities in decarbonisation and considering the potential role for fiscal policy to transition (Huwe and Rehm, 2022). Politt's (2019) argument establishes further scope for this Keynesian avenue of fundamental uncertainty to be explored in the frame of driving climate and wider societal ambitions, wherein the role of finance and the development and transfer of technology as a driving force is understood.

2.3   The moment

The climate challenges evinced at the turn of the 2010s were manifold yet not as acute as the situation as seen in the early 2020s. This section contextualises the stark messages in Marglin's Manifesto that stimulated the ensuing response from Harcourt and situates the context of the environmental movement as seen from the global policy vantage of the mid-2010s.

Today, in 2023, the most recent conclusions from the sixth round of the International Panel on Climate Change (IPCC) show 'widespread and rapid changes in the atmosphere, ocean, cryosphere and biosphere have occurred. Human-caused climate change is already affecting many weather and climate extremes in every region across the globe' (IPCC, 2023, p. 5). The panel argues that such climate change impacts, attributable to human activity, are expected to intensify. Moreover, decisions today will shape the impact on current and future generations. As the Climate Crisis Advisory Group have argued, this is the final warning bell, the sixth round findings show the world overshooting the 1.5°C threshold set out in the Paris Agreement and deterioration in the climate risks facing the planet (CCAG [Climate Crisis Advisory Group] 2023).

Prior to the Paris Agreement in 2015, however, the fifth IPCC assessment clearly outlined the clear influence of humans on the climate system and that has 'had widespread impacts on human and natural systems' (IPCC [Intergovernmental Panel on Climate Change], 2014, p. 2). The authors were clear that atmospheric concentrations of greenhouse gases like carbon dioxide are at levels 'unprecedented in at least the last 800,000 years' (IPCC, 2014, p. 4).

Moreover, inaction would 'long-lasting changes in all components of the climate system, increasing the likelihood of severe, pervasive and irreversible impacts for people and ecosystems' (IPCC, 2014, p. 8). To that end, a more sustainable development would be required to assist with the adaptation to a mitigation against climate change. Both Marglin and Harcourt's efforts can be understood through this lens.

Both authors responded to the planetary boundaries framework outlined by the Stockholm Resilience Centre—an influential framework which has shaped key papers like the Dasgupta Review (Dasgupta, 2021, p. 106) and works from the European Environment Agency (EEA and FOEN [Federal Office for the Environment], 2020). This framework outlines key thresholds beyond which nonlinear processes could lead to potential impacts on other systems and humans (Rockström et al., 2009, p. 472). The authors identify nine key systems, in which three already exceed planetary boundaries (rate of biodiversity loss, climate change and human impacts on the nitrogen cycle) (Rockström et al., 2009, p. 472).

The framework was later augmented by other authors to explicate three key systems which could alter the Earth system if surpassed (Steffen et al., 2015). The authors of the revised framework concluded the frame is not a prescriptive account of how to manage these systems. That, instead, is a political decision which must 'include consideration of the human dimensions, including equity, not incorporated in the PB framework' (Steffen et al., 2015, p. 736). It is to the answers to the political and equity response to this framework that the remainder of the chapter now turns.

3. Harcourt, climate economics and the 'Marglin Manifesto' (Harcourt, 2014a, p. 548)

3.1 Puzzles, plurality and protest

It is not altogether surprising, upon a rich career of applying multi-dimensional approaches to analysing first-principle problems, that Harcourt was caught by the renewed effervescence in ecological thought and climate policy impetus. This section brings to the fore Harcourt's *ELRR Special Issue*, which we can interpret as Harcourt's most cohesive contribution to the climate question—arguably Harcourt's *magnum opus* on the matter, despite being a minor footnote to his academic legacy and representing an intellectual response rather than creation. Echoing the premise of 1.1, this section explores three characteristic dimensions of Harcourt's intellectual approach which he applies to the climate question: commitment to real life problem-solving through economic theory, plurality as a core methodological tenet of resolution and a willingness to advocate and probe difficult questions across the gradient of orthodoxy and heterodoxy.

Harcourt's unimpeachable proficiency as an economic theorist, demonstrated throughout his career in his 30 books and over 400 articles, chapters and reviews, places him well to make good on his well-documented view that theory should be real, rather than simply neat. He believed that theory should be applied with judgement, utilising first principles and accounting techniques to tackle problems, such as environmental degradation and climate change, that 'threaten the world economy' (Nevile, Harcourt and Kriesler, 2015). In a 2016 interview with Dr. Constantinos Repapis, Harcourt observes, in a remark on Joan Robinson, that the best economists have the aspiration 'to try and create a more just and equitable society' (Harcourt and Repapis, 2016). Moreover, Harcourt's understanding of theoretical first principles was steeped in historical context, mapping chains of influence and the evolution of the various permutations of observation and belief applied to elemental approaches to value, capital and the like. Active in the quest for progressive and evolutionary economics, including the so-called heterodox approaches, Harcourt is credited for his significant contributions to the once-unpopular subject of the history of economic thought, which Harcourt saw as an essential part of economic theory, and indeed, the *responsibility* of the able economic theorist. He placed crucial value of understanding first principles in the context of their formulation so that one is able to

> relate it not only to what was relevant for when it was first produced, but also to the modern day . . . and it's fair, because it's giving credit to where the ideas came from. That's just elementary scholarship.
>
> (Harcourt and Repapis, 2016)

Referring to Hicks' description of the subject as sharing boundaries with both history and science (Harcourt and Repapis, 2016), Harcourt showed willingness to dive into either side to understand the climate problem. Committed, then, as he was, to problems of social justice with a core motivation for applying theoretical principles judiciously and led by values, the magnitude of the climate problem was not lost on Harcourt. Yet, in terms of Harcourt's approach, we may understand as yet another puzzle—albeit an existential one—to solve by unpicking the fundamental premises of the problem and convening dialogue to apply a *complete* rather than partial or representative understanding of each of those premises.

In the same breath, plurality in perspective is worth noting as a visible dimension of Harcourt's approach to the climate problem in the *Special Issue*. Alongside depth of understanding of the economic tenets, Harcourt valued the breadth and multidisciplinary approaches. Indeed, as his daughter Wendy Harcourt[3] attests in Harcourt (2022, p. 27), though they approached climate and environment policies from divergent angles, her discussions with Harcourt on climate change were fundamentally both pluralistic and optimistic. He recognised that a complex problem shared, empirically presented and intellectually dismantled—across perspectives, disciplines and schools of thought, as needed—was the critical pathway to its resolution. Wendy Harcourt recalls their conversations about the pressing environmental challenges facing modern capitalism as characterised by

> searching for justice, sharing your puzzles, and valuing connections with others who were equally concerned by the disruptions caused by environmental, climate, health, economic, and political crises.
>
> (2022, p. 33)

The 'Marglin Manifesto' (2014, p. 548), as Harcourt called it, and the ELRR *Special Issue* it inspired captured this primacy of plurality in Harcourt's economic thinking to tackle this existential puzzle. Marglin (2013) had delivered an economist's deductive, first-principles take-down of prevailing economic theory. This was framed upon the cogent and empirical consensus of 18 leading sustainability professionals: a 'quest' or 'challenge' (Harcourt, 2014b), essentially, to economic theorists. In answer, Harcourt's collaboration with Editor-in-Chief Anne Junor saw the release of a special issue of the *Economic and Labour Relations Review*, which rose to that challenge: to deliver the 'basic principles that might guide the quest to combine ecological sustainability with equitably redistributive development' (Harcourt, 2014b, p. 548). This was presented as a 'symposium' (Ibid.) of carefully curated voices—and crucially, to Harcourt's approach—not necessarily in perfect symphony and all the stronger for it.

Finally, Harcourt's personal involvement with advocacy and protest[4] is visible in his commitment to pursue difficult questions surrounding the climate challenge, where he considered real-world outcomes were failed by economics if considered a 'science'—something he did not accept (Harcourt and Repapis, 2016). The binary character of orthodoxy and heterodoxy was not one Harcourt recognised in any theoretical sense; this much is clear, both in his approach to economic theory and how he applied this in his post-Keynesian manifesto[5] (Nevile, Harcourt and Kriesler, 2015). Moreover, this is shown in his involvement with the progressive economics movement, where he frequently played the role of rapporteur for the underdog, not only willing but intellectually proficient to truly debate the fundamentals, even as they arguably distanced him from the mainstream.

It is worth considering precisely what quality of Marglin's—whether as an individual or as a thinker or both—might have inspired Harcourt to respond with the gusto he did. A surface-level, speculative assessment of the degrees of separation suggests the two were likely in acquaintance. Certainly, Marglin was an associate of Wendy Harcourt's, who recalls, in her *Development* editorial, becoming acquainted with Marglin in 'the days of the early global sustainable development movement' (Harcourt, 2011, p. 1) and whose influence on the *ELRR Special Issue* is tangible.[6] Yet equally, there are distinct intellectual parallels, in substance and approach, that we can draw between Harcourt and Marglin. Both had cemented their reputations relatively early in their careers, in a context governed by the prevailing approaches. In Harcourt's case, in a firmly Keynesian Cambridge under Joan Robinson whose environment was changing around him, and in Marglin's case, another steadfastly neoclassical Cambridge having 'won tenure in 1967 as a "straight," but who emerged as a closer[sic] Marxist shortly after' (Lee, 1975). Both used their platforms to query, question and problem-solve across schools of thought. Armed with both theoretical understanding and human acceptance of uncertainty in economic theory, both invited the radical consciousness of plurality to sense-check the direction of intellectual travel. In this vein, Marglin's economist's elucidation of the output of the Stockholm Resilience Centre (i.e., Rokstrom et al.) spoke powerfully to Harcourt, given his description of their collective voices representing 'an overall blueprint for the modern world' (Harcourt, 2014, p. 548).

Overall Harcourt indicates close sympathy with Marglin's aims, relevating Marglin (2013) as 'the Marglin Manifesto' and indicating its importance in reflecting 'the most pressing and difficult [issues] facing the entire world' (2014b, p. 548), and indeed, the act of reprinting in *ELRR*.

Together with this affinity for challenging status quo, protest and outreach, Harcourt's response to Marglin can equally be attested to the sizeable gap that remained (and arguably still remains) in post-Keynesian perspectives on climate issues. As Politt (2019) identifies and as delineated earlier, attempts to cohere and engage in the climate economics discussion from this lens had not taken real shape and effectively countered neoclassical approaches which did not capture Harcourt's values. Harcourt espoused, both through his own endeavours and personal reflections including in the introduction to the ELLR *Special Issue* (Harcourt, 2014), the importance he placed on the values—and therefore, the people—underpinning economic assumptions, methods and modelling and the critical role this played in evidencing the policy lifecycle. Wendy Harcourt highlights this as a fundamental motivation anchoring Harcourt's wider approach and driving his lifelong prominence in the post-Keynesian economic community. She recalls intensive discussions with Harcourt on the divisive question of demographics, and in particular, Dasgupta's *Time and the Generations: Population Ethics for a Diminishing Planet* (2019), which deliberately utilises the singular lens of economic modelling to understand the production-consumption-environment nexus to establish the numbers and identify 'where we probably should be' (Dasgupta, 2021, p. 218). Harcourt's approach was distinct in identifying this type of approach as a partial one which emphasises the objective science but, in doing so, 'eludes the complexity and erases the position of the person producing the knowledge' (Sasser, 2018 in Harcourt, 2023, p. 27) and where they stand on core values including human, civic and reproductive rights, freedom of choice, social equity, economic prosperity and sustainability standards.

This is consistent then with Harcourt's approach in galvanising a response to Marglin, in the form of a set of voices who shared Harcourt's problem-solving mindset, who represented plurality of discipline and brought their distinct values to the *ELRR Special Issue*. Amongst those voices were that of the late industrial economist Ajit Singh—a Cambridge contemporary of Harcourt's at the Department of Applied Economics and fellow stalwart of the post-Keynesian school—and that of one of the authors, Shachi Amdekar, Singh's erstwhile Research Assistant. The following recounts the lesser-known intellectual origins of this rare collaboration between Harcourt, Singh, King and others.

3.2   The premises for a new symposium

Combining an understanding of Harcourt's oeuvre with a recollective, autoethnographic approach,[7] this section first sheds light on the process by which Harcourt's leadership ignited a collective, multi-disciplinary and diverse effort to analyse the core tenets of climate economics. It reflects the process of the article's development within the *ELRR Special Issue*, from its inception involving back-and-forth with Harcourt, Wendy Harcourt, Anne Junor and its expansion into a blended approach across social commentary, spiritualism and scientific candour and incorporating climate policy and technology expertise.

This is, moreover, an opportunity to record some part of the intellectual back-story that led to the publication of Amdekar and Singh (2014) in Harcourt's ELLR *Special Edition*. We cannot speak for the experiences of the other authors that Harcourt convened but offer a case study of how Amdekar and Singh (2014) was developed. This specific article is the standing outcome of an unlikely collaboration between Harcourt, his Cambridge post-Keynesian contemporary Ajit Singh, pre-eminent physical chemist and former Government Chief Scientific Advisor and then the UK Foreign Secretary's Special Representative on Climate Change Professor Sir David King and myself, then a PhD student working on industrial development at Queens' College, Cambridge and Research Assistant to Ajit Singh. In retrospect—and quite aside from both the author's personal involvement and any bias accompanying such an autoethnographic exposition—as a Venn diagram, this coalescence of characters should be a remarkable one to anyone's standards.

And yet, little substantive commentary has followed the publication of either article or the *ELRR Special Issue*. Alongside featuring late in their respective intellectual thought, the otherwise relative absence of both Harcourt's and Singh's written body of work on climate change certainly might invite a degree of disbelief of their strength of feeling on this existential matter (Saith, 2018). Attesting, however, to Sen's (2015) obituary of Singh,[8] this narrative based on the author's experience of the project lends to the image of these intellectual behemoths applying their métier to fashion a call to arms against 'ecological destructions' (2015, p. 75), which they each saw as a future-facing, empirically measurable and multi-dimensional economic problem for the generations. This relish in tackling an issue so large and complex that propensity for problem-solving was visible in my very first encounter with Harcourt in person, at Singh's home-based office, where I had been fortunate to be spending several days a week working with Singh.

It started, naturally, with a cup of tea during a balmy Newnham summer. Over the course of one of Harcourt's then-regular annual visits to Cambridge. Harcourt had cycled over to Singh's Newnham home to catch up, reminisce, and this time, discuss Marglin's paper that Harcourt had sent over some days or weeks prior. Anyone who knew Harcourt and Singh would attest to not only their vast continued productivity as academics but also to their agile thinking, which was at ludicrous odds with their advanced respective ages and, in Singh's case, declining health. The exchange that I was drawn into was a high-octane, activist one, in no way heated but ignited with a contagious energy that, at this brainstorming stage, invited both reaction as well as informed opinion. Harcourt introduced Marglin (2013), as his gateway into serious, first-principles analysis of the climate challenge, then the mainstay of climate scientists and mainstream environmental economists. Marglin's universality and lack of hedging in his stark messaging shifted the conversation into a social dimension. It enabled, Harcourt asserted, the evaluation of the very *premises* on which mainstream economists routinely depended and which had not been interrogated from diverse perspectives. Marglin had identified an analytical gap, Harcourt argued, that post-Keynesian economic theorists and political economists had not known they had in the analysis of modern capital ('the man's got a point', or something to that effect).

Instinctively, industrial economist Singh, with whom I had spent some time discussing the core principles already, was drawn into Marglin's work due to its fundamental implications for growth and productive capacity—in particular, the complexities through which natural limitations to these could arise and what this meant for both developed and developing nations. Ann Zamitt,[9] also present and herself a gifted analyst, took the angle of development policy and the political difficulty of Global North and Global South dynamics, while I was interested[10] in how rationality, expectation and social investments might enable an exploration of restructure rather than outright reduction of productive capacity. Imbued in this early discussion and how Harcourt channelled this discussion was the combination of Marglin the individual and his approach, on the one hand, in manoeuvring and challenging the conversation and opening it up to others. On the other hand was the force of the conclusions Marglin came to (including the likes of exploring planetary boundaries), opening a door to and engendering what would become a chain of analytical perspectives. In the act of inviting others into this dialogue, Harcourt was following the spirit if not the letter of Marglin's manifesto.

The climate problem, Harcourt assured us, was sufficiently monumental for anyone to have at it; every economic theorist had a 'right' to analyse it. Indeed, such a problem necessitated precisely this diversity of thought—a view which Wendy Harcourt echoes in her reflections (2023). This framing of Harcourt's reaction to Marglin and how it came to define the character of the *ELRR Special Issue* is essential to establish, as his pluralism created space for and engaged Singh and myself—and, no doubt, others—to delve into the economics of climate science (see 3.3). Indeed, the fact that we were none of us—in Singh's living room that stifling August afternoon—environmental economists did not trouble anyone but myself, the early-career junior academic navigating the modern and siloed world of research sub-disciplines, schools of thought and the boundaries the mainstream ceded. Contending, however, with two polymathic post-Keynesians whose every instinct was to tackle such a challenge *because* of these very silos, the value of reframing the argument to the fundamentals of resource and allocation and grounding those principles in policy and people, was powerfully visible. Perry's (2013) argument, citing the relative paucity of post-Keynesian thinking on environmental economics, explains Harcourt's direction, to some extent, as argued earlier. Alongside this theoretical blind spot, another angle to consider is the combination of personalities in Harcourt and Singh themselves, of whom every obituary quite rightly describes as some combination of 'Renaissance man', 'all-rounder', 'iconoclastic' and 'boundary-pushing' (see for example, Hatch (2021), Stilwell (2021) and Cosh and Hughes (2015)). Each being master of a significant proportion of extant JEL classifications, that very subject came up in discussion when canvassing the sheer breadth of Marglin's scope and the angles by which to explore it.

The writing process and the exchanges thereafter between myself, Singh, Harcourt, and later, in the process the editor-in-chief of the ELRR, Anne Junor, demonstrate the trajectory of the paper's development from first principles, towards the social policy implications, towards climate science. Illustrating this point, the first set of notes that reflected and immediately followed the in-person discussion with Harcourt and Singh consisted of the following—notably, distinctly Galbrathian in theme—four strands of summarised thought, forming the basis of Amdekar and Singh (2014):

a) The production-consumption-welfare nexus requires exploration, given the necessary compatibility of economic security and sustainability and the difficulty of political bifurcation of Global North and South. In particular, the urgency of physical and psychological demand, respectively, has implications for redistribution and continued innovation to that end.

b) Conventional axioms warrant first-principles exploration; namely, the impossibility of satisfying human wants and that the economist (as the allocator of resources) has no role in questioning their origin. We can draw here upon Keynes (2012 [1936]) and Minsky (1975) on the concept of comparative living and Galbraith (1969) on the origin of wants and utility, respectively.

c) A Keynesian understanding of long-run rationality and expectation has implications as a toolkit for behavioural and attitudinal changes; however, this will, upon considering labour market dynamics, throw into relief the need for a well-designed, structurally robust and well-policed welfare state wherein the individual is an agent for change, assumed able to make consistent and resilient decisions to align with environmental goals.

d) The social investment angle brings to the fore Minsky's understanding of equity and the purpose of economy to promote social justice. When considering what *kind* of output is to be produced, *why* and *for whom*, we are concerned with not the premises for a new economy but a new society. Investment outcomes that incentivise the likes of consumption trends and perennial warmongering maintains employment, not welfare (Minsky, 1975).

Evident even from the brief foregoing summary is the early emphasis in discussion on the origins of thought and exploration of alternative underpinning values and dimensions of economic thought in a purpose-led understanding of the climate challenge. The article might have been left there as a cogent exposition of theory underpinning Marglin's arguments from a loosely post-Keynesian approach. However, the contagious excitement of the discussion Harcourt had begun led to wider consideration of two further angles: consideration of the policy instruments that might be brought to the fore and of the spiritual and community dimensions associated with the premise of collective utility and welfare. Harcourt encouraged exploration of both angles, emphasising authors' free reign to think wildly outside the box, and Singh considered the balance of these, in the argument, essential. To explore the policy angles and instruments and draw cross-disciplinary expertise, I discussed, in parallel, Marglin's (2013) paper with a close associate and development policy specialist from the Centre of Development Studies (University of Cambridge), Jane Lichtenstein, whose encouragement and input brought out in particular implications for state-led industrial policy in the Global South.

The conversation snowballed decisively, as Lichtenstein, in turn, brought in David King, Cambridge-based physical chemist, former Chief Government Scientific Advisor and then the UK Foreign Secretary's Special Representative on Climate Change—who had been closely engaged in the recent Paris negotiations.

South African-born King, whose aims and unpretentious approach to scientific discipline I considered sympathetic with both Singh's and Harcourt's vision for the article and *Special Issue*, accepted and amplified the powerful messaging driving Marglin's premise but offered important scientific critique. In particular, he framed the analysis of economic concepts with a coherent context of where, in scientific terms, political economy had progressed the climate debate and where it had failed it, effectively harnessing Harcourt's grounded approach. King, moreover, brought out the critical role of innovation and technology in the fundamental framing, citing live examples as indicators of positive, socialised investment and output, which he considered fundamental to the argument to restructure the production-consumption-welfare nexus. These, he argued, could foster a circular economy, and in this frame, balanced Singh's considerations of spirituality and community. Debate and disagreement concerned the economic understanding and valuation of existential risk, which King considered less developed. Reviewing the three-way exchanges[11] emphasises, moreover, King's aligned approach to that of Harcourt and Singh on what could be considered scientific and the role that context plays in the development of economic models to fit empirical data. Validating Harcourt's approach to the climate question, in this sense, King held that ignoring the context in which research was created led to situations in which, conversely, empirical data was made to fit the prevailing economic model, resulting in starkly different policy outcomes.

Even as a small component of the *ELRR Special Issue*, the case study of how Amdekar and Singh (2014) came into existence—in particular, by the cross-disciplinary inclusion of King's input—sought actively to take the baton of plurality from Harcourt, who, in turn, took it both from Marglin, Robinson and a powerful post-Keynesian tradition. Pluralism, to Harcourt (and, by extension, to Singh and King), did not mean a lack of specialism, or indeed, a lack of debate, but a simple refusal to adhere to silos, whether methodological or disciplinary. Extending this principle, we explore in the following section the benefits—and diversity of perspectives—that Harcourt's pluralistic approach to the climate question contributed.

3.3   *The special edition as a toolkit*

The previous sections have highlighted the *ELRR Special Issue* as a lesser-known case study within Harcourt's wider work, offering something of a paradox. On the one hand, it is undoubtedly dwarfed by Harcourt's groundbreaking analyses of capital and Keynesian theory and a small proportion of the reams of broader subject matter on which Harcourt engaged; on the other hand, if there were a 'Harcourt approach' of grappling with a puzzle, this work stands as its methodological microcosm. The following section goes on to analyse the curation and overall message of the *Special Edition* as Harcourt's methodological toolkit for pluralistic problem solving by introducing a spectrum of eight perspectives across the institutionalist and post-Keynesian traditions. The section concludes with an assessment of the impact of the *Special Issue* as a collaborative effort.

Outwardly, Harcourt relegates himself to the role of mere rapporteur in the *ELRR Special Issue*. Beyond attesting to the importance both of Marglin's (2013) message (based on that of Rockström et al., 2009) and of the diversity of perspective on this existential issue, Harcourt's introduction is a succinct summary (Harcourt, 2014). Yet, there was plenty to Harcourt's seemingly backseat role, as Junor attests both on the occasion of Harcourt's 90th Birthday and following his passing. She describes how

> Always thinking broadly and ahead of trends, as early as the December 2014 issue (ELRR 25[4]), Geoff organised a themed collection on the dilemma of reconciling decarbonisation with economic development and equitable global wealth redistribution in the face of catastrophic climate change.
>
> (Junor, 2021)

Junor reiterates Harcourt's intellectual prescience in engaging on the climate challenge in Junor (2022). She attests, moreover, to his hands-on approach to his advisory role to the Board of Editors of the *ELRR*, which was founded by Harcourt's close associates Nevile and Plowman incidentally, to take a post-Keynesian lens on economic and social justice. Indeed, the editorial and curational process was an involved one. It was not, after all, a single response or even joint paper that Harcourt selected to undertake here but a collective of voices representing a community of post-Keynesian and wider thinkers, in the spirit of Marglin's work. Upon an intellectual backdrop of plurality, Harcourt's convening of a powerfully argued set of articles across disciplinary boundaries presented a natural first step in the reconciliation of the challenges of economic development and growth, global redistributive justice and the future of the planet.

It is clear, from the diverse authorship of the *ELRR Special Issue*, that Harcourt intended for the piece to bring out those core dimensions of the climate debate that he deemed inadequately captured in mainstream analysis (Harcourt, 2014). Of the latter, there were clearly sufficient articulations, given Harcourt did not approach mainstream environmental economists for contributions. In their stead and in addition to Amdekar and Singh (2014)'s focus on new economy and new culture, expounded earlier, a clear—if dissonant—set of voices emerge:

a) Bradford's (2014) treatise laud's Marglin's premise but highlights, drawing upon classical economics and philosophy in a manner Harcourt considers powerful (Harcourt, 2014), the realities of the challenges involved in effective sequencing in policy approach, without root-and-branch change, to drive equitable outcomes.
b) Fischer (2014) offers a set of practical next steps to Marglin (2013), focusing on the redistributive elements, highlighting the financing gaps surrounding capital infrastructure, resource ownership and control across the Global North and South, and population and commensurate labour dynamics faced by the Global South.

c) Bartolini (2014) focuses on the individual and the community, characterising welfare through interaction and utility through social capital. These, he argues, provide a blueprint on a politically amenable set of measures to realise Marglin (2013).

d) Wendy Harcourt (2014) brings Marglin's message into today rather than tomorrow, narrowing the frame of uncertainty on his messaging, and draws upon interconnectivity, community networks and meshworks to incorporate resilience—both feminist and otherwise—at this level into policy response.

e) Bagchi (2014), again, puts community in the fore in response to Marglin's call to arms, warning of a 'new complicity between corporations and non-democratic political regimes and failure of workers worldwide to make common cause' (612).

f) Troy (2014) discusses the distribution of consumption in response to Marglin, emphasising the role of inequality, redistribution and well-defined property rights.

Through this diverse collection of voices, there exist, nonetheless, thematic spokes across global development policy and redistribution, gender and feminist dimensions, industrial policy and production, community, identity and spiritualism. On the one hand, capturing the spirit of Marglin as Harcourt saw it necessitated his approaching a set of diverse, and yet, on the key principles, like-minded scholars known to him. On the other hand, a clear dimension for establishing a pathway to social justice and redistribution is carved out as part of this curation process, likely also demonstrating Wendy Harcourt's influence on the work, given the characteristic cross-pollination across a spate of interlinked socioeconomic, contextual analyses and policy solutions in addressing the climate debate.

As Harcourt's toolkit, then, to approach climate and environmental issues, the *ELRR Special Issue* is demonstrative of that primacy he gave to plurality, perspective and positionality. Indeed, Harcourt's involvement in the evolutionary economics community, including the likes of the Association for Evolutionary Economics and European Association for Evolutionary Political Economy, over this period and the years that followed, is indicative of this influence. This might be considered, here, the natural successor of the post-Keynesian tradition to context-focused economic analysis of the climate challenge. The impact of taking such an approach highlights the multifarious means by which an economic problem—especially a high-stakes one—could be looked at and enables different policy levers to be scoped (i.e., not only net-zero and carbon-emissions capture and trading). Capturing the voice of the collective, who, in turn, brought people and community within the intellectual framework, carries significance here. Harcourt shifted the community from the challenge to the source of the solution.

4.   Concluding thoughts

We have explored, in this piece, the engagement of post-Keynesian and pluralist Geoff Harcourt in the climate debate, emphasising his contribution, as a rapporteur, in convening a set of diverse voices in response to Marglin (2013). At the heart of this work is a visible commitment to bridging across sustainability with social justice and an equitable, sustainable and redistributive form of development and growth.

The first part of this chapter outlines the context and relative maturity with which Harcourt came to oversee the *ELRR Special Issue*. We emphasise, first, Harcourt's role as an advocate for plurality, given his staunch belief in the need for economic theories, frameworks and datasets to be adapted to the context and phenomenon in question. Inherent in this is Harcourt's well-documented emphasis on being explicit on the values underpinning economic assumptions, straddling accountability and equity. A brief overview of the tradition through which Harcourt's methodology was influenced follows, emphasising key elemental understandings of capital, growth and uncertainty. Finally, we sketch the existential policy moment that engendered both Marglin's and Harcourt's work in the year prior to the landmark Paris Agreement and the gradual development of existential risk analysis and the Planetary Boundaries framework, which articulated a new understanding of resource limitation analysis.

The second part of this chapter explores the inception and development of the *ELRR Special Edition* and analyses this as an embodiment of Harcourt's methodological toolkit, fostering a pluralistic, multi-dimensional debate. Combining plurality with characteristic economic rigour in tackling Marglin's challenge, Harcourt took the baton in offering challenge to the mainstream with plurality to tackle a challenge greater than the mainstream might adequately service.

In solving the problem through the New Symposium, Harcourt amassed a range of authors, including Ajit Singh and one of the authors of this chapter. This case study emphasises Harcourt's contagious energy, which, in turn, drew in the climate expert David King, a pluralist like Harcourt, who helped to ensure that outcomes could meaningfully enhance policy design. Ultimately, we argue, what Harcourt left was a toolkit. While nominally the 'rapporteur', or 'editor', Harcourt opened a space for a fuller query, enabling questions to be asked from across wider dimensions, contexts and schools of thought.

Through this endeavour, we argue that Harcourt took the decisive first steps towards what might have become a fuller conversation, which embraces, marshals and unifies a range of perspectives to apply their context-driven knowledge to an existential challenge. This chapter is, in turn, a first step—a single lens by which to understand Harcourt's multifaceted contributions. In doing so, we demonstrate that, while environmental economics was 'not his discipline', addressing it as he did was entirely characteristic of his approach and values.

Notes

1 Shachi Amdekar is a policy professional and economist by background, having worked on industrial development and international technology transfer at the University of Cambridge. Matthew Fright is an independent researcher whose doctorate on the origins of national income accounting was awarded from the Centre of Development Studies in Cambridge.

2 We acknowledge, with tremendous gratitude, Dr. Jane Lichtenstein and Professor Sir David King, who have each been engaged in this important dialogue throughout the

development of the ELRR Special Issue and this chapter and whose respective expertise and continued efforts guide and inform a multi-disciplinary, policy-oriented approach to tackle climate and environmental challenges. We are, further, grateful to Professor Shailaja Fennell at the University of Cambridge for her advice, guidance and ever-present support and to Professor Wendy Harcourt for encouraging us to record this avenue amongst the later works of both Professor Geoff Harcourt (1931–2021) and Professor Ajit Singh (1940–2015). Any and all errors in this work are those of the authors alone.

3 Professor of Gender, Diversity and Sustainable Development at the Erasmus University Rotterdam.

4 Harcourt's well-documented opposition to the Vietnam War is a presence in almost every obituary of his.

5 The piece was explicitly called as such, in an early version published as UNSW Australian School of Business Research Paper No. 2013–36.

6 Wendy Harcourt writes, 'If we are to reach sustainability, then we require methodological pluralism' (2023, p. 27).

7 This narrative style recalls Harcourt (2023) and Cohen (2003), as, in parts, it draws upon Amdekar's own reflections of contributing to it, alongside early chapter notes, drafts and email exchanges.

8 Who sadly passed away the year following publication. Alongside Sen (2015), see, for example, Saith (2018).

9 Singh's partner and long-time collaborator, whose experience at Geneva-based organisations complemented her research interests in labour and gender angles to global workforce analysis in development policy.

10 Far too intimidated, of course, at least initially, to simply react with instinct, as my present company was wont to do, given their respective encyclopaedic knowledge of macroeconomic theory and production models.

11 At this point during the development of the paper published as Amdekar and Singh (2014), these exchanges were between King, Singh and myself. King, though acknowledged, could not co-author due to his official designation.

Bibliography

Amdekar, S D., and Singh, A. (2014) 'Climate Change and the Premises for a New Economy', *The Economic and Labour Relations Review*, 25 (4): 563–573.

Arestis, P., Palma, G., and Sawyer, M. (eds.) (1997) *Capital Controversy, Post Keynesian Economics and the History of Economic Thought: Essays in Honour of Geoff Harcourt*. Vol. 1. London: Routledge.

Arestis, P., and Sawyer, M. (2011) 'The Economic Policies of the Political Economy of the Australian Patriot and Cambridge Economist', *Intervention: European Journal of Economics and Economic Policies*, 8 (1): 129–145.

Bagchi, A. K. (2014) 'Earth-grab by Corporate Feudalism and How to Go About Resisting It', *The Economic and Labour Relations Review*, 25 (4): 612–618.

Bartolini, S. (2014) 'Building Sustainability Through Greater Happiness', *The Economic and Labour Relations Review*, 25 (4): 587–602.

Bird, P. (1982) 'Neoclassical and Post Keynesian Environmental Economics', *Journal of Post Keynesian Economics*, 4 (4): 586–593.

Bradford, W. (2014) 'Quo Vadis: Does Economic Theory Need a Sustainability Makeover?', *The Economic and Labour Relations Review*, 25 (4): 551–562.

Brown, W., and Shaw, W. (1983) 'Neoclassical and Post Keynesian Environmental Economics: An Addendum', *Journal of Post Keynesian Economics*, 6 (1): 140–142.

CCAG (Climate Crisis Advisory Group) (2023). *The Final Warning Bell: The Most Important Assessment of Humanity's Future on Earth to Date*. Cambridge (United Kingdom).

Cohen, A. J. (2003) 'Afterword: Who Is (Your) Geoff Harcourt?', in Cohen, A. J., Harcourt, G., 'Retrospectives Whatever Happened to the Cambridge Capital Theory Controversies?', *Journal of Economic Perspectives*, 17 (1): 199–214.

Cohen, A. J., and Harcourt, G. (2003) 'Retrospectives: Whatever Happened to the Cambridge Capital Theory Controversies?', *Journal of Economic Perspectives*, 17 (1): 199–214.

Cord, R. (2017) *The Palgrave Companion to Cambridge Economics Volumes I & II*. London: Palgrave Macmillan.

Cosh, A., and Hughes, A. (2015) 'Ajit Singh: The Radical Economist Who Carried Out Groundbreaking Work on Corporations and Stock Markets', *The Independent*, 20 July.

Dasgupta, P. (2019) *Time and the Generations: Population Ethics for a Diminishing Planet*. New York: Columbia University Press.

Dasgupta, P. (2021) *The Economics of Biodiversity: The Dasgupta Review*. London: HM Treasury.

Davis, J. B. (1997) 'Harcourt as a Historian of Economic Thought', in P. Arestis, G. Palma and M. Sawyer (eds.), *Capital Controversy, Post Keynesian Economics and the History of Economic Thought: Essays in Honour of Geoff Harcourt*. Vol. 1, pp. 401–410. London: Routledge.

European Environment Agency and FOEN (Federal Office for the Environment) (2020) *Is Europe Living Within the Limits of Our Planet?* EEA Report No. 1/2020. Copenhagen: European Energy Agency.

Fischer, A. M. (2014) 'Redistribution as Social Justice for Decarbonising the Global Economy', *The Economic and Labour Relations Review*, 25 (4): 574–586.

Galbraith, J. K. (1969) *The Affluent Society*. London: Hamish Hamilton.

Green, R., Harcourt, T., and Junankar, P. N. (2023) 'Geoff Harcourt and Economic Policy: Horses for Courses?', *The Economic and Labour Relations Review*, 34: 15–25.

Harcourt, G. (1972) *Some Cambridge Controversies in the Theory of Capital*. Cambridge: Cambridge University Press.

Harcourt, G. C. (1965) 'A Two-Sector Model of the Distribution of Income and the Level of Employment in the Short Run', *The Economic Record*, 41 (93): 103–117.

Harcourt, G. C. (1969) 'Some Cambridge Controversies in the Theory of Capital', *Journal of Economic Literature*, 7 (2): 369–405.

Harcourt, G. C. (2006) *The Structure of Post-Keynesian Economics: The Core Contributions of the Pioneers*. Cambridge: Cambridge University Press.

Harcourt, G. C. (2013) 'Why Myths in Neoclassical Economics Threaten the World Economy: A Post-Keynesian Manifesto', *UNSW Australian School of Business Research Paper No. 2013–36, and in the SSRN Electronic Journal*. Available at: https://papers.ssrn.com/sol3/papers.cfm?abstract_id=2374960

Harcourt, G. C. (2014a) 'Symposium: A New Global Economics? Environment, Development, Equity', *Economic and Labour Relations Review*, 25: 548–550.

Harcourt, G. C. (2014b) 'Climate Challenge Calls for a Rethink of Economics', *The Conversation*, 16 November. Available at: https://theconversation.com/geoff-harcourt-climate-challenge-calls-for-a-rethink-of-economics-34250

Harcourt, G. C. (2023) *Some Cambridge Controversies in the Theory of Capital*. 50th Anniversary ed. Cambridge: Cambridge University Press.

Harcourt, G. C., and Repapis, C. (2016) Interview. 'Geoff Harcourt on Keynesian Theory'. *Economics*. Interview. Goldsmiths, University of London. Available at: https://www.economicsppf.com/geoff-harcourt.html

Harcourt, T. (2021) 'Geoff Harcourt (27.6.1931 to 7.12.2021)', *Australian Economic Papers*, 61: 207–212.

Harcourt, W. (2011) 'Editorial: The Times They Are A-Changin'', *Development*, 55: 1–4.

Harcourt, W. (2014) 'A Feminist Response to Stephen Marglin's Premises for a New Economy', *Economic and Labour Relations Review*, 25 (4).

Harcourt, W. (2023) 'Conversations with GC Harcourt on Social Justice in the Face of Economic and Ecological Uncertainty', *Economic and Labour Relations Review*, 34: 26–34.

Hatch, J. (2021) 'Obituary: Geoff Harcourt: Scholar, Sportsman and Humanitarian', published on *The University of Adelaide—School of Economics and Public Policy*. Available at: https://able.adelaide.edu.au/economics-and-public-policy/news/list/2021/12/22/obituary-geoff-harcourt-scholar-sportsman-and-humanitarian

Huwe, V., and Rehm, M. (2022) 'The Ecological Crisis and Post-Keynesian Economics—Bridging the Gap?', *European Journal of Economics and Economic Policies*, 19 (3): 397–414.

IPCC (Intergovernmental Panel on Climate Change) (2014) *Climate Change 2014: Synthesis Report. Contribution of Working Groups I, II and III to the Fifth Assessment Report of the Intergovernmental Panel on Climate Change*. Geneva, Switzerland: IPCC.

IPCC (Intergovernmental Panel on Climate Change) (2023) 'Summary for Policymakers', in Core Writing Team, H. Lee and J. Romero (eds.), *Climate Change 2023: Synthesis Report. Contribution of Working Groups I, II and III to the Sixth Assessment Report of the Intergovernmental Panel on Climate Change*, pp. 1–34. Geneva, Switzerland: IPCC.

Junor, A. (2021) 'Anne Junor', in *Testimonials and Greetings, A-L*. Available at: www.geoff-harcourt.com/testimonials-and-greetings-a-l/#Testimonials

Junor, A. (2022) 'Vale G. C. Harcourt AC FASSA FRSN', *The Economic and Labour Relations Review*, 33 (1): 3–4.

Kaldor, N. (1967) *Strategic Factors in Economic Development*. New York: Cornell University Press.

Keynes, J. M. (2012 [1936]) *The General Theory of Employment, Interest, and Money*. Collected Writings of John Maynard Keynes. London: Cambridge University Press.

Kriesler, P. (2023) 'Introduction to the Second Symposium in Honour of Geoff Harcourt', *The Economic and Labour Relations Review*, 34: 199–202.

Lee, T. (1975) 'The Radicalization of Stephen Marglin: Profile', in *Harvard Crimson*, May 12. Available at: www.thecrimson.com/article/1975/5/12/the-radicalization-of-stephen-marglin-pbcbambridge/

Marglin, S. (2013) 'Premises for a New Economy', *Development*, 56 (2): 149–154.

Minsky, H. (1975) *John Maynard Keynes*. New York: Columbia University Press.

Nevile, J. C., Harcourt, G. C., and Kriesler, P. (2015) 'Macroeconomic Policy for the Real World: A Post-Keynesian Perspective', *Economic Papers: A Journal of Applied Economics and Policy*, 34 (3): 108–117.

Perry, N. (2013) 'Environmental Economics and Policy', in G. C. Harcourt and P. Kriesler (eds.), *The Oxford Handbook of Post-Keynesian Economics, Volume 2: Critiques and Methodology*. Oxford: Oxford University Press.

Politt, H. (2019) 'The Contribution of Post-Keynesian Economics to Climate Policy and Meeting Global Decarbonisation Targets'. Presented at the *Post-Keynesian Economic Society*. Available at: www.postkeynesian.net/downloads/events/Pollitt_2019.pdf

Repapis, C. (2014) 'The Scholar as Reader: The Last 50 Years of Economic Theory Seen Through G. C. Harcourt's Book Reviews', *Cambridge Journal of Economics*, 38 (6): 1517–1540.

Rockström, J., Steffen, W., Noone, K., et al. (2009) 'A Safe Operating Space for Humanity', *Nature*, 461: 472–475.

Saith, A. (2018) 'Ajit Singh (1940–2015), the Radical Cambridge Economist: Anti-imperialist Advocate of Third World Industrialization', *Development and Change*, 9 (2): 561–628.

Sasser, J. S. (2018) *On Infertile Ground: Population Control and Women's Rights in the Era of Climate Change*. New York: NYU Press.

Sen, S. (2015) 'Ajit Singh: Obituary', *Social Scientist*, 43 (7–8): 73–75.

Steffen, W., et al. (2015) 'Planetary Boundaries: Guiding Human Development on a Changing Planet', *Science* 347 (6223): 1–10.

Stilwell, F. (2021) 'Geoff Harcourt: Rapporteur, Raconteur, Political Economist Extraordinaire', *The Journal of Australian Political Economy*, 17 December 2022. Available at: www.ppesydney.net/geoff-harcourt-rapporteur-raconteur-political-economist-extraordinaire/

Tran-Nam, B., and Harcourt, G. (2016) 'A Note on a Conversation with Geoff Harcourt', *Australian Economic Papers*, 55: 491–509.

Troy, P. (2014) 'Climate Change Response: Linking Research, Policy and Action', *Economic and Labour Relations Review*, 25 (4): 619–628.

Velupillai, K. (2021) 'Geoff Harcourt: A Portrait (27 June 1931–7 December 2021)', *Australian Economic Papers*, 61: 213–216.

Velupillai, K. in Cord, R. (2017) 'Geoffrey Harcourt', in *The Palgrave Companion to Cambridge Economics Volumes I & II*. London: Palgrave Macmillan.

William, B., and Shaw, W. (1983) 'Neoclassical and Post-Keynesian Environmental Economics: An Addendum', *Journal of Post Keynesian Economics*, 6 (1): 140–142.

Part III

Economic development

8 Reflections on economic development and environment[1],[2]

Alessandro Roncaglia and (late) Paolo Sylos Labini

The problem of the relationship between economic development and the environment is too vast to permit a full discussion here. We will therefore limit ourselves to a few brief considerations.[3]

1. Faced with environmental problems, many scholars—economists and non-economists—wondered whether economic growth is sustainable or whether the negative effects on the natural environment are such as to question the very survival of mankind. Harsh criticism was directed, in particular, at what has been called the 'mania for quantitative growth', which assumes the expansion of national income as the central aim of economic policy. Yet, very few economists have—or have had—such a simplistic view of economic development.

Consider, for example, the most famous of classical economists, Adam Smith. Undoubtedly the idea of *per capita* product is at the centre of his reflections on the 'wealth of nations'; that is, on the stage of development reached by a country. But, for those who read his *magnum opus* carefully, it is clear that it is a simplification that allows economic science to take a decisive step forward. In fact, by identifying the 'wealth of nations' with *per capita* income, Smith establishes a relationship between economic development and the progress of human societies which is different from the one that had prevailed until then—think, for example, of William Petty in the 17th century—when the wealth of nations was identified with the overall product of the country: that is, with the economic strength of the nation, considered the basis of the military power and therefore of the political strength of the nation itself (that was the epoch of the full affirmation of national monarchies) rather than with the well-being of citizens, as has been the case since Adam Smith onwards. The identification of social development with the 'wealth of nations' and of this with *per capita* income focuses precisely on this decisive change of concept—from the strength of the state to the well-being of the citizen—as a central object of economics. It is clear, however, that we are facing a simplification: Smith's own hints to the problems of psychophysical impoverishment connected to the division of labour, which is also at the basis of productivity growth, show how other factors besides *per capita* income contribute to determining the well-being of the citizen. But simplification is still useful, given the high correlation that can be found both in the path of different national economic systems and in the comparison between different countries at a given moment in time; between *per capita* income and other

DOI: 10.4324/9781003375425-11

148   *Alessandro Roncaglia and (late) Paolo Sylos Labini*

measures of civil progress such as life expectancy or infant mortality, illiteracy and the like.

In fact, focusing attention on *per capita* income means, especially in the conditions of the Smith era, highlighting an element that constitutes the essential precondition for social progress.[4] As Smith says, 'Opulence and Commerce commonly precede the improvement of arts and refinement of every sort. I do not mean—Smith adds—that the improvement of arts and refinements of manners are the necessary consequence of commerce . . . only that it is a necessary requisite' (Smith, 1983 [1776], p. 137).

It is enough to look at the statistics of the World Bank, for example, to see that *per capita* income has a strong correlation with other indicators of social well-being, such as the level of education, the average length of life and infant mortality. This correlation concerns both the historical series within each country and the comparisons between different countries at a given moment in time. Thus, in Italy, infant mortality rate fell from 44 per 1,000 in 1960 to 10.1 in 1987, while *per capita* income roughly quadrupled. And if we compare the Italian experience with that of a country that in the first decades of the century[5] had a *per capita* product and a standard of living similar to ours—Argentina—we can see that, when the trend of the national product diverges, as it has happened since about 1950, other indicators also begin to diverge; and the differences, modest from one year to the next, become important within a few decades. Thus, in 1987, the *per capita* product in Italy was about three times that of Argentina, and at the same time, infant mortality in Italy was about one-third (the figure for Argentina is 29.7 per 1,000).[6]

Of course, the correlation is anything but rigid: many other factors, in addition to *per capita* income, affect the indicators of social well-being. Particular importance is given to inequalities in the distribution of income; moreover, sudden changes in a country's income (such as those occurred in 1973–74 in low-population crude oil producing countries, from Saudi Arabia to Kuwait) only gradually translate themselves into an improvement in other welfare indicators, given the time needed, for example, to adapt sanitary infrastructures.

The very existence of these correlations, however, leads us to reject the thesis that halving economic growth would be a goal of civilization. Social development is not identifiable only with economic development, and the latter cannot be identified only with the quantitative growth of *per capita* income; but economic growth still constitutes a decisive basis for improving living conditions. Among other things, if, by hypothesis, in a given country, the overall production remained stable, the increases in productivity allowed by scientific progress (essential in reducing labour sacrifices, and in any case, necessary in order not to retreat due to competition from other countries in which productivity continues to grow) would largely translate themselves into increases in unemployment, which is, itself, one of the main factors of social malaise. (The reduction in working hours, which has, in fact, halved in the space of a century, can absorb only a share of the productivity increases.)

If 'the zero-growth economy' constitutes a regressive utopia, therefore, the problem of environmental constraints on development must be tackled not in the sense of favouring policies that curb economic development but in the sense of favouring 'sustainable growth'—i.e., a growth that does not damage the natural environment in which we live.[7]

2. The notion of 'sustainable growth' has attracted more and more attention in recent years; from our point of view, the main problem does not concern its concrete definition, which is entrusted to rapidly developing scientific fields generically indicated with the term ecology, but the way in which it can be ensured that the choices of economic operators move in the desired direction. The relevant issues, from this point of view, concern the conflict between private interests and public interest and between the market and the state. These are questions that have been at the centre of the debate since the birth of economics[8]; in our brief considerations, we will once again adopt Adam Smith's point of view as a reference.

The distinction between private interest and public interest becomes an opposition, an irresolvable conflict, only if private interest is interpreted in a restrictive sense, as 'selfishness' rather than as 'self-interest'. Simplifying drastically, we can say that the first of the two meanings characterises the utilitarian roots of the marginalist approach that has dominated economic theory for more than a century; while the second meaning was explicitly placed at the basis of Smith's analysis. In other words, Smith's liberal theses are based on a double assumption: that, commonly, everyone knows their own interests better than the others; and that everyone's interests include the desire to be appreciated by others, and therefore, respect for the well-being of others. The first assumption explains the refusal of a centralised management of the economy, and therefore, the preferability of the market economy over the 'command' economy; the crises of the Eastern European countries[9] confirm the correctness of this Smithian thesis. The second assumption is, from our point of view, more important and complex. In fact, it constitutes, in the Smithian construction, an essential precondition for the pursuit of private interests by a multitude of economic subjects in competition with each other to lead to valid results for the well-being of society; however, in the developments of the same classical school of political economy, this assumption was submerged by the growing influence of utilitarianism.

In Smith's construction, the pursuit of private interests cannot conflict with public interest if each economic subject is bound in his choices to respect the 'moral principle of sympathy'. According to this principle, developed by Smith in the *Theory of Moral Sentiments*, individuals evaluate their own actions from the point of view of an 'impartial spectator' who, given all the elements known to them, judges them as an 'average citizen'. Legal institutions, whose proper functioning is essential to guarantee the security of exchanges in the market, find an essential concrete support in this moral principle. Thus, Smith's famous statement, according to which 'it is not from the benevolence of the butcher, the brewer, or the baker, that we expect our dinner, but from their regard to their own interest', should not be considered in isolation but in the context—which is vital for the functioning of a market economy—of the assumption of a civil society, founded on the general acceptance of the moral principle of sympathy and endowed with administrative and judicial institutions necessary to deal with cases of violation of a common ethics.

These foundations of civic culture and public institutions are necessary for the defence of the environment: both in a market economy as in a planned one; both in the presence of economic growth or decline. Just as a market economy cannot function if the butcher and the baker were free to adulterate their goods, it would not be possible to avoid the degradation of the natural environment without a civic conscience of its importance for social welfare and without institutions capable of intervening to impose respect for environmental constraints in cases of violation of the moral norm. However, it should be emphasised that—as the experience of tax evasion teaches—the strictest legal rules and the harshest sanctions are merely paper tigers in the absence of a sufficiently widespread civic sense. Precisely for the diffusion of this perception of the importance of the environmental issue, schools— and certainly not only in the context of the teaching of civic education—play an essential role.

3. The problem of the relationship between public intervention and free, private initiative in the context of a market economy thus begins to appear as a matter of complementarity rather than opposition. But this does not only apply to legal and administrative macrostructures: it also applies to more specific economic policy interventions. As an example, let's consider some problems related to the energy sector.

Growth and change have characterised the history of the energy sector over the last half century. The decline in the use of coal was accompanied, in the 1950s and 1960s, by the impetuous expansion of oil, while, in recent years, there seems to be a growing differentiation of energy sources: coal shows a slight recovery, oil shows a certain readjustment, natural gas increases, solar power and a variegated set of 'alternative energies' appear, while nuclear power disappears in some countries after the Chernobyl accident, although continuing to play an important role in others.

At the same time, in most countries, population and *per capita* income are growing; and energy consumption often rose even more rapidly, at least up to the 1974 crisis. What happened in more recent years seems to show that the oil crisis has, indeed, led to a change of course in several ways, but not a reversal of direction; and something similar seems to be happening today, in face of a public opinion that suddenly acquires an awareness of the risks of environmental catastrophes and of a gradual but cumulative and irreversible deterioration of the environment.

The growth of the energy sector and the changes in its internal structure are linked to the evolution of the economy as a whole by complex relationships of cause and effect. Thus, it is clear that overall energy consumption strictly depends on the trend of production and income; and it is equally evident that an increasing availability of energy is a prerequisite for economic development. In other words, economic development is conditioned by the supply of energy, but at the same time, it determines its demand.

We must not neglect the role of technological change; on the one hand, the growing mechanisation and the increase in the *per capita* product push in the direction of an expansion of energy consumption; but, on the other hand, technical progress, in the constant pursuit of reducing production costs, is also the source of a reduction in energy requirements per unit of product and of greater efficiency in the overall use of energy. The net result of these two opposing forces probably depends, to a decisive extent, on the price trend of the various forms of energy: there is a process of 'dynamic substitution' in periods of growth of these prices, in which businesses and households devote greater attention to the development and practical applications of new technologies which allow energy savings[10], while, in periods of declining energy prices (not necessarily in absolute terms, but with respect to the prices of other means of production and consumption), the drive towards a reduction in energy consumption is lower, the latter tending to closely follow the trend of production and income. On the contrary, energy consumption can grow faster than production and income, both for the reasons indicated previously (increasing mechanisation, and therefore, an increasing 'energy intensity' of production) and because household energy consumption corresponds, to a significant extent, to goods and services satisfying higher-order needs, which, by their nature, absorb an increasing share of income.

Technical progress, which proceeds at an unequal speed in several fields, is also the main factor in determining changes in the internal structure of the energy sector. Its importance is confirmed by two circumstances. First, the sequence wood-coal-oil-nuclear-fission and natural gas, solar and nuclear fusion, which indicates the succession of dominant energy sources (where the last link in the chain indicates the most likely scenario for the second half of the next century),[11] appears as a sequence of improvements in mankind's technological capacity to extract energy from nature, characterised by very strong increases in the supply of energy at decreasing average costs. Secondly, there is the growing penetration of electricity— i.e., the increase in the share of energy consumption satisfied by electricity. This trend ensures greater flexibility in energy supply,[12] given that electricity can be produced using different primary sources, and therefore, ensures greater energy policy autonomy for the various countries, which can make different choices according to their endowments of natural resources; moreover, in modern industrial systems, electricity allows for a more flexible use of energy as well as constituting the necessary support for the diffusion of information technology in manufacturing industries (automation) and in services.

Faced with a situation of continuous technological change, the choice between alternative energy sources cannot be analysed as a problem of 'static substitution', departing from an equilibrium situation in which various energy sources are used simultaneously because their marginal costs are equal—i.e., the cost of the last dose of energy produced by each source; relatively modest changes in the relative price of the various energy sources would, then, cause adjustments such as to bring the situation to a new equilibrium, distinguished by a reduction in the use of the energy source whose price has increased and vice versa.

In reality, the coexistence of different energy sources depends not only on the natural segmentation of the market (the fuel demand for automobiles is 'technologically' distinct from that of an enterprise's machines) but also on the presence of residual technologies alongside the first developments of modern technologies. Once built, a power station runs for 20 to 30 years; and when machinery goes out of use, it is often advisable to replace it with more modern ones of the same type, leaving the basic characteristics of the plant unchanged; finally, there is often a rather long interval of time between the moment of choosing the type of investment to be made and its realisation: more than five years, as a rule, both in the case of a nuclear power plant and in the case of putting an offshore oil reservoir into production. So, it is no wonder if, for example, the costs of producing electricity, at any given moment, differ from one plant to another and from one technology to another.

The path of energy consumption has posed very serious problems for the protection of the natural environment. These are problems which, as mentioned previously, are addressed by the public authorities. In fact, the effects on the environment of the production and utilisation of the several energy sources are a classic case of 'externality'—i.e., the effects of the activity of a specific group of producers or consumers which do not constitute costs or benefits for the individual producer or consumer but advantages or disadvantages for a wider group of economic agents, sometimes for society as a whole. In the case of a 'negative externality' (e.g., emissions of pollutants), the enterprise or consumer which are responsible for it have no economic incentives to limit its scope. Therefore, traditionally, economic theory suggests counterbalancing the 'negative externalities' through appropriate taxes or through specific rules that impose limits or purification interventions.

However, in practice, the difficulty in identifying the environmental effects of many human activities—and, in particular, those connected to the production and use of energy, and then, the difficulty of determining precisely their extent—have favoured a lax attitude in the past. No one cares about problems, the existence of which is largely unknown. In fact, it is now evident that the environmental consequences of energy production and consumption were underestimated, if not completely ignored, in the decades following the Industrial Revolution and until very recently.

In the current age, the growth of scientific knowledge and its widespread dissemination through an increasingly aware public opinion raises the understanding and sensitivity for environmental issues. Issues such as the greenhouse effect, which were completely ignored a few years ago, are now in the spotlight. We can safely predict, therefore, that environmental problems will have an increasing importance in strategic choices of the energy industry.

The list of negative effects associated with the production of energy is very long, particularly if we consider—as logically we must do—also the collateral effects of the 'upstream' production activities, such as the extraction of coal in mines or the transport of crude oil and natural gas. (It's not just about accidents, albeit very serious ones, such as the pollution produced by the sinking of an oil tanker like Exxon Valdez in Alaska; sometimes it's about real catastrophes, like explosions and fires caused by gas leaks in Ixhuatepec in Mexico in 1984 and along the Trans-Siberian Railway in 1989.) Every source of energy has its own problems, and often, more than one: among the factors which are responsible for the greenhouse effect, we find coal in the first row, followed by oil and, even further back, by natural gas; then, it is enough to recall the risks of catastrophes such as Chernobyl and the enormous, hitherto underestimated, problem of radioactive waste for thermonuclear power plants and the risks of catastrophes such as that of Vajont in the case of hydroelectric energy. (By the way, these catastrophes are much more common than is generally believed: the collapse of a dam causes disastrous flooding, and often, fatalities almost every year in some part of the world.)

A decisive role in the choice between the several energy sources, especially if we consider nuclear energy and renewable energy sources (solar, wind, biomass . . .) alongside fossil fuels, will be played by public interventions, which will be increasingly guided by the need to favour choices compatible with respect for the natural environment. This means ever more precise and binding legislation regarding the several energy sources (for example, on the safety of nuclear power plants or on polluting emissions arising from the use of fossil fuels) as well as a decisive stimulus for technological research aimed at improving the environmental impact of the various sources of energy and a policy of specific taxes, even very high ones (such as that on petrol consumption). A strong policy, in this sense, can contribute to reduce the income elasticity of energy consumption, and in extreme cases, to make it negative (as was the case for some years of oil consumption or total energy consumption in the United States after the oil crises of 1973–74 and 1979–80), thus allowing for an increase in income accompanied by a reduction in energy consumption (see also footnote 10).

However, if the reduction of energy consumption is feasible in some countries, such as the United States or Canada, where the intensity of *per capita* energy consumption is particularly high (about two times more than in a country as Italy), such an extreme result is hardly achievable for the world as a whole. In fact, many developing countries have very low *per capita* energy consumption, which are destined to grow if—as everyone wishes—their *per capita* income rises towards the current one of today's industrialised countries. Consider that the *per capita* consumption of energy is (data for 1986, taken from World Banks' *World Development Report* 1988, pp. 240–41) equal to 532 Kg. o.e. (oil equivalent) in China, 208 in India, 231 in Indonesia, 134 in Nigeria, 46 in Bangladesh, 7,193 in the United States and 2,539 in Italy (where there was an increase of 62% compared to the *per capita* consumption of 1965, which was equal to 1,568 Kg. o.e.).

If we take into account the expected population growth for the next few decades, especially in Asia, Africa and Latin America, world production needs to grow to avoid a general impoverishment; and the increase of production must be more rapid than that of population if things are to improve in the most backward areas of the globe. It is difficult for economic development not to be accompanied by a growth in energy consumption, even if technical progress and decisive economic policy interventions could help to contain this growth. Energy policy will therefore have to ensure that the availability of energy sources does not constitute an obstacle to economic development; the compatibility of development with environmental protection must be ensured not only by curbing energy consumption per unit of product but also by favouring the most appropriate choices among the various sources of available energy as well as ensuring compliance with environmental demands in the use of each of them.

In the absence of public interventions aimed at promoting energy saving, the income elasticity of energy consumption in the coming decades would be approximately equal to or slightly higher than one, as happened in past decades; and this means that the growth of energy consumption will go hand in hand with that of income. A world product growth rate of 3% per year (which is far from high, in face of the problems of economic backwardness existing today) entails a production level which will equal to 6.25 times the current one in 2050; in the absence of interventions, as has been said, energy consumption will tend to grow at the same rate. But if we are already facing very serious environmental problems with the current levels of energy consumption, how will we be able to bear a six- or seven-fold growth? It is clear that, in these conditions, the effort required to prevent energy problems from constituting a constraint on economic development is too high. Massive public intervention—based on taxes and incentives, regulations and direct interventions or research subsidies—is indispensable and must be extremely incisive in various directions: the search for energy saving, which is also a priority objective, must be accompanied immediately by interventions aimed at favouring the use of energy sources which are as respectful as possible regarding the natural environment and through a modification of the current composition of energy sources (for example, limiting the use of coal in favour of natural gas— much less dangerous from the point of view of the greenhouse effect) and through the development of technological improvements that make the use of fossil fuels less polluting and which favour the development and diffusion of 'new' or 'brand new' technologies, such as solar and nuclear fusion. Each of these directions of intervention must not be considered as excluding each other but as complementary.

4. We spoke mainly of the problems posed for the environment by the production and use of energy sources, since it is from this sector that the most serious and widespread problems arise, given the central role that energy sources play in the process of development. However, the environmental problems deriving from certain industrial productions are also serious, in the chemical sector above all, both due to the characteristics of certain processes and the effects of certain production goods (such as pesticides in agriculture, which can cause to the pollution of groundwater) and for the effects of the use of certain consumer goods. It is possible, in some cases—as we mentioned—to drastically reduce the damage to the environment through taxes or restrictive regulations, which aim to limit the 'negative externalities' as much as possible. In other cases, the only way to avoid damage seems to be that of prohibition, with the consequence that other processes and other products will be used. In all these cases, two types of contrasts emerge: between businesses and citizens and between workers (as well as businesses) and citizens. Sometimes, these contrasts turn into real conflicts, which the public authority is called upon to mediate. The solution may not be found within the enterprise or sector that causes the damage but in a broader context; for example, public authorities may be induced to promote substitute activities to mitigate the economic damage of workers who lose their jobs.

Another type of contrast emerges at the international level: if enterprises in a certain country are forced to adopt costly measures to reduce or eliminate pollution, these companies may find themselves at disadvantages in international competition, when these obligations have not been introduced in other countries. Conflicts of this kind can be reduced through international agreements establishing common obligations. On the international level, conflicts become serious or even too serious when it is recognised that the use of certain consumer goods must be drastically reduced or prohibited in all countries—or, at least, in all industrialised countries—to avoid ecological damage which affects the whole world. Conflicts of this kind recently emerged at an international conference held in the United States, where, among other things, the problem of the 'hole in the ozone layer' was discussed, this being, apparently, caused by the use of certain consumer goods which give rise to gaseous emissions. In this circumstance, we have seen how difficult it is to reach a sufficiently broad agreement.

The environmental problems associated with economic development are too diverse: problems related to the pollution of the air, water and land emerge. Particular problems are those of noise pollution and those coming from radioactive waste, which we try to make harmless by burying them at great depths and in uninhabited places. Then, there is the oldest and most extensive problem of municipal solid-waste, which has become increasingly serious as productive activities, especially industrial ones, have grown; and, since many wastes are, by nature, toxic, regulations have been introduced to prevent them from causing damage; these regulations, however, involve costly operations, enterprises not infrequently trying to hide the waste or to transfer it to countries where controls are less strict, so as to avoid such costs; often, these are backward countries. Therefore, waste has become a problem of enormous dimensions, which sometimes becomes an international issue.

Connected with economic development is also the problem of the progressive destruction of large tropical forests, especially in Latin America and Africa. Among the various causes at the origin of this problem are enterprises in developed countries that intend to obtain timber or local companies that intend to carry out gigantic speculations, even for the construction of roads; and there is the push, especially vigorous in certain African countries, of hungry people who intend to obtain land to cultivate.

5. While, as has been said, the so-called zero growth is not desirable, a slower growth than that experienced in the last four decades is, instead, fully acceptable for the most advanced countries; the situation is different in Third World countries, where it is vital, instead, to try to accelerate growth. In both categories of countries, however, what really matters is not so much the speed as the qualitative content of growth: for the developed countries, the maintenance of the advantages obtained up to now is at stake, but for the rest, their very survival is probably at stake. If we reflect on the fact that the development process, where it has taken place, has been driven by scientific and technical progress, we must conclude that it is from this progress that the answers to the tremendous environmental problems can come, both for developed and backward countries. In other words, a great effort of an international nature is needed to modify production methods and make them compatible with 'sustainable growth' and to identify methods capable of progressively

reducing the damages that have already occurred where these are not irreversible. More precisely, it is necessary to unify and to decisively intensify the efforts of all countries, especially the more developed ones, also with the creation of large international research institutes, not only in the field of experimental sciences but also in the fields of the human sciences.

Let us consider only two examples, the first especially concerning the developed countries; the second, the backward ones. First example: if we assume that automobiles cause serious pollution in cities, including noise, then it is necessary to give a strong impulse, in agreement with the large manufacturing companies, to studies and projects that may turn the electric automobile cheaper in the short run. Second example: in agreement with the governments of certain Third World countries, it is advisable to promote technical and economic programmes which may be able to halt deforestation and to give a strong impulse to researches which are capable of producing other 'green revolutions'; that is, which are able to increase rapidly agricultural productivity without causing environmental damage, also making forest conservation profitable. By now, it is clear that, in order to tackle environmental problems, especially those concerning Third World countries, the effort to be made is both a scientific as well as an economic one, since it also involves evaluating the costs and the financial resources that need to be employed.

Pollution and the volume of municipal waste have grown and are growing at an exponential rate, hand in hand with industrial production, whose overall volume has grown no less than 20 times over the last hundred years. The growth of environmental problems, such as that of production, has been gradual; only recently, however, have they exceeded a certain critical threshold, which has led to a rapid aggravation of those problems, and therefore, of their perception, not by a limited number of scholars—this had happened several decades ago—but by a large and growing number of people, including many politicians. As has happened with other human problems, once the critical threshold of perception has been overcome, after a more or less long interval, humanity must overcome the critical threshold of action.

By now, it is evident that, if Third World countries developed along the path followed by today's industrialised countries, the effects would be catastrophic for everyone; and since a lack of development or a too slow development would aggravate the calamities afflicting those countries—considering the demographic trends in progress—it is essential that the characteristics of the development process change in significative terms, as regards both production methods and the composition of production. It is literally vital to prepare an international strategy for a 'sustainable growth' of all countries, starting with those of the Third World; a strategy that has its driving force in the United Nations and that contemplates a reorganisation of financial relations—including the issue of foreign debts and the financial and technical assistance to developing countries—and a work of promoting international agreements for environmental protection—a strategy supported by science and technology through the creation of large research institutes, not only in the fields of physical sciences but also in the fields of social sciences. It is from knowledge—and then, from action based on knowledge—that salvation can come.

Notes

1 Presentation given at the European Summer University, Frascati, 15–20 October 1990, published in Italian in *Scuola e società*, n. 12, dec. 1990, pp. 532–8.
2 Translated from Italian by Vitor Eduardo Schincariol.
3 In what follows, we resume some ideas already proposed in previous works. See particularly Sylos Labini (1989) and Roncaglia (1989a, 1989b [from which part 3 is partly taken]).
4 It should be remembered, however, that the causal relationship between economic growth and civil development of a country is not unilateral: economic growth itself is favoured by a set of institutions and values often generically referred to as a country's 'degree of civilization'.
5 Editor's note: the authors refer to the 21st century.
6 Data on National Net Products are available in Maddison (1989, p. 19); data on infant mortality in World Bank (1989). The claim that economic growth presents a foundational precondition for the development of civil society is reproposed, with strong support from statistical data, in World Bank (1990).
7 See the Brundtland Report (The World Commission on Environment and Development, 1987).
8 An interesting analysis of the pre-Smithian phase of the first of the two debates is that of Hirschman (2013 [1979]).
9 Editor's note: crisis given at the beginning of the 1990s, as the former socialist bloc disappeared.
10 Accordingly, in Italy, oil consumption fell by more than 10% after the first oil shock, going from 97.2 million tons in 1973 to 87.7 in 1975, while the gross domestic product remained substantially unchanged. See Sylos Labini (1985). Several estimates of the price elasticity of energy demand are reported in Pireddu (1990).
11 Editor's note: 'next century' here meant the 21st century.
12 In Italy, according to ENEL, electricity consumption went from 13.3 Twh in 1938 to 38.3 in 1958 and to 220.4 in 1988; in the world, the share of electricity in energy consumption, which was insignificant at the end of the First World War and still less than 10% at the threshold of the Second World War, is around one-fifth around 1960 and around one-third in recent years.

References

Hirschman, A. O. (2013 [1977]) *The Passions and the Interests. Political Arguments for Capitalism Before Its Triumph*. Princeton: Princeton University Press.
Maddison, A. (1989) *The World Economy in the 20th Century*. Paris: OECD.
Pireddu, G. (1990) *L'energia nell'analisi economica*. Milan: Franco Angeli.
Roncaglia, A. (1989a) 'Italian Economic Growth: A Smithian View', *Quaderni di storia dell'economia politica*, 7 (2/3): 227–234.
Roncaglia, A. (1989b) 'Energia tra presente e futuro', in F. Reviglio, A. Roncaglia, et al. (eds.), *Uomo, Ambiente, Energia: Il Futuro*. Roma: ENI.
Smith, A. (1983 [1776]) *Lectures on Rhetoric and Belles Lettres*. Edited by J. C. Bryce. Oxford: Oxford University Press.
Sylos Labini, P. S. (1985) 'Dimensione energia', *Effetto prezzo*, 3: 39–42.
Sylos Labini, P. S. (1989) 'Sviluppo economico e sviluppo civile', *Moneta e credito*, 167: 291–304.
World Bank. (1989) *World Development Report 1989*. Oxford: Oxford University Press.
World Bank. (1990) *World Development Report 1990: Poverty*. Oxford: Oxford University Press.
The World Commission on Environment and Development. (1987) *Our Common Future*. Oxford: Oxford University Press.

9 Celso Furtado on natural resources, the environment and ecology

Economic development between myth and utopia

Vitor Eduardo Schincariol

1. Introduction[1]

Celso Furtado's *The Myth of Economic Development* (Furtado, 1974) is often remembered as a landmark in terms of reevaluating the classical ideas around economic and social development in light of ecological dimensions. It was published two years after the well-known *The Limits to Growth* (Meadows et al., 1972), which influenced Furtado's subsequent research. As Furtado showed interdisciplinary concerns, ecological aspects already existed in his work before, although in a limited form; at the same time, they reappeared in some of his subsequent intellectual output, with different tones. This chapter aims to revisit and to discuss Furtado's legacy with an eye on its environmental and ecological aspects. Particularly, the paper has the following goals: (1) to describe and to contextualise how ecological themes were taken by Furtado and to show how they evolved over time; (2) to suggest new lines of interpreting some of Furtado's most used economic categories in light of ecological concerns. The first goal bears more of a historical dimension; by its turn, the second goal aims to discuss some of the most important economic categories of the structuralist theory of accumulation. The chapter concludes that, although the bulk of Furtado's legacy was concentrated on analysing and overcoming 'underdevelopment', he showed progressive awareness of the human threats to the environment as well as the physical limits to the achievement of so-called 'development'. Additionally, it is claimed that a renewed ecological perspective of economic development can benefit from revisiting Furtado's theoretical framework, provided that adaptations are introduced in his original framework.

2. The colonial model

Furtado's first important academic work consisted in his PhD thesis, titled *Colonial economy in Brazil in the XVI and XVII centuries* (*Economia colonial no Brasil nos séculos XVI e XVII* [Furtado, 2001]),[2] which was presented at the University of Sorbonne (Paris) in 1948. Furtado was 28 years old. This work, which was to be published in Portuguese only in 2001, was followed by some short works on the Brazilian economy (a list can be found in Oliveira, 2003; Furtado, 1997c), and then, by Furtado's well-known *The Economic Growth of Brazil: A survey from colonial to modern times* (the original title being *Formação Econômica do Brasil;*

DOI: 10.4324/9781003375425-12

Furtado, 2006 [1959]). Both works—and particularly the later—were important chapters of the progressive development of the social sciences in Brazil in the last century, particularly with regard to historical analyses, which still suffered from prejudices that came from the 19th century. Together with Caio Prado Junior, Nelson Werneck Sodré and other modern Brazilian economic historians, Furtado wished to understand *underdevelopment* and searched for historical explanations for this condition.[3] Going against deterministic or racial explanations of the Brazilian backwardness, Furtado focused on the nature of the Portuguese colonisation of Brazil, which was marked by slavery, monoculture and large states. Today, these perspectives are common sense, but it was an intellectual victory against the conservative analyses that marked social sciences in Brazil in the first half of the last century (for a contextualisation, see Love, 2008 [1995]).

Furtado's PhD thesis stressed that the several stages of Brazil's economic history since the 16th century were all marked by the upsurge and then decline in exports of what we use to define nowadays as *commodities*; that is, agricultural goods and other raw materials. In other terms, the several steps of Brazil's economic history since colonial times were marked by the exploitation and exportation of primary goods and natural resources, sold to the markets of the old colonialist nations according to their needs. This condition, which was taken as a 'natural' one for the followers of the 'comparative costs theory', was rejected by Furtado and the Brazilian generation marked by so-called 'national-developmentalism', which argued for industrialisation and economic sovereignty.

> The great drop in the sugar prices by the end of the 18th century and beginning of the 19th will hit the Colony hard. The discovery of gold and diamonds in Minas Gerais will open, however, a new cycle to the economy of the nation [*sic!*]. . . . The mining cycle of the XVIII century would have the same importance as that of sugar in the previous century, but it would not differ significantly from sugar monoculture. The same could be said regarding tobacco, cocoa, cotton, coffee and rubber. From the gold mining to the rubber exploitation in the XX century, we will have a repetition of what we told before regarding sugar and pau-brasil [as the *Caesalpinia echinata* tree is popularly known]. It will always be characterised by the power of foreign trade over the interests of collective producers [*coletividade produtora*]. This is the fundamental vice of the colonial economy, or quasi-colonial: its movement around an axis which is outside it.
>
> (Furtado, 2001 [1964], p. 145)

It is interesting to note that Furtado had stressed the environmental consequences of the colonial economic model already in his PhD thesis of 1948. The following excerpts show how Furtado was far from being an economic historian whose preoccupations only revolved around conventional statistical data. Furtado had already expressed an awareness of the environmental aspects of the colonisation of Brazil in 1948, although this was not the main tone of his narrative. The colonial model of sugar production for exportation relied on a *physical* basis which

mixed humid coastal lands, abundant water and sunlight, and adequate temperature, together with the cheap labour given by indigenous and African slaves. The
setting up of the Portuguese colonial model in the Northeast led immediately to
deforestation.

> The sugar industry developed mainly in the Bahia Recôncavo [deep hollow]
> basin—next to the first capital of Brazil—and in the coastal strip of the North-
> east. This last region, which had rich tropical forests in the beginning of the
> colonisation, was devastated by fires which went ahead of crops [*plantações*].
> (Furtado, 2001 [1948], p. 98)

As the colonial model advanced, the original vegetation would be increasingly
destroyed by rudimentary tools of cultivation.

> The inexperience of farming in tropical lands led the Portuguese to imitate
> the indigenous. Therefore, the practice of coivara was introduced—the burn-
> ing of forests with the aim of cleaning the fields. It is easy to imagine the
> harmful consequences of this method which often led to the useless sacrifice
> of wide forestall areas [*trechos*].
> (Furtado, 2001 [1948], p. 153)

Furtado still stressed the fact that the rudimentary agricultural methods soon
exhausted its soils, which were quickly abandoned by new virgin ones. Methods
of land recovery were not implemented, and this led to the devastation of many
agricultural lands of the Northeast. The only legal measures which the Portuguese
implemented to protect the coastal forests aimed at safeguarding wood for building royal ships (Furtado, 2001 [1948], p. 154). The practice of rapidly exhausting
agricultural lands and then cultivating new virgin ones would be repeated in the
'purple lands' [*terras roxas*] of the Southeast, now used for coffee plantations.
'The monoculture of coffee, a true policy of "scorching land" [*terra arrasada*], will
leave a huge scar of infertile lands in one of the most fertile lands of the nation'
(Furtado, 2001 [1948], p. 155).
The prolongation of this 'land-using' economic model would lead to soil erosion.

> The action of monoculture can be observed in land and in man. It absorbs
> the best arable lands, promotes the indiscriminate devastation of forests, and
> turns the stockbreeding unfeasible. By being implemented on the basis of ru-
> dimentary methods of work, it dries up [*esgota*] the best lands in a relatively
> short time. On the other hand, by monopolising the control of the workforce,
> monoculture prevents any other form of economic activity, or reduces them
> to the most miserable conditions. It will be the case of stockbreeding.
> (Furtado, 2001 [1948], p. 121)

As we see, some aspects of Furtado's historical analysis of the environmental consequences of the Portuguese colonial model in Brazil could be defined as

vignettes of an 'environmental history' *avant la lettre*, given their relative scarcity at that time. The foregoing excerpts show that Furtado described the environmental consequences of the colonial model, describing what was essentially an extremely easy access to huge resources of low entropy in the colony, which had never been used in large-scale by the indigenous people. Today, we could say that this model of extracting abundant natural resources for short-term economic gains essentially increased the *entropy* of the Brazilian environment and territory, without creating an organised and autonomous agricultural system as well as an industrial apparatus that could help to partially revert or delay this entropic degradation by means of technical improvements and a more rational utilisation of resources.

Furtado's classic *The Economic Growth of Brazil* (*Formação Econômica do Brasil*, Furtado, 2006 [1959]) was written during his postdoctoral stage at Cambridge (United Kingdom). An aspect that differentiated this work was the handling of Keynesian tools of analysis in order to enlighten not only the nature of colonisation but its subsequent economic stages, from sugar plantations in the Northeast of Brazil to the coffee upsurge in the Southeast over the 19th century. Under the influence of Keynesian economics and his contacts with authors such as Joan Robinson (for his personal account, see Furtado, 1997c), Furtado adapted the Keynesian categories to understand the flows of wealth in Brazilian economic history. He intended to investigate questions such as the roots and impacts of the successive declines in sugar production and gold mining as well as the reasons of the internal migratory flows and the specificities posed by the coffee plantation in the Southeast over the 19th century. However, here, he was clearly more concerned with analysing the roots of underdevelopment with the new tools of modern Keynesian macroeconomics, environmental and ecological aspects not being emphasised. However, it is clear that these were obviously part of many important economic events, such as the economic involution of gold mining as soon as reserves were exhausted by their extensive exploitation (Furtado, 2006 [1959], chapter 15). Similarly, the abundance of land in the Southeast prevented improved methods of cultivation and capitalisation, which could be exchanged by pure extensive incorporation of new lands. In any case, natural resources were integrated into his historical explanations.

> The destruction of land, which can be taken as unforgivable [*inescusável*], is perfectly conceivable from the entrepreneur point of view, whose goal is to obtain the maximum profit from his capital. The preservation of the soil only matters to the entrepreneur when it has an economic ground. In fact, the economic incentives induced him to extend his plantations, to increase the quantity of land and labour force by unit of capital.
>
> (Furtado, 2006 [1959], p. 234)

By its turn, the extensive use of land and soil erosion led to a negative economic legacy left to the next generations.

> The situation [concerning the extensive use of land for coffee plantation] can be perfectly compared [*assimilada*] to the extractive industries, for the

depletion [*esgotamento*] of a mineral reserve account for an alienation of a patrimony whose absence may be regretted by the next generations. However, if the utilisation of the non-renewable reserve is used for starting a process of economic development, not only the present generation but the future ones—who will receive these reserves transformed into reproducible capital—will be benefited. The problem around soil is somewhat less serious because it is often possible to restore it.

(Furtado, 2006 [1959], p. 234)

Maybe because his memories of the war destruction—which he experienced in Italy as a soldier during the Second world War—had now partially faded and because, now, Furtado was to directly take part in the struggle for the Brazilian economic development over the 1950s and 1960s, *Economic Growth of Brazil*—as well as Furtado's subsequent works on Brazilian economy and economic development over the first half of the 1960's—do not show much environmental concerns. That work was concerned with understanding the flows of wealth over Brazilian history over time. However, Furtado's personal struggle as a policy maker for developing a specific Brazilian region—the Northeast, where he was born—would lead him to develop more deeply the relations between economic development and environmental issues.

2.1.   The underdevelopment of Northeast of Brazil as a mix of economic and environmental causes

After his stage at the Economic Commission of Latin America and the Caribbean (ECLAC) since 1950, Furtado returned to Brazil at the end of the 1950s, being, now, particularly engaged in the struggle for developing the Northeast of Brazil—whose economic performance was being put increasingly behind that of the Southeast. Albert Hirschman then defined this region as becoming 'familiar to newspapers readers and even to television viewers in the United States as an area where over 20 million people, close to one-third of Brazil's population, live in great poverty and perhaps in imminent danger of take-over by Castro-Communist inspired peasant leagues'. On the other hand, more realistically, to Brazilians 'the Northeast has become a national problem area for at least eighty years, ever since the long and cruel drought of 1877–79' (Hirschman, 1963, p. 13). The underdevelopment of the Northeast was a complex and long-term phenomenon which mixed a permanent decline of sugar prices in world markets with the transition from slavery to capitalism without full labour mobility, social reform and land distribution—these being aggravated by increasing population growth. The region was divided between a humid coastal strip where sugar production for exportation existed since the 16th century and an interior dry area, known as the *sertão*, where stockbreeding and subsistence agriculture prevailed. Population growth was not accompanied by a rise in the local food production, and periodic droughts caused deep social crises from time to time, as local subsistence agriculture dropped without proper water supply. However, the government actions until the 1950s were marked by the construction

of dams by public works, without structural reforms towards land restructuring—
the use of humid lands for food production—and adequate irrigation, which were
appropriated by landowners so as to feed cattle (as discussed by Callado, 1960).
Additionally, Furtado called attention to the fact that the (then) current Brazilian
industrialising policies by means of import substitution were negatively affecting
the Northeast: the region was a net exporter which supplied the South with hard
currencies but had to bear the devaluation the Brazilian currency *vis-à-vis* the dollar (which fostered the Southern industries) as well as higher prices for the goods
produced by the South (when compared to formerly imported goods). In short: the
(under)development of Northeast was a complex and multivariate phenomenon.

As a Northeastern (he was born in Paraíba, one of the Northeast states), Furtado
had a special interest in studying the roots of the region's underdevelopment and in
proposing new economic policies to overcome it. Still, a young economist in 1959
(he was not 40 years old), Furtado was able to explore the popular commotion
around the social conditions of the Northeast as well as the political trends towards
developmentalist in Brazil at that time, in order to rise to the position of influenc-
ing the decisions of president Juscelino Kubitschek (1956–1961). Now joining the
National Bank for Economic Development of Brazil (then BNDE), Furtado came
up with a new structuralist, multivariate approach to the development of the area,
by means of a technically rigorous study, which became a landmark in terms of
regional planning in Brazil. This was called 'A policy of economic development
for the Northeast' *(Uma política de desenvolvimento econômico para o Nordeste*;
Furtado, 1959). It summarised the bulk of Furtado's achievements at that time. It
was divided between an economic analysis of the area and policy recommendations, which culminated with the proposal of a new developmentalist federal entity,
the Superintendency for the Development of the Northeast (SUDENE).

This progressive experience in policy-making, which would last until the military dictatorship of 1964 in Brazil, was well documented by Albert Hirschman
(Hirschman, 1963) as well as by Furtado himself (Furtado, 1997a, 1997b); there
are also many specific studies and compilations (see; Cohn, 1978; Barros, 1975;
Oliveira, 2003; Mallorquin, 2005; D'Aguiar Furtado, 2009). However, the fact that
Furtado's study involved not only an economic approach but an environmental one
has not been adequately stressed by these studies. In fact, Furtado's approach for
the Northeast by means of a new federal entity as the SUDENE was a pioneer in
terms of mixing environmental and developmental approaches to underdevelopment problems. The novelty in the approach relied on the fact that the author described the underdevelopment of the area as a phenomenon which was caused by
multiple aspects: historical, economic and environmental ones.

Furtado observed that it was useless to merely construct dams and dig wells
by means of public works in order to avoid the worst consequences of periodic
droughts, which were manifested in the drop of the subsistence sector of the *sertão*,
and consequently, in aggravated misery. Accordingly, Furtado's explanation, firstly,
departed from the 'ecological' fact that, in comparative terms, the region was not
endowed with soils as fertile as in the Southeast as well as with natural resources
and a fully adequate water supply. These resources did exist in the region but on a

lower *per capita* relation if compared to more developed areas, particularly with regard to fertile lands. These previous environmental differences between the North and South of Brazil were intensified by the economic decline of sugar production in the Northeast as well as by the lack of significant social changes after the end of the slavery regime in 1888—contrary to the structural dissemination of wages with coffee production in the Southeast (especially in São Paulo state). Subsequently, the type of industrialisation adopted in Brazil since the 1930s resulted in internal transfers of wealth from the North to the South by means of higher domestic prices for the Southern manufactured goods *vis-à-vis* imports as well as by successive devaluations of the Brazilian currency, which fostered domestic industries but raised import prices. This hypothesis was carefully demonstrated with the use of official data.

During the 1960s, it was still not so common to define some types of economic policies as being guided by explicit 'environmental' criteria; but today, we can certainly claim that they were a central piece of Furtado's approach and a model for economic planning concerned with ecological limits to development. The author departed from the fact that there were, indeed, physical limitations to the development of the region—i.e., 'relative scarcity of arable land, inadequate rainfall [and] the predominance of subsistence sector in the stockbreeding of the semi-arid *hinterland*' (Furtado, 2006 [1959], p. 84). He then added the demographic dimension to the problem: 'if population grows fast [*com intensidade*] and the bulk [*constelação*] of natural resources is not much favourable, [the possibility of economic development] becomes a hard one, or even unfeasible' (Furtado, 2006 [1959], p. 86). However, the lack of water was not the main environmental limit for the development of the area: the *sertão* was not a desert, and much water was already available by new dams. But merely stocking water and implementing large-scale public works without a permanent supply of food with its corresponding adequate irrigation—as the federal policies still did up to 1958—were useless. Therefore, he argued, structural change in land structure, a relocation of the surplus population towards the more humid lands of Maranhão and an industrialising policy to absorb part of the unemployment should all be pursued as a new type of struggle against regional underdevelopment.

> Droughts constitute a production crisis caused by physical factors, and short-term policies cannot, of course, attack the root of the problem. They limit themselves to create artificially a demand for food which can only be satisfied by external supply. The long-term policies have been guided by the construction of dams [*açudes*], which constitute a mere preliminarily step for a better exploitation of lands and water in the region. Both short and long-term policies have indirectly contributed to hold a growing surplus population in the region, without changing the main aspects [*dados*] of the problem.
>
> (Furtado, 2006 [1959], p. 88)

This meant that there were limits to the economic growth of the region, even if 'correct' economic policies were implemented. Accordingly, if the basic variables behind the underdevelopment of the Northeast were a 'relative scarcity of land and lower capital accumulation' (Furtado, 2006 [1959], p. 90)—that is, 'unevenly climate, less favourable bulk of natural resources and the hidden or even open transfer of resources outside the region' (p. 105)—the main path to develop the Northeast should be to 'adapt the economy to the physical conditions of the environment' (p. 145), by means of a more 'rational utilisation of natural resources and lower use of cheap workforce' (p. 146), through the creation of work posts in other regions of the nation. In more specific terms, Furtado's policies for the development of the Northeast by means of the Sudene involved:

(i) A relocation of part of the surplus population that depended on landowners and which lived on the subsistence sector of the *sertão*, towards the more humid lands of Maranhão state.

(ii) Land restructuring in the humid coastal strip, by means of the economic exploitation of idle lands and eventually by reducing the area devoted to sugar production.

(iii) Transition from small-scale subsistence agriculture to food production channelled by market distribution.

(iv) The maintenance of food buffers and stocks so as to prevent supply crises during droughts.

(v) The use of the (eventually large) stocks of water to boost more food production, diverting a share of water supply from stockbreeding, with a penalisation of those who benefited from dam constructions in order to enrich themselves.

(vi) The introduction of more drought-resistant native plants in order to adapt agriculture to local environmental conditions.

(vi) Budgetary incentives towards industrialisation, which should absorb surplus population both in rural as in urban areas.

Furtado concluded his study with strong assertions and a gloomy prospect.

With a limited supply of land, the only way to raise the local wealth consists in raising the quantity [*dotação*] of capital per man employed, be it in agriculture or other sectors. On the other hand, given the impossibility of raising the exportation of agricultural products because of natural disadvantages, supply can only be diversified by means of diversifying production. . . . The only way of raising supply is to boost the exportation of agricultural goods or to industrialise. Thus, in face of scarcity of adequate land, the only way is industrialization. . . . If this solution is not feasible, the alternatives to the Northeast would involve to depopulate or to remain as a poor region.

(Furtado, 2006 [1959], p. 124).

Reflecting upon the failures of the previous policies to the region years after the military coup of 1964, which ended the progressive role of the Sudene, Furtado claimed that his approach was able to 'relate ecology with economic structures', something which helped to elucidate the phenomenon of 'drought'—*seca*—'as being a part of these structures' (Furtado, 1997b, p. 71). However, Furtado's environmental and, at the same time, industrialising approach to the region took only arable land and capital as scarce factors of production, neglecting a broad 'entropic' scarcity which would arise from an eventual fast economic growth in the region. His planning approach involved the environment but was still done under 'classical' developmental premises. The approach was clearly more realistic and adequate than the previous ones to the region, which took the apparent lack of water as the main problem of the region, but the promotion of industrialisation prevents us to define Furtado's approach as a full 'environmentalist' one by present standards. The problem with his approach was not that 'power through economic planning is legitimised by technique, by its manifestation in the form of social control' (Cohn, 1978, p. 154)—an odd claim against Furtado's sincere wish to promote general well-being in the Northeast. If it is true that development policies here should, indeed, depart from local environmental conditions, we could not ignore that the eventual success of industrialisation would create other environmental problems, typical of industrialised nations or regions poorly endowed with natural resources, as Japan. The lack of natural resources of the area would eventually lead to more net imports of energy and raw materials; maybe water reserves would dry up and nuclear energy would be taken as a solution for the energy dependence. Underdevelopment would disappear, but environmental problems would reappear on a larger scale.

For obvious reasons, Furtado did not take these eventual problems into account. His experience as a regional policy maker preceded his definition of 'development' as a 'myth'. Be that as it may, the military dictatorship in Brazil since 1964 led to the revocation of his political rights, his forced exile and, on a broader scale, to the end of developmentalist policies exposed by him and many of his generation.

3.   From the 'myth of economic development' to the 'preface to new economic policy'

During his exile, Celso Furtado initially settled in the United States for a short period (teaching at Yale University); he then moved to the University of Paris in 1965, being the first foreigner to be appointed as an academic professor in France (Furtado, 1997a, p. 13). Being in charge of teaching and research in economic development and free from bureaucratic and institutional activities, Furtado's academic work would thrive thenceforth. Among his main books—which were written in parallel with several shorter articles for specialised journals—we could mention the following ones (some of them translated in English): a historical review of theories of economic development (Furtado, 1974 [1968]); a magistral economic history of Latin America (Furtado, 1970); critiques to the economic policies of the dictatorship in Brazil (Furtado, 1972, 1981, 1983); analyses in international political economy (Furtado, 1982, 1987, 1998); an autobiography (Furtado, 1997a, 1997b, 1997c); critiques to neoliberal policies adopted in Brazil (Furtado, 1999, 2002). Most of these works do not tackle ecological and environmental issues directly, many being concerned with short-term critiques of stagnationist economic policies in Brazil, where Furtado's main concerns were related to the more 'conventional' themes of economic policies, economic activity and the employment level as well as critiques to monetarist economics. Furtado's subsequent ideas on ecology and environmentalism appear in his more academic works as *The Myth of Economic Development* (Furtado, 1974), *Preface to New Political Economy* (Furtado, 1976) and *Creativity and Dependence in the Industrial Civilization* (Furtado, 2008 [1978]). The article now turns to a summary of the author's remarks on environment and ecology presented in these works.

Furtado's *The Myth of Economic Development* (*O mito do desenvolvimento econômico*, Furtado, 2000 [1974]) marked his attention with ecological issues, but it was not properly a work on ecological economics *per se*. This short book, contrary to his previous contributions, does not show original ideas around the theme. Furtado was influenced by Meadow's *Limits to Growth* (1972) and decided to criticise one its main premises; that is, to make a critique of the anti-structuralist supposition that 'as the rest of the world develops economically, it will follow basically the US pattern of consumption—a sharp upward curve as output per capita grows, followed by a levelling off' (Meadows et al., 1972, p. 109). The original Brazilian edition of Furtado's book was divided into four chapters: it brought an opening short essay, which was followed by a chapter discussing the 'fundamental connections between development and underdevelopment'; by its turn, this was followed by a chapter on 'the Brazilian model of underdevelopment', and finally, by a brief conclusion titled 'Objectivity and illusion in economics' (see Furtado, 2000 [1974]). Only the first chapter dealt directly with environmental problems, which was interpreted under the traditional ECLAC's perspectives on economic history and economic theory.

Furtado attacked the idea that the modern trends in the world economy were leading to a universalisation of the 'American way of life'. He took the trouble of retaking economic history, economic theory and international political economy to reassess that underdevelopment still marked most nations outside the 'core' of the world economy, constituted by Western Europe, United States and Japan. Meadow's supposition obviously contradicted the structuralist framework of a 'core' and a 'periphery', with the former permanently showing a higher wealth in per capita terms as well as its capacity to retain the benefits of industrialisation and modernisation. The ongoing disparity between domestic productive capacity and the pattern of demand in the periphery, determined by the 'demonstration effect' and then import dependence, meant that 'peripheral capitalism engenders cultural mimesis, requiring permanent wealth concentration so that minorities can reproduce the consumption patterns of the centre' (Furtado, 2000 [1974], p. 45). Furtado's main argument was that underdevelopment—constituted by declining terms of trade, coupled with import dependence and unproductive expenditure of domestic economic surplus, all driving to low rates of investment—only allowed for a limited number of people enjoying the Western patterns of consumption. But 'as they adopted the collection [*panóplia*] of consumption goods of wealthier nations, peripheral nations were forced to raise the rate of exploitation, that is, to concentrate wealth still more' (Furtado, 2000 [1974], p. 93). The 'superfluous consumption of privileged minorities'

(p. 115) led to an obvious waste of resources that could be otherwise invested, not to mention to a higher environmental impact.

After exposing this argument with a historical and theoretical summary of the structuralist perspectives, Furtado then additionally argued that the universalisation of the 'American way of life' was physically impossible. The 'myth' relied on the false believe that 'poor people can someday enjoy the way of life [*formas de vida*] of rich nations' because 'the costs, in terms of the destruction of the physical world, are so high that all attempts to generalise it [*generalizá-lo*] would lead to the collapse of civilization' (Furtado, 2000 [1974], p. 75). The waste of resources now gained a new critical dimension: the environmental one. In reality, the conclusion that it was impossible to universalise the Western patterns of consumption to the whole world was a more or less obvious inference from the type of reflections that Kenneth Boulding and Georgescu-Roegen were already doing at that time (in fact, the latter is quoted by Furtado in footnote 6). However, it was a shocking argument in light of the previous pretensions of the classical theories of economic development.

On the other hand, as the fast dissemination of *Limits to Growth* led Furtado to his critical review; this was made almost exclusively with the goal of reinstating the structuralist perspective on the roots of economic underdevelopment, which he saw as a permanent phenomenon. His treatment of environmental issues was a brief one, focusing on non-renewable materials and defining the 'pressure on resources' as constituted by only 'two types' (lack of arable land and higher consumption on a per capita basis; Furtado, 2000 [1974], p. 68). There were no relevant incursions into externalities, intertemporal allocation of resources and operational suggestions around the need for a new system of national accounts. The question of 'why to ignore the collective costs arising from the destruction of natural resources, soil and forests (hardly renewable) in the GDP measuring?' (Furtado, 2000 [1974], p. 116) was made at the end of the work more on rhetorical grounds, as it was not discussed in concrete or operational terms. Sylla also argued that Furtado's claim that 'LTG's "catastrophic conclusions" should be rejected was not entirely justi-fied'. According to him, Furtado's *Myth*

> did not really address the question of the impact of the industrial civilization, from its origins until then, on the carrying capacity—the biocapacity—of the Earth. Indeed, even if economic growth may not be limited by the avail-ability of natural resources for a long time to come, as he argued, it may be limited by the saturation of the "sinks".
>
> (Sylla, 2000, p. xxii)

It could be added that Furtado also did not tackle the problem of *scale*: even a poor but large population has a high environmental impact, on several dimensions (water consumption, waste disposal, etc.). This still moderate position would give place to a more pessimist one over the following years.

However, Furtado's reinstatement of the idea that 'economic development' by Western standards was physically impossible—as well as his broader critique to the role that conventional economics was assuming in Brazil during the military dictatorship—helped to introduce important changes in the original structuralist goals of achieving 'development' by industrialisation. Furtado's critiques would help to change the tone in some fields of Latin American social sciences, particularly the 'heterodox' trends in economics, as it could be seen in ECLAC's new academic production around the term 'styles of development' (see, for example, the anthology edited by Sunkel and Gligo, 1980, with articles of Raúl Prebisch, Osvaldo Sunkel and other structuralists). When exploring the political economy of natural resources, Furtado also added new perspectives around the question of the declining terms of trade, stressing the fact that peripheral nations could exert their influence on international matters by means of protecting their domestic resources—although their utilisation 'as an instrument of power requires an articulation between nations that is absolutely not easy' (Furtado, 2000 [1974], p. 64). Despite its limited pretension, it was a new step towards a more comprehensive perspective.

The work *Prefácio a Nova Economia Política*—'Preface to new political economic'[4]—was released in Portuguese in 1976 with the self-declared high hopes of reverting the alleged 'diminishing returns of theorization inside the structuralist framework', given that, allegedly, the 'relatively higher flow of information has not been followed by effectiveness of our explanatory capacity [*plano explicativo*]' (Furtado, 1976, p. 14). With this new book, Furtado proposed new lines of further theoretical developments for what he thought that should be a renewal of social sciences, this based on a mix of classical political economy and Marxian and Weberian sociological categories, enhanced by structuralist and post-Keynesian new theoretical achievements. The useful tools of neoclassical economics should also be adopted when there were no substitutes.[5]

In terms of economic theory, Furtado referred particularly to the need for a 'broader notion of the concept of accumulation'. This discussion was not a novelty. For example, since the beginning of the 1970s, Joan Robinson was already asking 'what employment should be for' (Robinson, 1978 [1971], p. 11). Since at least *The Myth of Economic Development*, Furtado was following this trend of revising the Keynesian (and also structuralist) framework, raising doubts around the usefulness or even the rationality behind a mere expansion of the gross domestic product. Accordingly, in line with the so-called 'surplus-approach', Furtado would also argue for a more specific theory of accumulation, where 'investment as a flow' should be distinguished from 'investment as a stock'; the former could help to boost nominal growth and the level of employment, but the latter led to Robinson's question: 'what is growth for?'. In other words, to differentiate investment as a flow and as stock meant to evaluate in qualitative terms what 'society'— particularly private enterprises and rich families, in capitalism—were doing with *surplus* resources. Furtado then defined economic surplus and its main allocative patterns. Surplus could assume the following allocations that surplus can assume: population growth; more short-term consumption or unproductive accumulation of durable goods; educational expenditures for improving labour as a production factor; state expenditures and expenditures to enlarge the productive system (Furtado, 1976, p. 28).

He then took the trouble of not only exploring theoretically the question around the nature of surplus and accumulation in light of classical political economy and economic history but he also dwelled on the Weberian-inspired 'two basic forms of appropriating surplus'—'mercantile' and 'authoritarian' ones—as well as differentiating 'capitalism' and 'capitalist mode of production'. He then reached the question of a *price system*, which he interpreted in Sraffian terms. His arguments around factor remunerations summarised the position, with surplus and profits being 'determined as independent variables of the economic system'. As Sraffa argued that the rate of profits (and wages) 'has a significance which is independent of any prices, and can well be "given" before the prices are fixed' (Sraffa, 1960, p. 33), this left the path open for a sociological interpretation of wealth inequality and the very price system, which functioned not only as a direct reflection of 'labour-values' but as 'mere regulator of for distributing surplus' (Furtado, 1976, p. 48).

> If we observe the social product [*produto social*] as a whole [*em seu conjunto*], we will see that a relevant share of it is constituted by wages, salaries [*ordenados*] and fees [*honorários*] which originate personal incomes which are higher than workers' wages. The access to surplus as a wage earner or as an independent professional [*profissional liberal*] also means to be a part of the power structure. Those who study wealth distribution argue, even if implicitly, that a relevant share of the social product seized by these groups correspond to a "labour remuneration" or the "compensation for a service", as if there were some *economic* reason for a notary or an advertising executive to earn ten times more than a teacher and maybe thirty times than a worker. . . . Well, prices are not independent of power relations which establish the differences between wages, interests and the other elements of "wealth distribution". When we measure the social product by the standard of "factor costs" we are referring to the result of collective work by the use of a specific value system, which is also a system of social domination.
>
> (Furtado, 1976, p. 51)

The theoretical essay which constituted the first part of the book was followed by an interpretation of the recent trends in world political economy, with an emphasis on the role of the American economy and the dollar; by its turn, this was followed by a discussion around the position of the 'peripheral nations' in the world system.

Furtado mentioned environmental questions in several passages of his book. But he did not connect them with the theoretical effort of reconsidering the notions around accumulation and surplus, although eventually interpreting them in operational terms when discussing the role of underdeveloped nations as exporters of non-renewable resources. The author also argued that the development of China under Western patterns was 'physically unfeasible' (p. 61) and that many tensions in the world capitalist system relied on the 'growing dependence of the core nations with respect to the non-renewable resources of the periphery' (p. 107). He now showed growing pessimism around environmental issues, eventually with the use of expressionist sentences. The private appropriation of natural resources (and its corresponding technological structure) was the main factor behind the trans-formation of our civilisation 'into an infernal machine of irreversible processes of degradation of the physical world' (p. 121).

In the last part of the book, concrete proposals were suggested for the under-developed nations. Underdeveloped nations should join together and organise themselves for a joint international agenda; the price system for raw materials and agricultural goods should eventually be altered so that 'the low cost of living was subtracted from its final price' (p. 120). With regard to the non-renewable resources,

> The labour costs directly employed in the process of price formation of min-eral resources constitute only a small share of it. But a non-renewable re-source is a heritage which should not be liquidated without having in mind the consequences for the future generations. The fact that these resources are explored based on criteria that reflect strictly the interests of private people constitute one of the serious fetishes [*taras*] of our civilization. . . . A measure that would certainly alter this picture would be to fix minimum prices to non-renewable resources, in line with the American policies regarding crude oil.
>
> (Furtado, 1976, p. 122)

At the end of the work, Furtado reached the question around the so-called 'styles of development'—a new theoretical notion that was being discussed at the Eco-nomic Commission of Latin America and the Caribbean at that time, as a part of a 'revisionist' approach. The term also expressed a new stage in the theoretical ef-forts of interpreting Latin America in light of the economic policies implemented by the several authoritarian regimes that ruled the region (for a contextualisation, see Sunkel and Gligo, 1980; Love, 2008 [1995]; Rodríguez, 2006). He retook the themes of *The Myth*, arguing once again that 'there is no doubt that the life-style that currently prevails in the core of the world-system is not within reach of the Periphery'. According to him, 'the myth of economic development, i.e., the mille-narism that promised to all peoples of Earth to the life-style of the current abundant societies, belongs to the past' (Furtado, 1976, p. 123).

> The awareness of this reality, which can be seen in the blatant [*gritante*] waste of scarce resources caused by the reproduction of the life-style of the Core by the privileged minorities of the periphery, is one of the factors be-hind the current attempts of organising a new world order. To change the style of development, in the sense of reaching a more equal society in the peripheral nations, implies planning consumption before rationalising invest-ments, i.e., giving priority to the ends instead of the means.
>
> (Furtado, 1976, p. 123)

4. Dependence and creativity in the industrial civilisation

Furtado seemed to have followed his own suggestions in his new work, titled *Crea-tivity and Dependency in Industrial Civilization* (*Criatividade e Dependência na*

Civilização Industrial, Furtado, 2009 [1978]), which was published in 1978 and consisted in a broad historical and philosophical essay on the roots and the nature of modernity, and particularly, contemporary capitalism. Alfred Bosi defined the task of this book as a 'vigorous historical and conceptual synthesis of the industrial civilization' (Bosi, 2008, p. 13). The themes around ecology, such as the role of natural resources and their relation with the accumulation process—as well as the effects of pollution, the nuclear threat, and the ecological movements—were placed inside the combined structuralist theoretical and historical interpretations of the modern world system. Accumulation and surplus were now more openly seen in light of environmental aspects.

Accordingly, the 'supplementary surplus' could be achieved by means of 'trade exchange with other human groups or simply by accessing more abundant natural resources' (Furtado, 2008 [1978], p. 111). The 'pressure on the internal ecological frontier—aggravated by intense accumulation—leads to higher costs of production, [and thus] adds obstacles to the process of reproducing social structures' (p. 135). These aspects should not be interpreted only in theoretical terms but also with respect to the specific histories of each nation and international relations, in line with the combination of theory and history that constitutes Furtado's structuralist framework. Therefore,

> a nation as Uruguay could adapt perfectly to the industrial civilization— showing off [*chegando a ostentar*] a consumption diversification similar to those most advanced nations in productive terms—given its relative abundance of natural pasturelands which sustained extensive stockbreeding.
> (p. 93)

At the same time, 'the exploitation of non-renewable resources of high economic value—under domestic control, even if a partial one—provides many possibilities [*horizonte de opções*] of struggling against [*economic*] dependence, but it does not assure its overcoming' (p. 148). With regard to the contradictory effects of technology, he claimed that:

> For many years, the technological advance in a planet which we were only beginning to know, created the illusion that the supply of these resources would be forever elastic. The hypothesis that someday most of natural resources, particularly metals, be recycled and partially reused, cannot be excluded. But the technological orientation of the industrial civilization was not oriented according to this line. As these resources are located in peripheral nations, which can use them, a new whole of issues arises. Right: powerful interests of the central nations are formed so that the awareness of these problems does not arise, and to maintain the illusion that technology can solve the problems that it creates.
> (Furtado, 2008 [1978], p. 157)

Furtado's perspective on the questions around the nuclear technologies mixed Marxian, Weberian and ecological influences as well as his philosophical readings, particularly in Existentialism and the 'Critical Theory' (Frankfurt School). Thus, the impact of technological innovations and their diffusion in society constituted a 'dialectical' process (Furtado, 1978, p. 209), as could be seen in the problems around nuclear technologies. The nuclear technologies, which could be theoretically used in order to increase society's productive capacities, had been, in fact, created to increase the 'destructive potentials of man' (p. 210). 'The thirsty of the American companies to explore these technologies were so high', Furtado argued, 'that the transition to a "pacific exploitation" of uranium was seen as a natural process, which would lead to a "proliferation" of plutonium over the Earth's surface' (p. 210). He argued that the problems involving the storage of radioactive elements were being superficially treated, undervaluing the uncertainty aspects related to contamination. 'The "logic of accumulation" imposed itself over everything else', with a massive diffusion of a technology which was not completely controlled by society, including for military ends. The nuclear race would be the proof of the 'inherent insanity of our civilization' (p. 211), a type of statement which clearly revealed the influence of 'Critical Theory' on him. The nuclear question would be 'the most dramatic example of a historical process where society [*homem*] is aware of the problems arising from its decisions, but without knowing beforehand how to handle them'. Society is free to see itself inside the 'wheels', but not to 'escape from them'.

At the last part of his essay on the nature of industrial civilisation, Furtado observed that economic growth has an uneconomic feature in psychological terms: 'it has been proved that, in those nations with higher wealth levels and higher apparent diversity of consumption patterns, approximately the fourth part of the population needs psychiatric assistance' (Furtado, 1978, p. 219). As a result, the neglect of the state functions would mean the 'destruction of the only sphere [*espaço*] where authentic creative activities flourished inside the industrial civilization' (p. 212). The ecological movements assumed a decisive role in this task by 'reintroducing in politics the initiative of direct associations, claiming for men his multidimensional role as a political agent [*ator*]' (p. 224). This seemed to be 'the last chance against the invasion of the bureaucratic power': to reinstate the 'awareness of the ends concerning the social whole in the political motivations of the citizens'. In other terms, Furtado detached the ongoing importance of economic planning to handle environmental problems and the importance of civil society in pressing for adequate solutions by means of state policies.

5.   Towards a structuralist perspective of ecology

It was seen that, in his *Preface*, Furtado retook the pessimist outlook which was seen in the *Myth of Economic Development*. He also focused on giving some operational clues to his critique, particularly as regards price policies for non-renewable resources. On the other hand, the first theoretical essay of the *Preface*, which reconsidered the notions around accumulation and surplus, did not include ecological categories in its core. But the theoretical step of exploring the differences between 'investment as a flow' and 'investment as a stock' opened the opportunity, which was incidentally explored by Furtado, of asking: what forms of consumption are more wasteful and polluting? What forms of investment create more negative externalities and higher discount rates of the future? The focus on the difference between flow and stock and of both depending on *surplus* was the clue to a reinterpretation of structuralism (and post-Keynesian) along environmental lines as well of all doctrines based on the 'surplus approach'. Furtado's *Preface* did not explore these notions completely, but it prepared the ground for these theoretical exercises.

The interesting fact about the *Preface* is that Furtado explicitly delineated the paths for reconsidering aspects of the structuralist theory of accumulation under ecological premises for subsequent works and also for other authors. The first part of the *Preface* was followed by a short final section titled 'Annex—Table of suggested contents', with ten suggested points to be deepened by subsequent reflections. These were: '1. Social formations and power structures; 2. Social activities and social product; 3. Production system; 4. Population reproduction and social structure; 5. The appropriation of surplus; 6. Accumulation and [technological] innovation; 7. Foreign relations; 8. The state and the coordination of socio-economic activities'. Finally, the ninth point was titled: '9. The advance (*avanço*) in accumulation and the tensions in the ecological frontier'. It was finally followed by '10. Typology of economic development in current times'.

As if Furtado was aware that the task of introducing ecological notions in the theory of accumulation—and, in broader terms, in the social theory which he was trying to delineate—was a complex one, the ninth section of the 'Annex' regarding the 'tensions in the ecological frontier' was the shortest among the others. With a telegraphic style, Furtado listed the following points:

> The increase of efficiency as a compensation [*contrapartida*] of a higher energy consumption. Irreversibility of energy degradation. Creation of entropy and disorganisation of ecosystems. Acceleration of accumulation under private appropriation of natural resources. Socialisation of damages [*danos*] caused in the ecological dimension. Compromised [*comprometimento*] of future options. Renewable and non-renewable resources. The perspective of private interests and the acceleration in the use of non-renewable resources. The effect of this trend on technical progress. The ecological costs of the reproduction of specific [*certas*] social structures. Destruction of arable land, large-states and small holdings [*latifundismo-minifundismo*]. Predatory mineral exploitations in the international labour division. Urbanisation as a complex of productive and unproductive forms. Consequences in the ecological sphere.
>
> (Furtado, 1976, p. 69)

In fact, most of these notions had already been partially explored by Furtado in his works, with the probable exclusion of the first (which has also a 'dialectical' feature, as the increase in efficiency lowers prices and leads to a higher energy consumption). These points were not exactly a novelty, although much theoretical work was to be done on these lines. The following lines briefly explore some possibilities.

Furtado defined economic surplus as 'all resources of society beyond those necessary to its reproduction, adopting as a parameter of these costs of reproduction the level of living of the mass of the population' (Furtado, 1978, p. 165). However, a more adequate notion, more attuned with the finitude of resources, would lead to a new definition: that the economic surplus is the difference between consumption and production made possible by a previous stock of low-entropy resources which becomes degraded over time. This definition embraces the *time* dimension which became so important to 'heterodox' economics.[6] In fact, the progressive decrease of low-entropy stocks makes it economically more difficult to obtain surplus as time goes by. The mitigation of externalities and the need for recycling both reduce the level of net surplus free for consumption or to be 'accumulated'. In this sense, Furtado's definition of the *forms* that the economic surplus can take should be slightly changed. Today it is easier to see that, as time goes by, an increasingly higher share of surplus will take the forms of *mitigating* activities of the environmental impacts of economic activities as well as recycling; these cannot be simply defined as mere 'productive accumulation', as they make up a (partial) compensation for the broader entropic features of most of economic activities. At the same time, we could even contest the meaning behind the expression 'accumulation in the productive system', given that accumulation of capital accelerates entropy.

In reality, all economic surplus refers to a physical stock of goods. In Ricardo's theory, from which Sraffa's model is derived, it can be thought of as a stock of corn that covers the seeds used and the salaries. In the industrial system, this physical surplus takes the form of money, but if translated into use-value terms, it would refer to a sum of products whose purchasing power in the market exceeds the purchasing power of inputs and goods necessary for the physical/energetic replacement of the labour factor used in their production (wages). Anyway, this is only a static definition of surplus, which does not seem to be adequate when entropy is introduced. The 'static' definition generally refers to the production of surplus in a period of time which is exactly necessary to produce a certain amount of surplus; but, in this determined period of time, the soil has degraded, the machines have worn out, the workers aged, etc. The same investment of capital will probably lead to a smaller surplus in face of growing decreasing returns in mining and agriculture (as in the case of a mine with scarcer stocks). In other terms, the passage of time exacerbates the diminishing returns which arise from scarcity, and so, entropy engenders a progressive difficulty in obtaining surplus. Dynamically, the increase in the degree of entropy demands more investment to maintain the same unit of physical production, not only because of decreasing returns but also because of the rising costs of mitigation. In short: the 'static' definition of surplus is inappropriate in entropic terms.

The same could be claimed to other structuralist notions. Just as we can adopt notions referring to the 'density' of capital with regard to a unity of labour employed in any economic process, we can refer to the 'energetic intensity' of this or that type of investment as well as to higher or lower levels of 'ecological footprint' of each type of consumption. The 'multiplier' of employment by means of economic policies cannot be taken anymore without an explicit reference to the different environmental impacts of this or that type of investment which is to be pursued; it is evident that some investments are less harmful than others in ecological terms. Similarly, population growth could not be taken as an 'exogenous' variable anymore; they should be explicitly treated as a question of public policies in all countries with fast population growth as well as all questions regarding waste disposal, pollution, nuclear waste, the rate of discount of the future, etc.

It is evident that decisions based on these notions cannot be left to the private decisions of families and enterprises; the ecological crisis reintroduces the need for overall state planning. As stressed by one of Furtado's main theoretical references, Gunnar Myrdal, 'we would deceive ourselves if we believe that the goals could be reached without administrative direct controls' (Myrdal, 1972, p. 106). This general notion regarding the role of the state is the final link between the 'old' and the 'new' structuralist approach to economic development—which could also apply to the only apparently so-called developed nations (for a modern 'developmentalist' approach to environmental issues, see Bielschowsky and Torres, 2018, especially chapter XIV).

7.   An assessment

Furtado's guide to the structuralist theory, *Introduction to the theory of development— a historical-structuralist approach* (Furtado, 2000), was the last of his works on 'pure' economic theory as such. The book was taken as an easy introduction to structuralist economic theory, but in reality, it was not so didactic. The short but often theoretically complex version of 2000 was the revised third edition of the original one, which had been published for the first time in 1980. At first sight, Furtado could have developed, still more deeply, some of the main categories presented in this book along ecological lines, as a continuation from the path opened in *Preface to new political economy* and *Creativity and Dependence*. But probably, the book's content was already prepared before the publication of *Creativity and Dependence*; this may explain why ecological themes were not stressed. The main theoretical categories discussed in this introduction were already found in previous works, more or less under the same approach. However, the *Introduction* is still useful as a summary of the main structuralist categories and premises, easing the way to further theoretical reconsiderations in light of Furtado's own past hints.

It was seen earlier that Furtado suggested in *Creativity and Dependence in the Industrial Civilization* that the 'suicidal' waste of natural resources in the 'core' nations of the capitalist system could not but reinforce the international position of the peripheral nations as exporters of raw materials, in the long run (Furtado, 1978, p. 148). In fact, this assertion deserves a broader qualification, given the other consequences of the so-called 'Dutch diseases' in the periphery. Overvalued exchange-rates and deindustrialisation have not been the only consequences of exporting raw-materials and other 'commodities', particularly in Latin America. Polluted rivers and soil, successive natural disasters and similar 'negative externalities' have also accompanied those 'economic' consequences (for a current overview of the Latin American conditions, see Gligo et al., 2020). In fact, 'economic' and 'ecological' consequences could not be split by a renewed structuralist analysis; when commenting on ecological issues, Furtado frequently focused more on non-renewable resources, but they refer, as we know, to multivariate aspects that go from negative externalities, global warming, pollution and extinction of species to the legacy left for the future generations.

At the same time, several of Furtado's works over the 1980s were written in the spirit of criticising the policies of the International Monetary Fund, given its management of the debt crisis in Brazil and Latin America. Here, Furtado stressed the negative consequences of IMF's policies in terms of the more 'conventional' parameters of employment and production levels (see for example Furtado, 1982, 1983). In this case, ecological aspects were absent in face of alarming unemployment, denationalisation, social crisis and the loss of the sense of nationality in Brazil after the implementation of neoliberal policies and the uncritical acceptance of 'globalisation'. This seems to be an apparent contradiction in the intellectual direction that Furtado's work was taking, and in fact, it is. But this is a broader contradiction that lies in the heart of all developmentalist theories, *id est*, the conflict between (1) raising production and employment levels, and so, material well-being and (2) their corresponding environmental costs and impacts. This contradiction permeates Furtado's work over the 1980s, but it relates to a more problematic relation between ecology and 'development'.

This kind of contradiction has often led many authors to a radical rejection of all past economic theory. Thus, Leff argued, in a recent book, that 'deconstructing the unsustainable economy implies questioning the ontological regime where thought, knowledge, science, and technology are inscribed, where the techno-economic process that drives the historical destiny of humanity has been institutionalised' (Leff, 2021, p. 213). This type of extravagant assertions may be interpreted as a suggestion that past economic theory is useless, given its 'postmodern' apparent overcoming. This is manifestly absurd; it is clear that economic theory can evolve through time so as to keep up with new realities. This possibility can be seen, for instance, in the absence of racial or sex cleavages in Furtado's previously mentioned theory of power. Racial and sex differences lead to corresponding different levels of 'ecological footprint' and access to energy and matter. Furtado's theory of power does not take into account this gap but can obviously be explored by structuralist accounts of ecological problems. The modern economic interpretation of ecological issues can benefit from tradition in economic theory, which, here, particularly refers to Furtado's structuralist framework.

6. Conclusion

This chapter aimed to recover aspects in the work of Celso Furtado which had been not detached or which have been even overlooked by the economic literature—a task which makes part of the broader goals of the history of economic thought. Our chapter has shown that Celso Furtado was aware of environmental themes in economic history and economic theory since the beginning of his intellectual output, although his perception of them has grown and developed over time. Furtado was influenced by the modern literature on environmental and ecological issues, even declaring that 'economic development' was a 'myth' as well by historical events related to these issues. This marked a departure from his original 'utopian' perspectives regarding the economic development of Brazil and Latin America. At the end of his life, Furtado observed, in one of his last works—*In search of a new model*—that:

> The development of the nations which are in vanguard of technological progress also seem to have taken a wrong direction [. . .]. More than twenty years ago I realised that the entropy of the universe rises, that is, that the global process of development has a considerable ecological cost. But only now this process shows itself as a threat to the very survival of humanity. The fact is that industrial civilization and its way of life have a considerable cost in terms of non-renewable resources. To universalise this model to all humanity, which is the promise of the so-called economic development, would mean to accelerate a world catastrophe which seems inevitable if the direction of this civilization.
>
> (Furtado, 2002, p. 78)

Even faced with this sad scenario—for the poor nations and for nature—Furtado has not rejected a sober style, never falling into despair. He continued to struggle for social justice and economic independence, which included political activities (for example, as a Minister of Culture between 1986–1988) and political writings (see for example Furtado, 1998, 1999, 2002). He has not adhered to postmodern nihilism or relativism. Accordingly, this work has also argued that Furtado's theoretical legacy is a point of departure for new structuralist interpretations of environmental and ecological issues, being able to evolve over time as new categories and new events arise in the management of those issues. In this sense, Furtado's critique of the 'myth of economic development' did not preclude new ideas and renewed utopias.

Notes

1 My gratitude to Fernanda Graziella Cardoso (Federal University of ABC, Brazil) for her detailed comments and suggestions. The chapter's title was kindly suggested by her.
2 All translations from Portuguese were made by the author.
3 'Development' being described by Furtado as a 'body of articulated social processes to which a positive sense is attributed' ('conjunto de processos sociais articulados ao qual se empresta um sentido positivo'); see 'O desenvolvimento do ponto de vista interdisciplinar', Furtado (2013 [1979]).
4 The Portuguese title does not have a definite article before 'political economy'. It was as if Furtado was trying to avoid dogmatism, leaving the door open to many and not only one 'heterodox' interpretation of his theoretical suggestions.
5 'My disagreement with the neoclassical economists always arose from the fact that the problems which interested them seemed to me trivial or simply false. My disagreement with the Marxist economists arose from the fact that they forbade *a priori* any use of the instruments of neoclassical economics, even when there were obviously no others' (Furtado, 1992, p. 199).

6 'The question which concerns the economist is related to some social problems that have been expressly simplified so as to be treated with specific methods. This process of simplification takes, in general, the elimination of the factor time' (Furtado, 1976, p. 11).

References

Barros, R. M. (1975) 'A experiência regional de planejamento', in B. M. Lafer (ed.), *Planejamento No Brasil*, pp. 111–138. São Paulo: Perspectiva.

Bielschowsky, R., and Torres, M. (2018) *Desarrollo y igualdad: el pensamiento de la CEPAL en su séptimo decenio*. Santiago de Chile: United Nations/Economic Commission for Latin America and the Caribbean.

Bosi, A. (2008 [1978]) 'Prefácio', in C. Furtado (ed.), *Criatividade e Dependência na Civilização Ocidental*, pp. 9–32. São Paulo: Companhia das Letras.

Callado, A. (1960) *Os industriais da seca e os 'Galileus' de Pernambuco*. Rio de Janeiro: Civilização Brasileira.

Cohn, A. (1978) *Crise regional e planejamento*. São Paulo: Perspectiva.

D'Aguiar Furtado, R. (ed.) (2009) *Arquivos Celso Furtado. O Nordeste e a saga da SUDENE. 1958–1964*. Rio de Janeiro: Contraponto/Centro Internacional Celso Furtado.

Furtado, C. (1970) *Economic Development of Latin America*. Cambridge: Cambridge University Press.

Furtado, C. (1972) *Análise do 'modelo' econômico brasileiro*. Rio de Janeiro: Civilização Brasileira.

Furtado, C. (1974 [1968]) *Teoría y política del desarrollo económico*. Mexico City: Siglo Veintiuno Editores.

Furtado, C. (1974) *O mito do desenvolvimento econômico*. 2nd ed. Rio de Janeiro: Paz e Terra.

Furtado, C. (1976) *Prefácio a nova economia política*. Rio de Janeiro: Paz e Terra.

Furtado, C. (1981) *O Brasil pós-'milagre'*. Rio de Janeiro: Paz e Terra.

Furtado, C. (1982) *A nova dependência, dívida externa e monetarismo*. Rio de Janeiro: Paz e Terra.

Furtado, C. (1983) *Não à recessão e ao desemprego*. Rio de Janeiro: Paz e Terra.

Furtado, C. (1987) *Transformação e crise na economia mundial*. Rio de Janeiro: Paz e Terra.

Furtado, C. (1992) 'Celso Furtado', in P. Arestis and M. Sawyer (eds.), *A Biographical Dictionary of Dissenting Economists*. Cheltenham: Edward Elgar.

Furtado, C. (1997a) *Obra Autobiográfica. Tomo I*. São Paulo: Paz e Terra.

Furtado, C. (1997b) *Obra Autobiográfica. Tomo II*. São Paulo: Paz e Terra.

Furtado, C. (1997c) *Obra Autobiográfica. Tomo III*. São Paulo: Paz e Terra.

Furtado, C. (1998) *O capitalismo global*. Rio de Janeiro: Paz e Terra.

Furtado, C. (1999) *O Longo Amanhecer*. Rio de Janeiro: Paz e Terra.

Furtado, C. (2000) *Introdução ao Desenvolvimento. Enfoque histórico-estrutural*. Rio de Janeiro: Paz e Terra.

Furtado, C. (2000 [1974]) *The Myth of Economic Development*. Medford: Polity Press.

Furtado, C. (2001) *A economia colonial no Brasil nos séculos XVI e XVII*. São Paulo: Hucitec.

Furtado, C. (2002) *Em busca de novo modelo. Reflexões sobre a crise contemporânea*. Rio de Janeiro: Paz e Terra.

Furtado, C. (2006 [1959]) *Formação econômica do Brasil*. São Paulo: Companhia das Letras.

Furtado, C. (2008 [1978]) *Criatividade e Dependência na Civilização Ocidental*. São Paulo: Companhia das Letras.

Furtado, C. (2009 [1959]) 'Uma política de desenvolvimento econômico para o Nordeste (GTDN)', in R. D'Aguiar Furtado (ed.), *Arquivos Celso Furtado. O Nordeste e a saga da Sudene. 1958–1964*, pp. 83–164. Rio de Janeiro: Contraponto/Centro Internacional Celso Furtado.

Furtado, C. (2013 [1979]) 'O desenvolvimento do ponto de vista interdisciplinar', in Rosa Freire D'Aguiar (ed.), *Celso Furtado Essencial*, pp. 96–113. São Paulo: Companhia das Letras.

Gligo, N., et al. (2020) *La tragedia ambiental de América Latina y el Caribe*. Santiago de Chile: Economic Commission for Latin America and the Caribbean/United Nations.

Hirschman, A. O. (1963) *Journeys Toward Progress. Studies of Economic Policy-Making in Latin America*. New York: The Twentieth Century Fund.

Leff, H. (2021) *Political Ecology. Deconstructing Capital and Territorializing Life*. Cham: Springer.

Love, J. (2008 [1995]) 'Economic Ideas and Ideologies in Latin America Since 1930', in L. Bethell (ed.), *The Cambridge History of Latin America*. Cambridge: Cambridge University Press.

Mallorquin, C. (2005) *Celso Furtado: um retrato intelectual*. Rio de Janeiro: Contraponto/Xamã.

Meadows, D., et al. (1972) *The Limits to Growth*. New York: Universe Books.

Myrdal, M. (1972) 'Economics of an Improved Environment', *World Development*, 1 (1–2): 102–104.

Oliveira, F. (2003) *A navegação venturosa: ensaios sobre Celso Furtado*. São Paulo: Boitempo.

Robinson, J. (1978) *Contributions to Modern Economics*. Oxford: Basil Blackwell.

Rodríguez, O. (2006) *El estructuralismo latinoamericano*. Mexico City: Siglo Veintiuno/ECLAC.

Sraffa, P. (1960) *Production of Commodities by Means of Commodities*. Cambridge: Cambridge University Press.

Sunkel, O., and Gligo, N. (eds.) (1980) *Estilos de Desarrollo y medio ambiente en la América Latina*. Mexico City: Fondo de Cultura Económica.

Sylla, N. S. (2000) 'Introduction', in C. Furtado, 2000 [1974], *The Myth of Economic Development*. Medford: Polity Press.

10 The evolution of the ecological perspective in Latin American Structuralism

Gabriel Porcile and Miguel Torres

1. Introduction

During the years following World War II, the global economy exhibited the highest rates of economic growth in the 20th century, with a leading role of industrial production. In this *golden age* of capitalism, the paradigm of development played a significant role, inspired by the United Nations and by influential economists associated with it, like Nurkse (1953), Rosenstein-Rodan (1943), Myrdal (1957), Hirschman (1961), Singer (1950), and Prebisch (1949). This paradigm sought to reduce differences in income per capita between advanced and laggard economies and reproduce the successful example of the developed world in terms of industrialisation and patterns of consumption. The ensuing increase in industrial production imposed greater pressure on energy resources and heightened the extraction of natural resources and the predatory exploration of nature. At the beginning of the 1970s, however, the negative environmental consequences of the prevailing growth and consumption patterns began to be fully recognised. An important step forward to address these issues was the reflection on the limits of growth (Meadows et al., 1972) and the creation of the United Nations Environment Programme (UNEP).

Looking more specifically at the Economic Commission for Latin America and the Caribbean (ECLAC), most of its work on the environmental dimension of economic development was made between 2000 and 2010, with pioneer contributions of Osvaldo Sunkel in the late 70s. Two reasons explain why: first, the increased sophistication of the analytical tools associated with the rise of environmental economics and ecological economics after 2000; second, the emergence of critical environmental phenomena, such as climate change and global warming, which sent a clear message about the limits of the planet to its predatory exploitation. We will argue that these analytical developments can be seen as part of a much longer tradition in ECLAC's thinking. They are built within the theoretical framework of ECLAC's centre-periphery theory and keep in place the central role of structural change as a condition for overcoming the peripheral condition.

This chapter discusses how the environmental dimension has been incorporated to and evolved within the Latin American Structuralist tradition. The chapter contains four sections besides this introduction and the concluding remarks. Section 2 briefly examines the early contributions of ECLAC and some key ECLAC

DOI: 10.4324/9781003375425-13

intellectuals, like Raúl Prebisch, Celso Furtado and Aníbal Pinto. The third section highlights the pioneer work of Osvaldo Sunkel and the interdisciplinary team he led in the ECLAC/UNEP joint project to study the links between the environment and 'development styles' towards the end of the 1970s. The results of this project were expanded through other studies that would be carried out during the 1980s. These historical milestones marked the full incorporation of environmental concerns to ECLAC's thinking on development. Section 4 presents advances in the analysis of the development-environment relationship during the 1990s and 2000s in the context of neoliberal hegemony and ECLAC's alternative vision based on neo-Structuralist ideas. Section 5 presents the three-gap model, which was formulated to discuss the conditions required of economic, social and environmental sustainability. This model synthesises the most recent environmental ECLAC analysis in the context of climate change and biodiversity degradation observed in the current phase of globalisation.

1.   Prebisch, Furtado and the 'classic' ECLAC structuralism

Latin American Structuralism is a strain of economic thought which is part of the heterodox schools in economics. The work of Prebisch (1949) conceives the global capitalist economy as a system of bipolar structures that interact asymmetrically (see also Rodríguez, 2006; Torres and Ahumada, 2022). He distinguishes two poles in this system: the centre and the periphery. In Prebisch's view, in the pattern of specialisation that characterised the first globalisation era, the economies of the centre specialised in the production and export of manufactured goods, with higher levels of technological progress. Thanks to this specialisation, the centre shows higher levels of productivity and economic growth compared to the periphery. Labour productivity tends to be more homogeneous across the diversified economic structure of the centre. In addition, labour unions are stronger and well organised, which allows workers to keep real wages in line with productivity growth (see Furtado, 1961). In contrast, peripheral economies specialise in the production and export of low-productivity primary goods, with little technological content. A production structure dominated by commodities gives rise to a superstructure with powerful rentiers, who are not inclined to invest in innovation and capital formation. Instead, they use the economic surplus to replicate the consumption patterns of the centre. These patterns of production and consumption constitute the imitative nature of peripheral capitalism—a type of capitalism that is centripetal as a result of the dynamics of surplus utilisation, as Prebisch (1981) argued.

The production structure of the periphery is highly heterogeneous, which led Anibal Pinto to elaborate the concept of structural heterogeneity (Pinto, 1965, 1970), considering both the productive structure and the occupational structure. Following Octavio Rodríguez (1998, p. 135):

> The productive structure is said to be heterogeneous when there coexist sectors, branches, or activities where labour productivity is high or normal . . . along with others where productivity is much lower. Aníbal Pinto also indicates that

this difference is much greater in the periphery than in the centres. This type of productive structure corresponds to a certain type of occupational structure. One mirrors the other. In a peripheral economy, there is labour employed under conditions of high or normal productivity . . . but there is also labour employed under conditions of greatly reduced productivity, which constitutes underemployment.

The definition of this 'peripheral condition' led Prebisch (1949) to derive one of the most prominent and controversial results: the thesis of the secular deterioration of the terms of trade, which was almost simultaneously developed by Singer (1950). This deterioration is explained by: (i) the low-income elasticity of the primary goods exported by the periphery, in contrast to the high-income elasticity of the technology-intensive manufactured exported by the centre, (ii) the inability of the workers in the periphery to retain as higher wages the increases in labour productivity, (iii) limited technological progress[1] and the absence or weakness of the institutions required to generate it and (v) differences in the amplitude of economic cycles between the centre and the periphery.[2]

The central ECLAC and Prebisch argument in the early postwar period was that overcoming the peripheral condition requires industrialisation. However, peripheral industrialisation is problematic, as it implies: (i) the need for simultaneous investments in multiple sectors and (ii) the need of international cooperation to finance the rise of investment and to open markets for the periphery's manufactured goods. Peripheral specialisation in raw materials and low-tech sectors limits the capacity to earn foreign currencies, which, in turn, causes imbalances in the balance of payments and domestic inflation.[3] This, in turn, constrains the capacity to import capital goods and the corresponding assimilation of technological progress, ultimately hindering the process of industrialisation in the periphery.

Within this analytical framework, Prebisch's manifesto offered Latin-American economies a state-led industrialisation; in the conditions of the early post-war period, in the heydays of the dollar shortage, this took the form of import-substituting industrialisation. Some of the economies that followed this pattern, including Argentina, Brazil and Mexico, and to a lesser extent, Chile, Colombia and Uruguay, achieved significant advances in structural change during the 1950s. However, by the early 1960s, there was a growing perception in ECLAC that import-substitution industrialisation had lost momentum and failed to produce the expected results (Bielschowsky, 1998).

It became necessary to reassess the initial program and propose structural reforms that would reinvigorate economic growth by addressing structural bottlenecks that the original structuralist works had not considered. One of these bottlenecks stemmed from the increasing migration from rural areas to the cities as industrialisation deepened. Prebisch (1963) observed that the new industrial establishments that were altering the landscape of the major urban centres in the region did not have the capacity to fully absorb the growing influx of labour from rural and agricultural areas. Prebisch referred to this incapacity as a 'dynamic insufficiency', which explained the extensive segments of urban marginality and underemployment emerging within the context of industrialisation. He highlighted the crowded and environmentally unsafe conditions to which these new pockets of urban poverty were exposed. Prebisch (1963) also noted that the agricultural sector exhibited a significant lag in productivity compared to other economic activities, primarily due to high levels of land concentration. Overcoming the peripheral condition required that diversification should go hand in hand with tax reforms to combat poverty and marginality, and agrarian reform, to deconcentrate land ownership, modernise agricultural techniques and provide better living conditions for rural populations.

As discussed previously, the early Structuralist formulations placed their greatest emphasis on the economic aspects of development through policies of structural change and industrial policy, and to a lesser extent, on its social aspects through the analysis of the employment dynamics (structural heterogeneity). However, they did not incorporate the dimension of environmental sustainability. According to Bárcena, de Miguel and Samaniego (2019), by the 1970s, the structuralist debate shifted its focus towards the role of natural resources. It was Enrique Iglesias, the Executive Secretary of ECLAC between 1972 and 1985, who opened the discussion about the role of the environment in the development process. This topic was subsequently addressed by Sunkel based on the idea of 'development styles'.

Nevertheless, it is possible to find some early reflections from structuralist authors on the link between development and the environment. Prebisch (1963) expressed concern about the destruction of nature because of unregulated private action and suggested the need for active state intervention in its conservation and rational use. Furthermore, his concept of 'dynamic insufficiency' introduced an aspect that Sunkel would later develop more explicitly: the relationship between the formation of marginalised human settlements and environmental deterioration. Prebisch also highlighted that the prevailing production patterns, resulting in congestion and pollution in cities, rivers and seas, had given rise to ecosystem imbalances that could not be addressed solely from the logic of the markets (Prebisch, 1970). In the same vein, Furtado (1974, 1975) emphasised the predatory nature of capitalism and proposed the need to modify this dysfunctional economic pattern through consumption planning (Furtado, 1977). In the next sections, it will be shown how sustainability was fully incorporated into the ECLAC thought tradition on development in a world highly asymmetric in terms of power, technology and finance.

2.   Development styles and environmental issues[4]

The 1970s saw the emergence of a strong environmental movement on a global scale. The first responses to these demands came from the Club of Rome, which outlined the vision of developed countries through the concept of the limits to growth (see Meadows, 1972), and from the United Nations through the 1972 Stockholm Conference on the Human Environment and the establishment of the UN Environment Programme (UNEP). These United Nations initiatives were a reaction to the approaches of the Club of Rome in that they incorporated the interests of underdeveloped countries into the analysis, seeking a balance between two objectives: conservation of environmental assets and poverty eradication.

In view of these positions, ECLAC enters this debate with an even more radical stance than the one raised by the United Nations, giving to the development-environment relationship a richer content in order to consider the goals of the developing economies. In this regard, Bielschowsky has argued that the approach of CEPAL 'was guided by the idea of altering the styles of development of each country in the region through strategies that would allow, at the same time, to combat poverty and inequality and to preserve the environment' (Bielschowsky, 2010, p. 69).

It is precisely by means of the concept of a development style that the analysis of the relationship between environment and development comes into the ECLAC's classic structuralist approach. As Bielschowsky (1998) points out, the guiding force of the CEPAL thought in the 1970s was the idea of 'enabling the [development] style that leads to social homogeneity' and to 'strengthen industrial exports'. In this context, Osvaldo Sunkel was called in 1978 again to the CEPAL to lead the newly created Environment and Development Unit with the aim of extending the approach of development styles based on the idea of sustainable development.[5] In these years, Raúl Prebisch was working on various documents that would constitute his final work (Prebisch, 1981). Prebisch and Sunkel, two of the most significant exponents of structuralism, working in parallel, converged in producing an articulated vision combining the transnational capitalism developed by Sunkel (1973) and the dynamics of capitalism in the peripheral economies highlighted in Prebisch's work.[6]

This confluence can be seen in Prebisch (1980). In this work, the author observed that that:

> The exceptional impetus gained over the last few decades, until recent times, is the consequence not only of impressive technical progress but also of irrational exploitation of natural resources—above all, of energy—which, in its turn, has had a marked influence on the orientation of technique. So, there has been an element of falsity in the system's operation which has had highly dramatic world implications.
>
> (Prebisch, 1980, p. 69)

For his part, Sunkel was leading the ECLAC/UNEP joint project on Development Styles and the Environment, having formed a prominent team of experts in these subjects, with Nicolo Gligo and Carlos Galopin among their main contributors. This project produced numerous publications and a major international seminar in 1979, which allowed for the identification of the main links between the socioeconomic and environmental dimensions of development and the generation of a methodology to deepen and expand the limits of these compressions. The result of these researches and debates are the works Sunkel and Gligo (1980) and Sunkel (1980, 1981).

Prebisch (1980) and Sunkel (1980) allowed for the establishment of a well-founded conceptual relationship concerning the economic, social and environmental dimensions of development through the lens of development styles. In terms of Pinto (1976), these growth styles represent a certain type of dysfunctional interaction between supply and demand patterns and distributive patterns. From the perspective of the production pattern, the progressive dynamics of technology fail to overcome the environmentally unsustainable 'path dependency' characterising hydrocarbon-intensive production processes, which generate various negative externalities. On the other hand, structuralism strongly criticised consumer society, highlighting that, as the benefits of technological progress extend to new social strata in terms of demand, the consumption patterns of the centre and the purportedly sovereign nature of individual preferences according to neoclassical creed, essential human values such as social equity, culture, collective life, and concern for the biosphere are relegated to a secondary position. The clear conclusion drawn from these arguments is that the periphery mimics this model at the expense of sustainable social and environmental development.

To conclude this section, it is useful to refer to the synthesis presented by Bárcena, de Miguel and Samaniego (2019, p. 222) regarding Sunkel's environmental thinking and the contributions that, based on his reflections, expanded the analytical toolkit of Latin American Structuralism. These authors highlight the following aspects:

1   **Economic growth and the environment**. Economic activity has concrete effects on the environment that lead to its deterioration through environmental pollution and the generation of waste that negatively affects the planet's ecosystem. Income accounting based on the circular flow of income does not consider these effects as costs (Sunkel, 1987).

2   **Environmental damage and poverty**. The environmental impacts of growth are felt more intensely by the poorest segments of the population, 'exacerbating their precarious situation and social injustices' (Sunkel, 1987, p. 170).

3   **The ecosystem's absorption capacity as an economic resource.** Sunkel observed that the environment is a productive input because it provides the material basis of production and plays the function of waste absorption. Sunkel stressed that nature should be amortised like other forms of capital to the extent that the ecosystem's absorption capacity constitutes an economic resource (see Bárcena, de Miguel and Samaniego, 2019, p. 222).

4   **Environmental deterioration as inefficiency in the economic development process**. Pollution and environmental degradation reduce productive capacity, increase production costs and exacerbate preexisting development constraints. Environmental deterioration, thus, tends to lead to environmental, economic and humanitarian crises.

5   **The environmental perspective is distributive in both inter- and intragenerational terms**. Based on this perception, Sunkel (1987) argues that the environmental dimension of development requires a political approach because the interests of different stakeholders, including different generations, come into

conflict, and the market experiences significant market failures in terms of re-source allocation. Equitable access to environmental benefits is necessary, with the costs and benefits distributed fairly among individuals of the present genera-tion and between them and the future generations.

6 **Environmental management and development styles**. Proper environmental management can be the foundation of a functional development style, combin-ing social inclusion, democratic strengthening, mitigation of ecosystem deterio-ration and a rationalisation of the basic needs of the population.

The work of Osvaldo Sunkel and his team at ECLAC left an important legacy, which would be recovered by the main authors of the so-called neo-Structuralism, a new phase in ECLAC thinking that emerged in the mid-eighties.

3. Structural change and technological change: neo-Structuralism and the response to the neoliberal challenge

As discussed in the previous sections, the environmental challenge as a critical dimension of development policy was firmly established in the ECLAC literature since the late 1970s. In the next decades, two aspects of the structuralist theory would become increasingly important in ECLAC thought. First, a more elaborated understanding of the links between structural change and technological change, which reflected the influence of empirical and theoretical developments in the field of industrial organisation, innovation and learning (Cimoli and Katz, 2003; Dosi, Riccio and Virgillito, 2022). Second, a growing concern with the importance of equality not only as an outcome of the pattern of specialisation but also as a barrier to technical and structural change. This renewed concern with equality entailed also strengthening the analysis of political economy variables in shaping economic policy. Subsection 4.1 deals with the contributions of ECLAC in the understanding of the determinants of technical and structural change, and subsection 4.2 focuses on the role of equality in sustainable development. The new ideas on technical change, combined with a new approach in the analysis of the problems of inflation and the exchange rate (not discussed in this chapter) are the basis of what would become known as New Structuralism.

3.1. Structural change and technology: the contributions of Fernando Fajnzylber

Fernando Fajnzylber offers a new approach to the problems of technical and struc-tural change in two works which are remarkable contributions to the Structuralist tradition; namely, Fajnzylber (1983, 1990). The focus in Fajnzylber (1983) is the 'old' structuralist concern with the inability of the region to overcome the depend-ence on exports of natural resources and low-tech commodities, leading to recur-rent external crisis, slow growth and structural heterogeneity—the latter defined as the coexistence of high-productivity jobs with a substantial share of the total labour force allocated in informal or subsistence jobs. For Fajnzylber, this dependence was a manifestation of the limits to growth posed by the absence of the leading sectors in technological innovation in the production matrix of the periphery. In his own words[7]:

> At variance with the crucial role that the industrial sector plays in developed countries, as a source of a surplus in foreign trade, in Latin America it explains the structural nature of the trade deficit, and as a result, its growing resort to foreign debt.
>
> (Fajnzylber, 1983, pp. 207–208, authors' translation)

Competitiveness stemming from mastering technological capabilities is a recurrent theme throughout Fajnzylber's 1983 book. This concern foreshadows the concept of 'spurious competitiveness' (1990, p. 65)—which is based on low wages and the abundance of natural resources—developed by Fajnzylber after he joined the Economic Commission for Latin America and the Caribbean in 1985, as opposed to the concept of 'authentic' or 'systemic' competitiveness (based on endogenous technological capabilities) The links between equality, technical change, competitiveness and growth are further unpacked in Fajnzylber (1990). Technological backwardness leads to the specialisation in sectors which are less dynamic from the point of view of technical change and international demand. As a result, such specialisation implies slower productivity growth and the emergence of the external constraint on economic growth. Both factors explain the insufficient creation of employment in sectors with high and/or increasing productivity. This establishes a crucial link between diversification, growth and equity. The transformation of the production pattern towards technology-intensive sectors is a necessary condition for curbing structural heterogeneity.

Although the environment does not figure so centrally in Fajnzylber's work as the problems of technical change, inclusiveness and competitiveness, he clearly understood the importance this dimension had acquired and the crucial implications it would carry for devising the development policies of the future. In Fajnzylber (1992),[8] he observed that competitiveness and environmental sustainability would be increasingly co-dependent and that the latter would represent a barrier to exports as significant as that represented by tariff and non-tariff barriers. For this reason, being environmentally responsible for Latin America is not just a matter of quality of life but a necessary condition for rising the income level and the dynamism of the economy. Although Fajnzylber did not develop further this idea, he placed on technical change a major responsibility in making compatible the demands for growth and equality with the necessity of protecting the environment.

In sum, the contributions of Fernando Fajnzylber showed, at the same time, a significant continuity with previous ECLAC contributions and a clear breakthrough by incorporating a more systematic and rigorous way the problems of technical and structural change. The key point he brought to the analysis was a well-articulated discussion of the links between sustainability, income distribution and competitiveness, in which technical change was the ultimate determinant. This approach was complemented with solid empirical evidence on how the pattern of specialisation compromised the incentives and momentum of learning and with an emphasis on the rentier nature of the Latin American international insertion—heavily dependent on spurious competitiveness rather than authentic competitiveness. He also clearly acknowledged that sustainability would be the key factor in competitiveness in the future—an insight that was validated in international economic relations in the past two decades.

3.2. Citizenship, equality and the environment: a response to the (dominant) neoliberal agenda

Political economy variables were never absent in ECLAC's analysis. How to approach the political economy of development was subject to intense debate within ECLAC itself. Weberians and dependentists competed to explain how different social groups and classes organised in coalitions that shaped economic policy, while the concept of styles of development sought to explain how these policies gave rise to certain patterns of production, consumption and redistribution of the gains in labour productivity. However, in the first half of the 1990s, the interest in the political economy dimensions faded in ECLAC work. In part, this may be associated with the era of triumphant neoliberal ideas, in which policy options appeared to be extremely limited—the 'There is no Alternative' (TINA) phase in economic policy. The possibility of thinking in different avenues for growth became extremely difficult in a period dominated by the strong version of the Washington Consensus and the rise of financial globalisation (Bértola and Ocampo, 2012).

In this rather unfavourable intellectual context, the ECLAC (2002) represented the response of the structuralists tradition to the new world created by the process of globalisation. The work recognised the new reality created by globalisation not only in terms of economic transformations but also in terms of social and political changes. The new role of financial globalisation and the constraints it imposes on macroeconomic policy (in particular, the fiscal and exchange rate policies) and financial stability are emphasised in the ECLAC document. At the same time, it pointed out that these transformations can and should be redirected in a direction less harmful for the environment, democracy and the full exercise of citizenship. ECLAC (2002) suggested what seemed unthinkable in many intellectual and policy circles at that time; namely, that there is more than one avenue for sustaining an open multilateral system and that this avenue should contemplate dimensions neglected in the TINA discourse, not least in the field of environmental sustainability.

ECLAC (2002) dedicates an entire chapter (chapter 9, pp. 273–306) to analysing the environmental dimension from different angles: the dependency of natural resources, the role of technology and regional and local capabilities to address environmental problems, the need to build institutions to monitor, assess and correct the environmental impacts of growth and the importance of foreign investment and international cooperation in a transition towards a greener economy.

In sum, it can be said that ECLAC (2002) recovers and advances the research agenda set forth by Fajnzylber between 1983 and 1990 and incorporates more fully the problems of economic and social rights (going beyond income distribution), the tensions of economic policy brought about by full financial liberalisation in a globalised world and how globalisation exacerbated environmental problems which should be addressed within a new growth trajectory.

4.   The three gaps of sustainable development

ECLAC (2010) inaugurated a new phase in its discussion of sustainable development. As it was the case of ECLAC (1990) and ECLAC (2002), this work shows strong elements of continuity with respect to the previous ECLAC contributions along with some important differences in emphasis and some new theoretical extensions. In the ECLAC tradition, elements of continuity are very strong since the very beginnings of Prebisch's centre-periphery theory to the developments of the first two decades of the 21st century (technological asymmetries, the technology-specialisation nexus and the reproduction of asymmetries, their impact on growth, distribution and structural heterogeneity). At the same time, new elements are gradually incorporated to the basic model, such as a more comprehensive discussion of technical change, the social and political implications of specialisation, the restrictions and opportunities associated with globalisation and the tensions created by rising inequality and the destruction of the environment.

ECLAC (2020) offers a simple, analytical framework that aims to put together the different parts of ECLAC narrative in a way in which interactions can be made explicit as well as potential synergies and contradictions between the three dimensions of sustainable development: economic, social and environmental. To build this analytical framework, three rates of growth are defined.

We start with the canonical balance of payments-constrained growth equation, which is part of both LAS (Latin American Structuralism) and Keynesian growth models (see Thirlwall, 2011).

The first is y^T, the rate of economic growth that keeps the current account in equilibrium, where ε is the income elasticity of exports, m the income elasticity of imports and y^W is the rate of growth of the rest of the world. It is assumed that the real exchange rate is stable in the long run and does not affect the equilibrium rate of growth. For a thorough review of this model see Blecker and Setterfield (2019, chapter 9) and Blecker (2022).

The second is the rate of growth of growth necessary for social equilibrium y^S. There is no clear-cut definition for y^S, except that it should allow for a redistribution process that encourages equality and the incorporation of the underemployed to formal labour markets at a rate that ensures political and social stability in the context of political democracy.

Finally, following Althouse, Guarini and Porcile (2020) and ECLAC (2020), we define the rate of growth with environmental equilibrium (y^L) as that which is consistent with the protection of the environment. We will use the reduction in CO_2 emissions as a reference for environmental sustainability. More specifically, we assume that x is the rate of growth of GHG (greenhouse gas) efficiency (units of GDP per unit of GHG emissions) that must be attained at a global level to keep the earth temperature below 1.5°C.

We define the centre-periphery environmental frontier (CPEF) as the combinations of the rates of growth in the centre (y^W) and periphery (y^L) that allows for a reduction of emissions equal to x. Formally:

$$(1) \quad y^L = \frac{1}{a}\left[\left(z^C - x\right) + a\left(z^P - z^C\right) - (1-a)\,y^W\right] \text{ with } 0 < a < 1$$

y^L is the rate of growth of the periphery compatible with environmental sustainability. The higher is the rate of growth in the centre, the lower is y^L. The intercept of the curve depends on the rate of growth of GHG efficiency due to green technical change in the centre (z^C) and the periphery (z^P), weighted by the share of the periphery in global GHG (a). The impact of green innovations in the centre is captured by the term $\left(z^C - x\right)$, which is growth of GHG efficiency in the centre, as compared with the target (the ceiling of 1,5°C) and the term $\left(z^P - z^C\right)$, which is the velocity with which the periphery catches up with green technological change in the centre (the change in the technology gap of the periphery with respect to the environmental technological frontier). Assuming that the centre is the technological leader, if $z^P > z^C$, then technical change is faster in the periphery (catching up in green technologies); if $z^P < z^C$, there is technological divergence in favour of the centre, as the periphery lags behind the green technological frontier.

Thus, there is a maximum rate of growth the periphery can attain (given the existing technology and the rate of growth of the centre) to keep emissions below the critical level identified by climate change science. This rate of growth is expressed in the y^L, y^W plane as the centre-periphery environmental frontier (CPEF). Growth in the periphery depends negatively on growth in the centre; the CPEF may shift towards the right due to innovation and catching up in green technologies, as discussed in the next section.

ECLAC (2020) offer some simulations that show that in Latin America the rate of growth require for social equilibrium is higher than the rate of growth consistent with external equilibrium, while the latter is higher than the one compatible with environmental sustainability—i.e., $y^S > y^T > y^L$. These inequalities yield three gaps: the social gap $\left(y^S - y^T\right)$, which is the difference between the required rate of growth for social equilibrium and that compatible with external equilibrium; the environmental gap $\left(y^T - y^L\right)$, which is the difference between the BOP-constrained rate of growth and the one that respects the environmental limits of the planet; and the sustainable development gap, which is the sum of both gaps, $\left(y^S - y^L\right)$. *An economy can be considered to be moving along a sustainable development path if and only if it is true that the equality $y^S = y^T = y^L$ is satisfied in the long run.*

Of the three rates of growth, only y^T emerges from market forces in trade and financing. There are no market forces working in favour of social or environmental equilibrium. Therefore, the equality between the three rates of growth should be attained through public policies that modify the intensity and direction of structural and technical change towards environmental protection, along with measures to redistribute income in favour of labour.

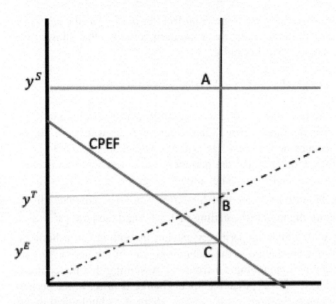

y^T: *rate of growth with external equilibrium.*

y^L_S: maximum rate of growth compatible with environmental sustainability.
y^S: minimum rate of growth required for social equilibrium.
AB social gap; BC environmental gap; AC gap of sustainable development.

Figure 10.1 The three gaps of sustainable development.

Source: author's elaboration.

Figure 10.1 presents the 'business as usual' scenario, which reinforces international asymmetries. The curve TB gives the rate of economic growth consistent
with a balanced current account; the curve CPEF is the centre-periphery environmental frontier that gives the rate of growth of the periphery required for reducing
GHG emissions at the rate x for each rate of growth in the centre; and the hori-
zontal line gives the rate of growth for social equilibrium. The centre grows at an
exogenous rate y^W. The distance between points A and B is the social gap, while
the distance between B and C is the environmental gap. The AC segment gives the
total gap of sustainable development.

In the BAU scenario, the centre heightens its efforts at green innovation, but
there is no international cooperation for the diffusion of technology nor green industrial policy in the periphery. Green innovation in the centre shifts the CPEF
to the right, but the shift is small because the periphery fails to absorb these new
technologies, leading to a higher environmental gap. If the periphery losses international competitiveness as a result of being left behind in technical change, y^T
falls and the social gap increases. The most likely result is, therefore, an increase in
the three gaps of sustainable development.

Closing the three gaps requires industrial, environmental and social policies simultaneously

Figure 10.2. The three gaps and the coordination of policies in a big push for sustainability. *Source:* author's elaboration.

In sum, the combination of poverty and underemployment, low levels of diversification and technological capabilities and the prevailing patterns of production and consumption gives rise to a scenario in which $y^S > y^T > y^L$. To make all the rates of growth converge to y^S needs changes in both the intensity and the direction of technical change.

To attain the necessary transformations required by sustainable development, ECLAC (2020) argued that a big push for sustainability would be required, in which the industrial, social and technological policies should work in close coordination to ensure the convergence of the three rates of growth. A strong redistributive effort would be necessary to reduce the rate of growth necessary for social equilibrium (this is why redistribution cuts vertically the triangle formed by the three rates of growth at the angles). In turn, technical change is at the basis of the whole policy efforts, implying not only a major acceleration in the rate of technical change in the periphery but also redirecting innovations towards eco-innovation and the protection of the environment—proxied in the figure by the commitments that developing countries made regarding the reduction of CO_2 emissions after the 1990 Paris Agreements. Such reductions are expressed in their National Determined Contributions.

In sum, there is a set of intertwined policies that should be embraced for having sustainable development: a) a major effort at eliminating poverty, reducing inequality and extending social protection; b) to encourage domestic investments and institutions for green technologies that boost decarbonisation while easing the external constraint on growth (see also Barbier, 2019). The political economy conditions necessary for the adoption of these policies, however, have been conspicuously absent. Moreover, in recent years, war and geopolitical rivalry implied a setback to the attention that inequality and climate change had gained in the previous decades. International cooperation to address global challenges, including that necessary to prevent a climate catastrophe from happening, is at the same time more urgent and more difficult to attain.

5.   Concluding remarks

The Structuralist tradition stresses the importance of structural change as a key instrument to overcome the peripheral condition. Structural change would allow the periphery to remove the barriers of the external constraint on growth and to create the formal jobs necessary to absorb underemployment and subsistence workers. This is also the key to converge in GDP per capita with the developed economies.

However, structural change and convergence cannot follow the same path of the developed economies, lest the world would be exposed to an environmental catastrophe. A new development path, based on new patterns of consumption and production, must be adopted. Such a transformation, to be viable in the long run, cannot leave behind the developing world. ECLAC was a pioneer in alerting the international community about the fact that 'business as usual' was no longer an option; and in suggesting new avenues for international cooperation, industrial policy and technological policy that could make sustainable development possible in both centre and periphery.

The three-gap model summarised in the last section helps visualise the interactions between the three dimensions of sustainable development (social, economic and environmental) and how to make policies in various fronts compatible. Some of these interactions may create higher tensions, but some of them are complementary and reinforce each other. The possibility of a virtuous circle of more equality, more green technical change and more employment and stability in the economic system exists. But to effectively move in this direction, a new political economy is required, both at the domestic and the international levels. The Structuralist tradition contributes to providing the economic and social rationale for aligning interests and policies in the pursuit of sustainable development.

Notes

1 Marini (2023) also explored this idea under the concept of labour superexploitation in his analysis of dependent capitalism.
2 This refers to the fact that boom cycles are shorter in the periphery due to their difficulty in sustaining high growth rates over time, while downturn cycles are more extended.
3 In relation to inflationary processes and their connection with peripheral development trajectories, Noyola Vázquez (1957) and Sunkel (1958), among other structuralist authors, argued in contrast to monetarist economists that inflation is not solely a result of monetary factors, but rather, stems from a distributive struggle of a structural nature with specific sources and mechanisms of propagation. These perspectives were referred to as the structural approach to inflation.
4 The elaboration of this section is based fundamentally on Bielschowsky and Torres (2018). This analysis has also been nurtured from the works of Bárcena, de Miguel and Samaniego (2019) and Bárcena and Torres (2019).

5 He held this position from 1978 to 1987; during this decade, Sunkel incorporated the environmental dimension of development into his traditional research themes of dependency and transnational capitalism.
6 For a complementary review of Prebisch (1981) on peripheral capitalism, see Pérez Caldentey, Sunkel and Torres (2012). The analysis of transnational capitalism developed by Sunkel in the early 1970s looked at the processes of integration of multinational companies and those of national disintegration in the peripheral context, also linked to the problem of structural heterogeneity. The compulsory reference of this author on this subject is Sunkel (1973).
7 Fajnzylber stressed the absence of a competitive sector producing capital goods in Latin America, which, in his view, limited the ability of the region to generate technical change (Fajnzylber, 1983, pp. 185–190)
8 'Progreso técnico y competitividad en América Latina, Conferencia CEAPL PNUD 25 al 27 de setiembre 1991 en Santiago de Chile', in 'Industrialización y Desarrollo Tecnológico', Informe 12, División Conjunta CEPAL/ONUDI de Industria y Tecnología, CEPAL' United Nations, April 1992.

References

Althouse, J., Guarini, G., and Porcile, G. (2020) 'Ecological Macroeconomics in the Open Economy: Sustainability, Unequal Exchange and Policy Coordination in a Center-Periphery Model', *Ecological Economics*, 172 (2): 1–29.
Barbier, E. (2019) 'How to Make the Next Green New Deal Work', *Nature*, 565 (7737): 6–7.
Bárcena, A., de Miguel, C., y Samaniego, J. (2019) 'Osvaldo Sunkel: un antes y un después para la dimensión ambiental del desarrollo en el pensamiento estructuralista de la CEPAL', in A. Bárcena y M. Torres (eds.), *Del estructuralismo al neoestructuralismo. La travesía intelectual de Osvaldo Sunkel*, pp. 201–239. Santiago de Chile: ECLAC.
Bárcena, A., y Torres, M. (2019) 'Osvaldo Sunkel: una semblanza intelectual', in A. Bárcena y M. Torres (eds.), *Del estructuralismo al neoestructuralismo*, pp. 15–46. La travesía intelectual de Osvaldo Sunkel. Santiago de Chile: ECLAC.
Bértola, L., and Ocampo, J. A. (2012) *The Economic Development of Latin America since Independence*. Oxford: Oxford University Press.
Bielschowsky, R. (1998) 'Evolución de las ideas de la CEPAL', in *Revista de la CEPAL*. Especial ed. Santiago de Chile: ECLAC.
Bielschowsky, R. (ed.) (2010) *Sesenta años de la CEPAL: textos seleccionados del decenio 1998–2008*. Buenos Aires: Siglo XXI.
Bielschowsky, R., y Torres, M. (2018) *Desarrollo e igualdad: el pensamiento de la CEPAL en su séptimo decenio. Textos seleccionados del período 2008–2018*, Colección 70 Años, N° 1. Santiago de Chile: ECLAC.
Blecker, R. (2022) 'New Advances and Controversies in the Framework of Balance-of-Payments-Constrained Growth', *Journal of Economic Surveys*, 36 (2): 429–467.
Blecker, R., and Setterfield, M. (2019) *Heterodox Macroeconomics. Models of Demand, Distribution and Growth*. Cheltenham: Edward Elgar.
Caldentey, P., Sunkel, O., and Torres, M. (2012) *Raúl Prebisch (1901–1986): un recorrido por las etapas de su pensamiento sobre el desarrollo económico*. Santiago de Chile: ECLAC.
Cimoli, M., and Katz, J. (2003) 'Structural Reforms, Technological Gaps and Economic Development: A Latin American Perspective', *Industrial and Corporate Change*, 12 (2): 387–411.
Dosi, G., Riccio, F., and Virgillito, M. E. (2022) 'Specialise or Diversify? And in What? Trade Composition, Quality of Specialisation, and Persistent Growth', *Industrial and Corporate Change*, 31: 301–337.

ECLAC. (1990) *Changing Production Patterns with Social Equity: The Prime Task of Latin American and Caribbean Development in the 1990s*. Santiago de Chile: United Nations.

ECLAC. (2000) *Equity, Development and Citizenship*. Santiago de Chile: United Nations.

ECLAC. (2002) *Globalization and Development*. Santiago de Chile: United Nations.

ECLAC. (2010) *Time for Equality: Closing Gaps, Opening Trails*. Santiago de Chile: United Nations.

ECLAC. (2020) *Building a New Future: Transformative Recovery with Equality and Sustainability*. Santiago de Chile: UN-ECLAC.

Fajnzylber, F. (1983) *La Industrialización trunca de América Latina*. Mexico City: Centro de Economía Transnacional/Editorial Nueva Imagen.

Fajnzylber, F. (1990, August) 'Industrialization in Latin America: From the "Black Box" to the Empty Box', *Cuadernos de la Cepal*, 60.

Fajnzylber, F. (1992) 'Progreso técnico y competitividad en América Latina, Conferencia CEPAL PNUD 25 del 27 de setiembre 1991 en Santiago de Chile', *Industrialización y Desarrollo Tecnológico*, Informe 12, División Conjunta CEPAL/ONUDI de Industria y Tecnología. Santiago de Chile: United Nations.

Furtado, C. (1961) *Desenvolvimento e subdesenvolvimento*. Rio de Janeiro: Fundo de Cultura Econômica.

Furtado, C. (1974) 'El mito del desarrollo y el futuro del Tercer Mundo', *El Trimestre Económico*, 41 (162): 407–416.

Furtado, C. (1975) *El desarrollo económico: un mito*. Mexico City: Siglo XXI.

Furtado, C. (1977) 'El nuevo orden económico internacional', *Investigación Económica*, 36 (139): 13–23.

Hirschman, A. O. (1961) 'Ideologies of Economic Development in Latin America', in A. O. Hirschman (ed.), *Latin American Issues: Essays and Comments*, pp. 3–43. New York: Twentieth Century Fund.

Marini, R. M. (2023) *The Dialectics of Dependency*. New York: Monthly Review Press.

Meadows, D., et al. (1972) *The Limits to Growth. A Report for the Club of Rome's Project of the Predicament of Mankind*. New York: Universe Book.

Myrdal, G. (1957) *Economic Theory and Underdeveloped Regions*. London: Gerald Duckworth.

Noyola Vázquez, J. F. (1957) 'Inflación y desarrollo económico de Chile y México', *Panorama Económico*, 170. Santiago de Chile: ECLAC.

Nurkse, R. (1953) *Problems of Capital Formation in Underdeveloped Countries*. Oxford: Basil Blackwell.

Pinto, A. (1965) 'Concentración del progreso técnico y de sus frutos en el desarrollo latinoamericano', *El Trimestre Económico*, 125: 3–69.

Pinto, A. (1970) 'Naturaleza e implicaciones de la heterogeneidad estructural de la América Latina', *El Trimestre Económico*, 37 (1): 83–100.

Pinto, A. (1976) 'Styles of Development in Latin America', *CEPAL Review*, 1. Santiago de Chile: ECLAC.

Prebisch, R. (1949) *The Economic Development of Latin America and Its Principal Problems*. Santiago de Chile: United Nations/ECLAC. Available at: https://hdl.handle.net/11362/30088/

Prebisch, R. (1963) *Hacia una dinámica del desarrollo latinoamericano*. Mexico City: Fondo de Cultura Económica.

Prebisch, R. (1970) *Transformación y desarrollo: la gran tarea de América Latina*. Mexico City: Fondo de Cultura Económica.

Prebisch, R. (1980) 'Biosphere and Development', *CEPAL Review*, 12. Santiago de Chile: ECLAC.

Prebisch, R. (1981) *Capitalismo periférico: crisis y transformación*. Mexico City: Fondo de Cultura Económica.

Rodríguez, O. (1998) 'Heterogeneidad estructural y empleo', *Revista de la CEPAL*, Special Issue: 315–321.

Rodríguez, O. (2006) *El estructuralismo latinoamericano*. Mexico City: Siglo XXI.

Rosenstein-Rodan, P. (1943) 'Problems of Industrialization of Eastern and South-Eastern Europe', *The Economic Journal*, 53 (210/211): 202–211.

Singer, H. W. (1950) 'The Distribution of Gains Between Investing and Borrowing Countries', *American Economic Review: Papers and Proceedings*, 40 (2): 473–485.

Sunkel, O. (1958) 'La inflación chilena: un enfoque heterodoxo', *El Trimestre Económico*, 25 (99–100): 570–599.

Sunkel, O. (1973) *Capitalismo transnacional y desintegración nacional en América Latina*. Buenos Aires: Ediciones Nueva Visión.

Sunkel, O. (1980) 'The Interaction Between Styles of Development and the Environment in Latin America', *CEPAL Review*, 12: 15–49.

Sunkel, O. (1981) *La dimensión ambiental en los estilos de desarrollo de América Latina*. Santiago de Chile: ECLAC/PNUMA.

Sunkel, O. (1987) 'Del medio ambiente al ambiente entero: bases para alternativas de desarrollo sostenible', in *El desafío latinoamericano: potencial a desarrollar*. Caracas: Editorial Nueva Sociedad.

Sunkel, O., y Gligo, N. (eds.) (1980) *Estilos de desarrollo y medio ambiente en América Latina*. México: Fondo de Cultura Económica.

Thirlwall, A. P. (2011) 'The Balance of Payments Constraint as an Explanation of the International Growth Rate Differences', *PSL Quarterly Review*, 64 (259): 429–438.

Torres, M., and Ahumada, J. M. (2022) 'Las relaciones centro-periferia en el siglo XXI', *El Trimestre Económico*, 89 (353): 151–195.

11 Bioeconomic and resilient development strategies in face of Covid-19 in the South

The example of Senegal

Abdourahmane Ndiaye and Muhammad Ba

1. Introduction

At a time when advanced capitalist economies (United States of America, Europe) have faltered in the face of the Covid-19 pandemic, voices have been raised to affirm that 'it is up to Africa to take the lead of a political initiative in proposing a roadmap to the international community, rather than waiting for it' (Yade, 2020). This proposal, which would have seemed to be a pure and simple provocation and dismissed as a rhetorical one, had a particular resonance in the context of the pandemic.

In the first place, the pandemic has vividly confirmed that prosperity does not inevitably rhyme with happiness or resilience. On the contrary, as suggested by Ulrich Beck, capitalism creates a risk society (Beck, 2001). Risk is inherent to capitalism. For example, by reducing health budgets, we jeopardise the full capacity of health systems to deal with a pandemic. The challenge of austerity policies, far from aiming to revise the functioning of institutions, only pursues the goals of making savings and satisfying the conditions of the so-called convergence criteria, and in particular, to abide by the neoliberal dogma of a public deficit capped at 3% of the GDP—an imperative, besides, which has no scientific basis. To maximise individual profits, capitalist dystopia imposes a collective risk on human societies so great that it could compromise their existence.

Then, faced with this capitalist dystopia, other paths supported by utopians have been posed since the 18th century, the age of nascent capitalism (Paquot, 2007).[1] Since the early 1970s, a resilient utopia based on the so-called bioeconomy has emerged and gained momentum (Meadows, Meadows and Randers, 1972; Illich, 1973; Georgescu-Roegen, 1978; Passet, 1979). During the 20th century, bioeconomy was defined through various academic fields: as a study of populations in biology, as natural resource management models or an entropic approach to economics, as in the work of Nicholas Georgescu-Roegen. Since the beginning of the 2000s, bioeconomy has been established as an institutional watchword under the leadership of the OECD and then the European Commission, which made it the spearhead of sustainable and clean growth, changing fossil resources by biotechnology. The introduction of bioeconomy in the European agenda was initiated by research-innovation policies, although their design and financing procedures were

DOI: 10.4324/9781003375425-14

strongly influenced by the industrial sectors of the financial oligarchy. Accordingly, the potential changes induced by bioeconomy in the primary sector of the economy generate tensions because they compete with other perspectives for the future of this sector (Pahun, Fouilleux and Daviron, 2018)[2] and also with broader perspectives related to natural and societal ecosystems.

By deepening this introductory statement, in the following sections, we will first clarify the notions of bioeconomy and resilience before subsequently arguing that, without a delinking, Senegal cannot restore hope to its population in terms of proper levels and conditions of life. In the third part, we discuss the conditions for a resilient development strategy based on extractive resources.

2. What is the conceptual framework for bioeconomy and resilience?

The bioeconomy, which is subject to a controversial debate nowadays, is, according to Pahun, Fouilleux and Daviron (2018), 'an expression that has flourished since the beginning of the 2000s'; it gave visibility to scientific research which tended to bring together economics and science through a rational and careful management of nature. However, the authors show that, currently, this term takes on another meaning and describes another reality, which is now supported by the lobbies of productivist agriculture, chemistry and biotechnology industries as well as being disseminated by international institutions such as the European Commission, the OECD or FAO. This semantic shift reflects, according to these authors, a change in the vision of agriculture (primary sector) and its governance, particularly within the European Commission. There is every reason to believe that this interpretation of bioeconomy tends to 'produce more with more', thanks to small factories and nature reduced to the condition of new resources to be exploited (Pahun, Fouilleux and Daviron, 2018).

For us, the meaning of 'bioeconomy' relates to that originally espoused by its founding fathers (Nicholas Georgescu-Roegen, René Passet, the Group of Ten, etc.) in connection with a rational and careful administration of resources for the benefit of a resilient development (Ancey, Pesche and Daviron (2017). This contrasts with the biocentric approach of the so-called weak sustainability, in which natural resources are considered as substitutable assets. This leads to confusion, since the notion of resilience resembles compassion and security—characteristics of a neoliberal ideology also leading to the weakening of public policies.

The anthropo-biocentric version of the bioeconomy (Magnaghi, 2003) here adopted is one of the sources of inspiration for thinkers of the social-ecological transition who propose a quiet degrowth (Latouche, 2007) and happy sobriety (Rabhi, 2010). The proponents of this paradigm argue for an urgent transition towards a humanist ethos which presupposes an organic link between humans and non-humans; namely, 'living things, ecosystems, histories and societies'. The perspective is not, strictly speaking, an economic problem in a narrow sense. In fact, its scope is a bioeconomic one because it concerns the particular way of life of humanity as a biological specimen[3] living in a physical universe governed by thermodynamic principles (Georgescu-Roegen, 1978).[4] While economic rationality was based on the convention of a stingy nature, although allowing for inexhaustible resources, humanity finds itself confronted with the strictly opposite conditions of the destruction of its natural resources through excessive production (Passet, 2011). This highlights nature's finite and limited character as well as its great generosity. Still, according to Passet (1979), life and its terrestrial environment must be understood as a unit—the biosphere. Kept in the biosphere, economic organisations must respect its laws and regulatory mechanisms. Thus, the paradigm that imposes itself is no longer that of mechanics but that of evolutionary biology and thermodynamic physics, notably through the law of entropy. Complex ecosystems ensure, through the law of entropy, the evolutionary survival of humanity through that of the biosphere to which it belongs. Only a viable bioeconomic economy is able to abide to the laws of nature and to listen to it carefully.

Senegal, having just discovered oil and gas mines, found itself challenged by the problem of rentier economies and the temptations of the so-called Dutch disease, or the curse of raw materials or natural resources abundance (Auty, 1990). Dutch disease is an economic phenomenon that provokes the decline of the local manufacturing industry as the inevitable consequence of the exploitation of natural resources. The increase in export revenues ultimately appreciates the domestic currency and makes exports from other sectors more expensive to the benefit of imports. The appreciation of the currency leads to a drop in the competitiveness of the entire economy; hence, the curse! Our reflection, as part of a bioeconomic scientific programme, leads us to question the orientations of the Emerging Senegal Plan (PSE) based on a type of economic growth whose main engine are the rents from mines and hydrocarbons. The debate, as posed, concerns open governance strategies such as the Extractive Industries Transparency Initiative (EITI).[5]

Recently discovered deposits of mineral resources (oil and gas) are seen as likely to bring unexpected trajectories to the economic growth projections of neoliberal emergence. How can Senegal forge an alternative and resilient development strategy based on fossil mineral resources in a world seeking to transition to a carbon-free economy? How can we build and develop energy security for Africa as a basis for the desired structural transformations? How can we pose possible solutions to go 'beyond senile capitalism' (Amin, 2001) and organise the exodus towards the new civilisation which can only assume a low-carbon, resilient, united and cooperative economy? This programme cannot be achieved without leaving behind economic determinism ('economism' or 'economic religion'); that is to say, a society entirely dominated by the imperatives of the productive apparatus and, more particularly, by its international financial sphere (Passet, 2003).

The notion of resilience, first elaborated and used in other scientific fields, benefits from the proliferation of its uses in scientific publications from the mid-1990s (Ancey, Pesche and Daviron, 2017).[6]

Bioeconomics, following the early publications of Nicholas Georgescu-Roegen (1971), was originally presented as a paradigm which had the ambition to replace Newtonian mechanics that prevailed in economics, especially after the so-called marginalist revolution. This paradigm suggests (re)thinking economic science and economic policy based on the principles of evolutionary biology and classical thermodynamic physics. Our intention here is to propose bioeconomics as a paradigm that can lead to a revaluation of Senegal's policies regarding the management of its extractive resources. Two reasons can justify this choice.

First and foremost, bioeconomics is a paradigm with the ambition of placing ecological concerns at the heart of economic thought and decision-making. Since the economic sphere is a subsystem of the Earth and the universe, economic processes cannot be narrowly defined within what Georgescu-Roegen calls the arithmomorphic dialectical logic (Georgescu-Roegen, 1978). More concretely, it involves utilising resources according to the logic of optimality and not of maximisation. To achieve this, the constraint of biodiversity equilibrium must always define the boundary of possibilities for resource exploitation.

The other reason justifying the choice of bioeconomics as a paradigm for public policies following the Covid-19 crisis is based on the fact that an 'all-oil' economy does not protect against exogenous shocks. From our perspective, there is a need to develop organic agriculture (organic agriculture, according to Georgescu-Roegen [1978, p. 372]), which should rely on a low degree of mechanisation, meaning appropriate technologies (Adair, 1984),[7] and the use of natural fertilisers. This may seem paradoxical at a time when achieving food security in the face of population growth is imperative. However, as the pioneers of bioeconomics believed, the bioeconomic programme must be associated with bioeconomic ethics, which calls for moving away from the 'everything, right now' logic inherited from the industrial revolution, with its relentless pursuit of productivity (Georgescu-Roegen, 1971). Instead, the logic of a just transition (Laurent, 2023) and moderation allows us to consider this organic agriculture for the medium and long terms.

In a few words, the bioeconomic programme, as a guide for the management of extractive resources, is primarily based on a change in ethics. It will involve exploiting our gas and oil resources outside the orthodox principle of economic maximisation. One might rightfully raise the argument of the choice criteria. Indeed, how can one define the effectiveness of a policy without this principle of maximisation? The answer, once again, can be found in Nicholas Georgescu-Roegen (1977, p. 270), who postulates 'the minimization of future regrets that present actions could provoke'. This programme cannot be implemented without a delinking in the governance of mineral resources.

3. Delinking as a mode of governance for mineral resources

The concept of delinking, as developed by Samir Amin (1986), does not imply a return to the Stone Age, nor does it seek self-sufficiency. Disconnection suggests a break from the dominant capitalist system. It entails a strategic shift in the perception of internal/external relationships as a response to the unavoidable requirements of self-centred development. Delinking promotes the reconstruction of a globalisation based on negotiation, rather than submission to the exclusive interests of imperialist oligopolies. It fosters the reduction of international inequalities. The primary form of current disconnection is defined by the challenge to the five privileges of contemporary imperialism: control of advanced technologies; access to the Earth's natural resources; management and subordination of the globally integrated monetary and financial system; domination of information and communication technologies; production, control and dissemination of weapons of mass destruction.

Emerging countries are on this path, with varying degrees of determination. Our goal is to identify the constants and emerging changes at work in Senegal, at the twilight of the Covid-19 pandemic and at the dawn of the 21st century. This work of analytical identification should lead to scenario proposals from which strategies can be defined and proposed at the national, sub-regional and continental levels. To do this, we draw upon two major lines of thought: Samir Amin's disconnection (1986) and bioeconomics, which underlie eco-socialist experiences located in the sense of the theory of the symbolic site (Zaoual, 1999; Machrafi, 2008).

Expressed in everyday language, delinking means deglobalisation, or disconnection. The neo-Marxist school of development (Samir Amin, Arghiri Emmanuel, André Gunder-Frank, etc.) has demonstrated that the Triad (United States, Europe and Japan) subjugates the peripheries to satisfy its needs at the expense of periphery populations. Delinking is, thus, a path that allows the internalisation of what constitutes the very essence of life, by returning to those values associated with one's own culture (Ndiaye et al., 2018). What some call the 'immediate economy' (Dione, 2020) enables distancing from global competition so as to build oneself intrinsically.[8] From our perspective, disconnection offers a different but convergent interpretation with the eco-socialist line of thought, when asserting that we must emancipate ourselves from the capitalist system so as to generate productive degrowth and break free from rampant consumerism—a source of obesity and cardiovascular diseases in developed countries and of malnutrition and hunger in the peripheral countries of globalised capitalism. Furthermore, the criticisms of consumerism (increasing waste, environmental pressures, resource exploitation, labour conditions in low-wage exporting countries, etc.) have intensified. These issues—especially ecological ones, health-related and inequality problems—have become more visible mobilisation targets. They have gradually led to a variety of potentially convergent reactions aimed at addressing these concerns (Rumpala, 2009). This emancipatory quest is linked to a reorientation towards the satisfaction of our essential needs. These factors will inevitably create social wealth. This is the perspective that Ivan Illich (1973) offers in his 'convivial society', which restores leisure time and puts tools at the service of human communities.

Rich in hydrocarbons, mineral resources and water, the African continent is still perceived in very limiting terms, given its low participation in global capital and goods flows. Still constrained by 'development partners' through their 'fatal aid' (Moyo, 2009),[9] African economies struggle to overcome the main cause of the weakness (or absence) of proper reflections on strategies for pro-poor, introverted, self-centred development strategies, which are capable of eradicating poverty and reducing inequalities that undermine social cohesion and a better living.

How to delink the governance of mineral resources? Governance is here understood as a search for compatibility between various modes of regulation, cultures, legitimacy and *a priori* non-convergent interests. It is worth noting that, in the 19th century, most natural resources from extractive industries were already being exploited in Africa. Copper, iron, gold, salt and other resources were produced in large quantities, with such quality that they could compete with products from Europe (Sodji, 2019). Driven by a desire to control raw materials, the elites in the former colonies hurried to establish political and legal frameworks to protect investments (Radmann, 1978). The short-term and outward-focused visions of leaders did not allow the states to pursue a path of self-centred economic growth (Austin, 2010) and initiate the necessary and desirable structural transformations.

4. Extractive industries, an outdated basis for desirable structural transformations?

In Senegal, mineral exploitation dates back to independence, although it remained marginal due to its limited contribution to the gross domestic product. The primary raw materials exploited at that time were mainly phosphate from Taïba and quarries in the Dakar region. In 2014, the sector contributed on average to less than 1 billion CFA[10] francs per year (IGE, 2014). The start of gold mining in 2009, followed by zircon mining in 2014 and the growth of cement factories have increased the sector's contribution, which grew to 35% of the total volume of exports in 2017, with a financial contribution of 124.5 billion CFA francs (CN-ITIE, 2019). According to the National Committee on Extractive Industries Transparency Initiative (CN-ITIE), the sector's contribution (mining and hydrocarbons) experienced a slight decline, dropping to 120.3 billion CFA francs in 2018, a decrease of 4.2%.

With the crisis in the extractive industries, we have witnessed a drop in the stock prices of most mining companies by more than 75%, when compared to their levels at the beginning of 2015—this being orchestrated by those who claim to be 'partners' in Africa's development. Neither the entry of the BRICS (Brazil-Russia-India-China-South Africa) nor the meagre new promises of the G20—mainly aimed at subsidising multinational corporations—can disguise the widespread stagnation in the most significant circuits of the global economy for Africa. In this context, global prosperity goes hand in hand with the mistreatment of the environment (Harvey, 2017) and societal health. Delinking leads us back to a centrality of ourselves in our relations with the rest of the world. It seems to us the only way of reconciling ecological urgency, economic challenges and societal issues.

While attempting to increase the efficiency of taxation mechanisms through mining code reforms, African states aim to enhance their mining and oil revenues and thereby strengthen their capacity for development intervention. However, these efforts must not be undermined by corruption practices and other kleptocratic schemes. Although Senegal is one of the countries that best adheres to the transparency rules, the state failed to prevent the Petro-Tim scandal. This alleged corruption scandal has shaken Senegal to its presidency. According to a BBC report published on 2 June 2019,[11] Aliou Sall, the brother of the President of the Republic of Senegal, is said to have received a bribe in exchange for the allocation of oil and gas concessions in Senegalese waters. While the Petro-Tim case has been known for years in Senegal, the British television channel goes further by claiming to possess confidential documents that, for the first time, would support these suspicions of corruption.[12] The idea is to make the exploitation of natural resources a lever for economic growth, provided that oil and mining revenues are managed rigorously and transparently, free from clans and other predatory motives. 'To be competitive, Senegal must [. . .] offer attractive conditions for potential players in the oil industry which are conducive to the development of exploitation or production investments in the national territory' (Law 98–05 of 8 January 1998, on the Petroleum Code—Preamble).

But conversely and symmetrically, this framework established for the competitiveness of states is also attractive to investors, which can deviate from (or compromise with) the official development objectives. When examining the oil and gas reforms in African countries, one cannot help but wonder if the aim of such reforms is not so much to provide the state with greater financial strength or to adequate governance frameworks to the benefits of large oil and gas firms. It is, in reality, a regulation of state ambitions by the market through the Extractive Industries Transparency Initiative (EITI). The Initiative seeks to 'moralise' or to foster the admission of reforms and resource governance for both national and international public opinion. This can be particularly explained, according to the innovative work of Patrick Bond and his team at the University of Johannesburg, because these reforms are mostly driven by donors or carried out under their control. Their unspoken objective is to facilitate the access of oil and gas firms to African natural resources on preferential terms, as reflected in the competitive approaches of mining codes (Bond and Garcia, 2015).

Even before the peak of commodity prices in 2011 and its collapse in 2015, the neoliberal strategy of a small open economy oriented towards exports had caused significant damage in terms of human development, gender equity and the environment (Bond, 2006). While data on poverty, mortality, morbidity and education improved somewhat (especially after the G7 debt relief program in 2005, which gradually eliminated the prohibitive operating costs of basic public services), the conditions for everyday life in Africa did not improve, especially since the start of the global recession in 2008 (Gumede, 2016). As shown by the poverty monitoring survey in Senegal, the incidence of poverty has only slightly decreased, from 48.3% in 2006 to 46.7% in 2011 (Republic of Senegal, 2013). Since the devaluation of the CFA franc in 1994, the reduction of poverty and improvements in living conditions have been slow to materialise (Ndiaye, 2008).[13]

In Senegal, production was expected to begin in 2022, according to the projections of the new Australian operator, Woodside Petroleum. Its production will span 25 years and reach a peak of approximately 100,000 barrels per day between 2030 and 2037 (*Réseau Sénégalais des Think Tanks*, 2020). According to a recent study by the International Monetary Fund, oil and gas revenues are estimated to account for 5% to 8% of GDP, an outlook based on the Senegalese Think Tanks Network, in its policy brief of 4 February 2020, titled 'Governance of Oil and Gas Resources: State of the Debate and Prospects'. The same source informs that production of natural gas is expected to reach 100,000 barrels of oil equivalent between 2026 and 2042 before gradually declining from 2043 (RSTT [*Réseau Sénégalais des Think Tanks*], 2020).[14]

5. Differences between oil and natural gas: avoiding throwing out the baby with the bathwater!

A significant distinction between oil and natural gas is needed here. In general, the difference between the carbon costs of oil when compared to that of natural gas is not always emphasised, most analyses considering them equally depletable and polluting fossil resources. Considered as the least polluting of fossil fuels, natural gas is a primary source of energy, naturally present in the subsurface, and undergoes no transformation after extraction. Natural gas is derived from the transformation of organic materials into gas. Its burning primarily emits water vapour and CO_2 without the emission of smoke or particles. The burning of natural gas carbon dioxide releases 25% less pollutants than the burning of oil and 50% less than the burning of coal, this condition making natural gas the cleanest, least environmentally impacting fuel as well as the most suitable for industrial and domestic needs (Engie, 2019). Senegal's energy sovereignty should rely on natural gas and open a new era for energy sovereignty of West Africa.

6. A delinked strategy, at odds with the model of the small open economy

How can these mineral resources become accelerators of structural transformations and allow CEDEAO (Economic Community of West African States) to become a prosperous and resilient economic zone? How can they generate energy sovereignty for African countries? We have strong reservations about the commonly accepted and proposed idea, even by progressive intellectuals, to align with the goals and mechanisms of the EITI (Extractive Industries Transparency Initiative), which formally democratises the governance of natural resources. Indeed, as important as this initiative may be for deepening the democratic governance of mineral and hydrocarbon natural resources or ensuring local development benefits for the populations, it does not break with the current predatory pattern that compels Global South countries to export unprocessed raw materials while importing high-value-added manufactured products. This perpetuates the deterioration of terms of trade. In addition to this first concern, there is another, even less acceptable, one, which suggests sustainable development in the Global North and growth in the Global South. This leads to climate migrations that provide indecent labour. Moreover, these flawed ideas orchestrate the invisible mobility of wealth from the South to the Triad and the control of natural resources by kleptomaniac transnational firms like Glencore. Finally, the majority of African countries affiliated with the Extractive Industries Transparency Initiative and stakeholders in export-led growth have not succeeded in transforming the advantage, if there was one. Bold proposals will need to be imagined in order to break this pattern, related to a serious and in-depth reflection on a sovereign governance of natural resources and their ability to strengthen the position of Southern countries in the new, post-Covid-19 global order.

The strategy here proposed consists of segmenting the markets for oil and gas and assigning them different functions. To achieve this, the highly polluting oil can serve as a source of foreign exchange, as it is easily exportable. The exploitation of gas could lead to the deepening of research towards smart cities, such as Masdar in Abu Dhabi—a model for ecological cities—the world's first city built for a zero-carbon and zero-waste lifestyle. Dongtan is another example of these ambitions, in China. Rather than treating these resources as a source of limited export revenues, as is already the case with phosphates, they should be seen as an opportunity to approach the future of Africa differently, by the investment in clean technologies that provide societal added value in terms of living standards and quality of life. Envisioning a future for Africa with little or less carbon is possible.

At this level, the implementation of the bioeconomy can be accomplished by following the scheme described in the following figure. It represents an economy that links different components of the economic chain, starting with agriculture. As mentioned earlier, the development of this sector should focus on an organic and harmonious path while respecting biodiversity requirements. Agriculture should also be a biomass-producing sector, which is the essential factor for structural transformation based on the bioeconomy. Instead of fossil fuels, which are, in the words of Nicholas Georgescu-Roegen, a capital factor, biomass is a flow factor that should serve as an input to the transformation chain, relying on the lever of biotechnology. The products and byproducts of biotechnology should be used in various sectors and even return to agriculture.

To turn extractive resources into a sustainable development lever, we propose decoupling oil and gas. Revenues from their exploitation will be the primary source of funding for research and development of clean technologies in the medium and long term (see the foregoing model). The axiom of biotechnology is, for us, a way

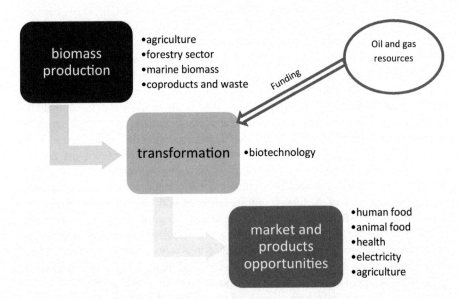

Figure 11.1 Model: biomass production chain.

Source: based on Delgoulet and Pahun (2015).

for sovereignty, provided that the research results foster the emergence and con-solidation of start-ups.

7. Conclusion

In the 'Anthropocene' context which human societies are experiencing, the trans-formation of lifestyles is a social-ecological urgency. We must revisit the exponen-tial dynamics triggered on all fronts: greenhouse gas emissions; use of fossil fuels; overconsumption of water; soil degradation; deforestation; depletion of fishery resources; erosion of biodiversity; dispersion of toxic and/or ecotoxic products; and more. To achieve this, we need to move away from the culture of 'no limits', distancing ourselves from the absurd spirit of Bernard de Mandeville's *The Fable of the Bees*, which posits that private vices are supposed to generate collective virtues (Mandeville, 2007 [1705–1724]), this justifying an apologetic approach to consumption and endless growth.

The time has come to change course, even to emancipate ourselves from the excesses of a growth society that struggles to achieve more growth. Worse still, it is built on a model of predation of natural and societal resources that continually shows its limits. More is not always better, especially in these times where the An-thropocene notion has gained a theoretical centrality (Revkin, 1992; Crutzen and Stoermer, 2000; Grinewald, 2012).

The option of a self-sustaining of the needs proposed by André Gorz, based on self-production, can be seen as an invitation to retake social intelligence as a source of wealth (both non-material and material) and resilience. To move away from the development perspective, seen as an attempt of a 'Westernization of the world' (La-touche, 2005), desirable structural transformations must be built on inclusive and solidarity-based domestic economies. This implies a conducive environment for the emergence of non-market, market and multiscale (local, regional, national and Afri-can) cooperation initiatives. This should lead to active state engagement to encour-age and support the creation of cooperatives, mutual organisations, activity groups, economic interest groups, associations and social and solidarity enterprises at the regional level. These transformations should be based on small production units in the form of companies by individuals or capital, following tax and remunera-tion regulations—this being a starting point for reclaiming lost sovereignty. Hassan Zaoual's (1999) approach to symbolic sites should count as one of the pillars of this strategy. Social and economic transformation must be 'embraced from within by local, autonomous, responsible, competent, organized, and deeply integrated actors within their symbolic sites of belonging' (Panhuys, 2013, p. 115). The other pillar of social transformation is the hybridisation of mechanical and organic solidarity, both inscribed in human communities and social relations of production. Resources derived from 'natural assets' could then initiate the financing of the transition to an ecological socialism, or ecosocialism. In short, it is about moving away from short-term calculations and gradually breaking free from relationships of submission to the interests of global financial capitalism. The post-Covid-19 era—the world to come—presents an urgency to refocus on endogenous concerns based on short circuits—a lever for local development (Ndiaye, 2016). This bioeconomic disconnection is not only possible but also revitalises the relocation of economic dynamics as well as promoting shorter routes and circuits and reinforcing autonomy, this acting as a lightning rod against increasingly complex exogenous shocks, such as the Covid-19 pandemic. The case study of mineral resources is, indeed, a relevant example to foster the bioeconomic approach proposed here. However, bioeconomics must reinvest in agriculture and other vital sectors for sovereignty, such as chemistry and medication (such as hybridisation of pharmacopoeia research and modern medicine), so as to avoid creating an economy of 'all-oil' with petrochemical industries that will undoubtedly contribute to environmental deterioration. It is time to put energy at the service of Africa (Eze, 2019) in order to make it an engine of endogenous development. The social-ecological transition we are calling for is an articulation between natural systems and human systems to build a new, resilient common narrative and robust institutions that will enable their anchoring (Laurent, 2017).

Notes

1 The work of the utopians foresaw the typical ideals of the so-called degrowth strategy, even though the term did not exist. Short routes, shared gardens, pooling of all kinds, work sharing, participatory housing, zero-interest loans, collective ownership of capital and production tools were all recipes proposed by the utopians since 1516 with the publication of *Utopia*, the work of Thomas More.
2 It should be noted that Senegal does not have an official programme for developing sustainable value chains on bioeconomic lines!
3 Based on the work of bio-anthropology taken up by Alfred Lotka, Georgescu-Roegen traces a distinction between living species according to so-called endosomatic and exosomatic instruments. Endosomatic instruments are means of acting on the world which relate to the basic individual needs. On the other hand, exosomatic instruments are tools which are not direct biological constituents of the individual. Man has the specificity of using exosomatic instruments to alter physical reality.
4 When a thermodynamic system is isolated without possible exchange with the outside, it can only evolve spontaneously towards the maximum of its entropy, this tending towards a state of definitive equilibrium (second principle); however, while the total quantity of its internal energy remains preserved, its quality is reduced (first principle).
5 The EITI, in English 'Extractive Industries Transparency Initiative', is an international non-profit organisation under Norwegian law responsible for maintaining and supervising the implementation of standards and legal norms regarding this industry. Launched in 2003, the aim of the norm is to assess how much revenue from a country's oil, gas and mineral resources are managed in a transparent manner. The Initiative aims to strengthen government systems by emphasising public and corporate governance. It is also a source of information to raise public awareness and promote public debate regarding stakeholders in the extractive sector and their use. The EITI departs from the principle that a country's natural resources belong to the citizens of that country. When the extraction of these resources is well managed, the wealth generated can contribute to developing the economic and social sector. Poor management of the sector quickly leads to armed conflicts.
6 'The exegesis of this notion has subsequently led to numerous publications that reflect the plurality it encompasses. Beyond its polysemy, the idea generally associated with the concept of resilience revolves around the capacities of adaptation and transformation of a "system" in the face of external shocks' (Ancey, Pesche et Daviron, 2017). For a

deep discussion of interpretations of the concept of resilience, one can read with interest Ancey, Pesche and Daviron (2017).

7 The approach of appropriate technologies and endogenous development is an invitation to break away from transferable models and mimicry and to consider that models should always be subject to local appropriation. As Joseph Ki-Zerbo aptly puts it, 'he who sleeps on someone else's mat sleeps under the open sky!'.

8 Much like China, Russia, India, Venezuela, Cuba and Vietnam, South Africa adds to this, since Apartheid led to a forced disconnection, resulting in embargoes from the rest of the world. This is reminiscent of Friedrich List's didactic plea for protectionism (1998 [1841]).

9 See also the review by Marc Raffinot (2009).

10 Franc of the Financial Community of Africa.

11 Available at www.youtube.com/watch?v=UlTXRWMYpzQ/

12 For further information see: www.lemonde.fr/afrique/article/2019/06/04/au-senegal-le-frere-du-president-soupconne-de-corruption_5471359_3212.html/

13 The statistics provided by the ANSD regarding the incidence of monetary poverty in Senegal show conflicting data. According to ESPS-II, the incidence of monetary poverty was 48.3% in 2006, while the Poverty Reduction Strategy Document-II estimated it at 50.5%. In any case, these data attest to the fact that poverty is not significantly decreasing. 'According to the results of the 2001 Senegalese Household Survey (ESAM-II), 48.5% of households live below the monetary poverty threshold, whereas during the 1994 Household Survey (ESAM-I), poverty affected 61.4% of households. As for the proportion of the population living below the poverty threshold, it stood at 57.1% of households in 2001/2002 compared to 67.9% in 1994/1995' (Ndiaye, 2008, p. 315).

14 Accordingly, the strategic thinking for the post-2043 period must be initiated right now. It is necessary to identify the drivers that will take over after the peak of oil exploitation in Senegal.

References

Adair, P. (1984) 'Développement endogène et technologies appropriées en milieu rural', *Économie rurale*, 162: 2.

Amin, S. (1986) *La Déconnexion*. Paris: Éditions La Découverte.

Amin, S. (2001) *Au-delà du capitalisme sénile*. Paris: Éditions Presses Universitaires de France.

Ancey, V., Pesche, D., and Daviron, B. (2017) 'Résilience et développement: complément, substitut ou palliatif: Le cas du pastoralisme au Sahel', *Revue internationale des études du développement*, 231: 57–89.

Austin, G. (2010) 'Développement économique et legs coloniaux en Afrique', *International Development Policy*, 1: 11–36.

Auty, R. (1990) *Resource-Based Industrialization: Sowing the Oil in Eight Developing Countries*. Oxford: Clarendon Press.

Beck, U. (2001) *La société du risque. Sur la voie d'une autre modernité*. Paris: Éditions Aubier.

Bond, P. (2006) *Looting Africa*. London: Zed Books.

Bond, P., and Garcia, A. (eds.) (2015) *An Anti-Capitalist Critique*. Johannesburg: Jacana Media.

Comité National de l'Initiative pour la transparence des industries extractives du Sénégal. (2019) *Rapport de conciliation 2018*. Ngor Almadies/Dakar.

Crutzen, P. J., and Stoermer, E. F. (2000) 'The Anthropocene', *Global Change/IGBP, Newsletter*, 41: 17–18.

Delgoulet, E., and Pahun, J. (2015) 'Bioéconomie: enjeux d'un concept émergent', *Centre d'étude et de prospective*. Paris: Ministry of Agriculture of the French Republic. Document de travail n°10. Available at: http://agriculture.gouv.fr/telecharger/77594?token=05 bf88d9a d030e48e51df1088782b870.

Dione, A. (2020) 'L'économie immédiate: baromètre et levier de résilience face à la pandémie du Covid-19', *Senplus*. Available at: www.seneplus.com/opinions/leconomie-immediate-barometre-et-levier-de-resilience-face-la/

Engie, S. A. (2019) *Gaz naturel: combustible et source d'énergie*. Available at: https://particuliers.engie.fr/gaz-naturel/conseils/types-gaz/gaz-naturel-source-energie.html/

Eze, P. A. (2019) 'Il est temps de mettre l'énergie au service de l'Afrique', *Financial Afrik*, 19. Available at: www.financialafrik.com/2019/09/15/il-est-temps-de-mettre-lenergie-au-service-de-lafrique/

Georgescu-Roegen, N. (1971) *The Entropy Law and the Economic Process*. Cambridge, MA: Harvard University Press.

Georgescu-Roegen, N. (1977) 'The Steady State and Ecological Salvation: A Thermodynamic Analysis', *BioScience*, 27 (4): 266–270.

Georgescu-Roegen, N. (1978) 'De la science économique à la bioéconomie', *Revue d'économie politique*, 88 (3): 37–382.

Grinewald, J. (2012) 'Le concept d'Anthropocène, son contexte historique et scientifique', *Entropia*, 12: 1–46.

Gumede, V. (ed.) (2016) *The Great Recession and Its Implications for Human Values*. Johannesburg: Real African Publishers.

Harvey, D. (2017) *Marx, Capital and the Madness of Economic Reason*. London: Profile Books.

Illich, I. (1973) *La Convivialité*. Paris: Éditions Seuil.

Latouche, S. (2005) *L'occidentalisation du monde. Essai sur la signification, la portée et les limites de l'uniformisation planétaire*. Paris: Éditions La Découverte/Poche.

Latouche, S. (2007) *Petit Traité de la décroissance sereine*. Paris: Éditions Les Mille et Une Nuits.

Laurent, É. (2017) *À l'horizon d'ici. Les territoires au cœur de la transition social-écologique*. Paris: Éditions Le bord de l'eau.

Laurent, É. (2023) *Économie pour le XXIe siècle. Manuel des transitions justes*. Paris: La découverte.

List, F. (1998 [1841]) *Système national d'économie politique*. Paris: Éditions Gallimard.

Machrafi, M. (2008) 'Introduction au paradigme des sites. Épistémologie et concepts', *Revue Repères et Perspectives*, 11: 81–92.

Magnaghi, A. (2003) *Le projet local*. Bruxelles: Éditions Mardaga.

Mandeville, B. (2007 [1714]) *La Fable des abeilles*. Paris: Éditions Vrin.

Meadows, D., Meadows, D., et Randers, J. (1972) *Halte à la croissance*. Paris: Éditions Fayard.

Moyo, D. (2009) *L'Aide fatale. Les ravages d'une aide inutile et de nouvelles solutions pour l'Afrique*. Paris: Lattès.

Ndiaye, A. (2008) 'L'initiative PPTE est-elle efficace pour la réduction de la pauvreté? Le cas du Sénégal', in G. Daffé and A. Diagne (eds.), *Le Sénégal face aux défis de la pauvreté. Les oubliés de la croissance*, pp. 301–322. Karthala: Éditions CRES.

Ndiaye, A. (2016) 'How Can Short Food Supply Chains Be a Lever for the Development of a Local Economy Based on Peasant Family Farms?', in *Review Policy in Focus, The International Policy Centre for Inclusive Growth*, pp. 24–27. Brasilia: United Nations Development Programme.

Ndiaye, A., et al. (eds.) (2018) *Rapport Alternatif Sur l'Afrique numéro zéro*. Dakar: Éditions Enda Tiers Monde/Forum du Tiers Monde/Codesria/Fondation Rosa Luxembourg.

Pahun, J., Fouilleux, È., and Daviron, B. (2018) 'De quoi la bioéconomie est-elle le nom? Genèse d'un nouveau référentiel d'action publique', *Nature Sciences Sociétés*, 26 (1): 3–16.

Panhuys, H. (2013) 'Rôle des socioéconomies dites informelles dans l'Afrique postcoloniale', in H. Panhuys, M. M. Mudjir and P. M. Mulumba (eds.), *L'économie sociale et solidaire dans le basculement du monde au Nord et au Sud*, pp. 113–154. De l'entreprenariat institué au partenariat situé. Paris: Éditions L'Harmattan.

Paquot, T. (2007) *Utopies et utopistes*. Paris: Éditions La Découverte.

Passet, R. (1979) *L'économique et le vivant*. Paris: Éditions Payot.

Passet, R. (2003) 'Introduction', in P. Merlant, R. Passet and J. Robin (eds.), *Sortir de l'économisme. Une alternative au capitalisme néolibéral*, pp. 9–16. Paris: Les Éditions de l'Atelier.

Passet, R. (2011) 'L'avenir est à la bioéconomie', *Libération*, 23 May.

Rabhi, P. (2010) *Vers la sobriété heureuse*. Arles (France): Actes Sud Éditions.

Radmann, W. (1978) 'The Nationalisation of Zaire's Copper: From Union Minière to Gecamines', *Africa Today*, 4: 25–47.

Raffinot, M. (2009) 'Dambisa Moyo, L'Aide fatale. Les ravages d'une aide inutile et de nouvelles solutions pour l'Afrique', *Afrique contemporaine*, 232 (4): 209–216.

Republic of Senegal. (1998) *Law 98–0508, 'Code pétrolier'*. Dakar: Ministère du Pétrole et des Energies.

Republic of Senegal. (2013) *Deuxième enquête de suivi de la pauvreté au Sénégal (ESPS-II)*. Dakar: Agence Nationale de la Statistique et de Démographie.

Republic of Senegal. (2014) *Rapport public sur l'état de la gouvernance et de la reddition des comptes*. Dakar: L'Inspection générale d'État (IGE).

Réseau Sénégalais des Think Tanks. (2020) *La gouvernance des ressources pétrolières et gazières: état du débat et perspectives*. Dakar.

Revkin, A. (1992) *Global Warming: Understanding the Forecast, American Museum of Natural History, Environmental Defense Fund*. New York: Abbeville Press.

Rumpala, Y. (2009) 'La "consommation durable" comme nouvelle phase d'une gouvernementalisation de la consommation', *Revue française de science politique*, 59 (5): 967–996.

Sodji, A. (2019) 'La gouvernance des ressources naturelles en Afrique', *Law World*, 28 March. Availableat:www.lawworld.fr/la-gouvernance-des-ressources-naturelles-en-afrique/#_edn1

Yade, R. (2020) 'Seule l'Afrique apparaît en capacité de penser la destinée collective de l'humanité', *Le Monde*, 6 April. Available at: www.seneplus.com/opinions/seule-lafrique-apparait-en-capacite-de-penser-la-destinee

Zaoual, H. (1999) 'Théorie des sites et organisation économique', in S. Latouche, et al. (eds.), *Critique de la raison économique. Introduction à la théorie des sites symboliques*, pp. 79–109. Paris: L'Harmattan.

Index

absentee ownership 90, 92, 97, 99, 100, 101, 102
accumulation by dispossession 59, 89, 90, 91, 96
accumulation of capital 7, 8, 9, 10, 19, 36, 38, 49, 89, 90, 102, 105, 108, 110, 115, 127, 158, 165, 169, 170, 172, 174, 175
Adams, H. 4
Adorno, T. 16
advertising 81, 82, 83, 85, 87, 170
Africa 91, 136, 153, 155, 160, 198, 200, 202, 203, 204, 206, 209; and Covid-19 198; West Africa 205
agriculture 6, 7, 8, 10, 49, 53, 57, 58, 65, 77, 79, 118, 154, 156, 160, 162, 165, 183, 184, 199, 201, 206, 209; and A. Smith's approach 29, 30, 31, 32, 34, 35, 36, 39, 40, 44, 45; and command over resources 41, 42; and surplus 50, 51, 52
Alier, J. M. 4, 12, 22, 29, 31, 70, 74; and his critiques to classical political economy 5
Anthropocene 207
anthropological studies 42, 77, 93, 97, 98, 101, 102, 104, 105
Association for Evolutionary Economics 138
austerity policies 198

backwardness 118, 154, 159; technological 188
balance of payments 190; constrained growth models 183
Bankovsky 77, 80
banks 115, 153
Barro, R. 114
Bielschowsky, R. 176, 185, 194
Big Push for sustainability 117, 118, 121, 193

bioeconomy 198, 199, 206
biomass 153; production chain 206
Blaug, M. 5, 14, 23
Boas, F. 97, 103, 104
Boulding, K. 4, 10, 17, 24n8, 168
Brazil 116, 122, 161; colonisation 158, 164, 166, 167, 168, 177, 178, 183; deforestation 160; droughts 163; Northeast 162; Sudene 163
Brundtland Report 157n7
Bureau of Home Economics 77, 79

Canada 153
capital 11, 15, 19, 36, 38, 52, 53, 91, 108, 109, 126, 183, 186, 206, 208; as a quantity 108; as a scarce resource 166; capital critique 20, 123, 134, 136; constant capital 9; and entropy 175; fixed capital and joint production 63n3; natural 114, 117, 119, 120; natural capital in Adam Smith's work 30
capital controversy 20, 123, 127, 134
carbon emissions 57, 58, 60, 61, 62, 205, 206; carbon-neutral economy 110; decarbonisation 118, 128, 137, 193; low-carbon economy 117, 119
carrying capacity 4, 34, 168; in Adam Smith's work 45
Carson, R. 18
center periphery model 167, 171, 176, 181, 182, 186, 188, 190, 191, 192, 194
class 57, 62, 189
Clausius, R. 4
cleanliness 74, 75
Club of Rome 184, 196
CO_2 emissions 120, 190, 193, 205
Coase, R. 17
Cobb-Douglas production function 199